The Man Who Adores
the Negro

The Man
Who Adores
the Negro

Race and
American Folklore

PATRICK B. MULLEN

UNIVERSITY OF ILLINOIS PRESS

Urbana and Chicago

Manufactured in the United States of America

1 2 3 4 5 C P 5 4 3 2 1

∞ This book is printed on acid-free paper.

Library of Congress Cataloging-in-Publication Data

Mullen, Patrick B., 1941–

The man who adores the negro : race and American folklore /
Patrick B. Mullen.

p. cm.

Includes bibliographical references (p.) and index.

ISBN-13: 978-0-252-03265-3 (cloth : alk. paper)

ISBN-10: 0-252-03265-9

ISBN-13: 978-0-252-07486-8 (pbk. : alk. paper)

ISBN-10: 0-252-07486-6

1. African Americans—Folklore—Research.

2. African Americans—Race identity.

3. Folklore—United States—Field work.

I. Title.

GR111.A47M85   2008

398.2089'96073—dc22   2007023279

"To us, the man who adores the Negro is
as 'sick' as the man who abominates him."

—Frantz Fanon, *Black Skin, White Masks*

Contents

Acknowledgments

My southern background has something to do with my interest in race, but I won't follow in the tradition of William Faulkner who dedicated *Go Down, Moses* to "Mammy Caroline Barr." My cultural ties to Faulkner are clear, however, in that Melissy, the woman who ironed clothes and did housework for our family, was the only black person I knew as a child.

Far more important in establishing my perspectives on race are the people I knew and learned from as an adult. I've known Darnell Williams since my first year of teaching at Ohio State, and we have remained close friends even after he returned to the South to teach and work as a college administrator. He has always delicately, humorously, and lovingly traveled back and forth across the boundaries between the races. The same could be said of our mutual friend Gwen Herrell, a Columbus schoolteacher who performed wonders for racial harmony in and out of the classroom. Knowing them has deeply enriched my understanding of African American culture.

The same year I met Darnell, I also became friends with several colleagues at the university who advanced my knowledge about cultural difference and commonality. Three specific instances come to mind: discussing Jean Toomer's *Cane* with Hortense Simmons, listening to Albert King's *King of the Blues Guitar* and going to B. B. King concerts with Art Thornton, and listening to and talking about *Jazz at the Philharmonic* with Carl Marshall.

And more recently, other university colleagues, students, and friends discussed various aspects of my research on race with me and read chapters from the book manuscript. Former graduate student Aaron Oforlea's citation of Frantz Fanon in a paper led me to the quote that became the title of this book. One of the first people I told about the title was English Department colleague Tony Libby, who enthusiastically supported it in spite of resistance from some quarters. In a graduate seminar on race, Mary Manning's interpretation of Bongo Joe's "What I Like About the Jungle" caused me to see it in an entirely different way (see chapter 5). Students in that seminar on race and folklore and another on race and literature provided insights that stimulated my thinking at a crucial time in the writing of the book. One of those students, Mickey Williams, became a collaborator in field research on African American children's rhymes (see chapter 7). A former student and current program coordinator at the OSU African American and African Studies Community Extension Center, Carla Wilks, was also an invaluable collaborator on the children's rhymes project. Brooksie Harrington's dissertation and subsequent research on Shirley Caesar have deepened my understanding of gospel music.

English Department colleagues Valerie Lee, John Hellmann, and John Roberts read individual chapters and helped immeasurably in determining the final shape of the manuscript. Ohio State colleague Ike Newsum read and talked to me about one chapter, but he helped me even more with many late night discussions about music, art, literature, politics, and race. Other Ohio State folklorists, Mark Bender, Katey Borland, Amy Horowitz, Barbara Lloyd, Tim Lloyd, Margaret Mills, Dorry Noyes, Amy Shuman, Martha Sims, and Sabra Webber, discussed folkloric issues relevant to the book with me on many different occasions. Martha was especially helpful in solving some problems in the chapter on Alan Lomax. Amy Shuman invited me to discuss my collaborative research with Reverend Jesse Truvillion (see chapter 8) in two of her graduate seminars, giving me even more perspectives on the ethics of fieldwork across racial lines. And I will always be indebted to Jesse Truvillion for sharing his family and personal history with me, adding greatly to my understanding of African American history and culture and contributing his unique perspective to chapters 3 and 8. Without the kindness and consideration of my friend Bob Russell who introduced the two men from East Texas to each other, I would not have met Jesse in the first place.

As with any folklore book, this one is dependent on the consultants I interviewed during my field research, specifically Son Brill, Junior Carter, George Coleman ("Bongo Joe"), Mollie Ford, "Lightnin'" Hopkins, and the dozens of children whose rhymes I recorded in 1971, 2000, and 2001.

At the beginning of my career, Roger Abrahams encouraged me to pursue my interests in African American culture when I was in one of his graduate seminars at the University of Texas. When I was approaching retirement, he agreed to be interviewed for my critique of his scholarship in chapter 6, providing a critical added dimension to the study. Other folklorists have influenced my research on African American culture through their books, articles, and personal communications, especially Meg Brady, Bob Cantwell, Cece Conway, Gerald Davis, David Evans, Bill Ferris, Trudier Harris, Rosemary Hathaway, Bruce Jackson, Bill Lightfoot, Barry Pearson, Jeff Titon, and Bill Wiggins.

Because of the importance of African American music to this study, the preceding list contains the names of several folk music scholars, and I need to add the names of other scholars and friends with whom I have talked music with over the years: David Brose, Charley Camp, Kathy Greenwood and Bob Jones, Charlie Jackson, Brian Lovely, Mark Lutz, Janice and Tom Mitchell, Dudley Radcliff, John Reese, Vic Rini, Jim Scarff, Curt Schieber, and Jack Shortlidge. Jack has been sending me material on music and race since the beginning of my research. Without them, my knowledge of American vernacular music would be much thinner.

John Stewart's reading of the first draft of the manuscript for the University of Illinois Press indicated areas that needed significant clarifications, especially fuller explanations of the ethnographic principles that underlie the study. His second reading let me know that I had cleared up those general problems but also indicated some specific work that still needed to be done. Both readings helped to make this a stronger and better book. An anonymous reader of the first draft encouraged me with an evaluation that gave me some useful directions to pursue in African American studies. Tom Green's positive evaluation of the second draft meant a great deal to me because of the respect I have for his scholarship in folklore and anthropology. Judy McCulloh helped me through the early phases of the publication process and Joan Catapano through the final stages; both of their efforts were necessary to the success of the project.

Traditionally, authors thank their spouses last, and while avoiding Faulkner's example at the beginning, I will follow literary ritual here at the end. My wife, Roseanne, shares the love of African American music with me, especially singers such as Arthur Prysock, Ella Fitzgerald, Ray Charles, and Aretha Franklin. She knows jazz standards from the first note, naming the title while I'm still struggling with the tune. She even adapted to my tastes in Texas swing and honky-tonk, and shares my love of dancing to rhythm and blues, soul, and Motown. Because of her aversion to loud smoky places, she didn't always go to hear music with me, but we made up for it with recorded music at home, dancing around our kitchen floor. She gave me emotional and intellectual support throughout the long process of doing the research and writing this book; her advice about the collaborative research chapter helped me work through crucial issues and gave it a new and more relevant direction. I thank her and everyone who helped me.

Folklore Research Across Racial Boundaries

But in my book when I teach my childrens,
I try to teach them all, we all the same color,
it don't mean nothing.
—Mollie Ford

Her name was Mollie Ford. She was an elderly black woman who lived on a small farm up a hollow off the Ohio River. She gave various dates of birth that would have made her 84, 97, or 103 when we talked in 1980. I was a 39–year-old folklorist doing field research in southern Ohio, and a local historian had suggested that I interview her. We sat on lawn chairs under a big tree near her house, and I recorded our conversation. The racial difference between us was not mentioned, but race did enter into our conversation. At one point she was telling me about the inner-city children in a program sponsored by the Catholic Church who used to come to her farm to learn about rural life:

"Because I got thousands and thousands of childrens all in various regions, all nations and nationalities, but in my book when I teach my childrens, I try to teach them all, we all the same color, it don't mean nothing . . ."
"I believe that. We're all brothers and sisters."
She screamed in response, "THAT'S what I'm trying to tell the world, child."
"And I know it."
"It's no difference."
"I know it, and I believe it."
"And I'm here to tell you: I'm a witness to it," she whispered, "the color of your skin don't mean nothing."
"I know that."

And a few seconds later, "It's the truth if ever I told it. I don't care what we call ourselves, what color we are, we are just God's creation, and one man, one man ain't made no different than the other one."
"I know it."
"Woman ain't made no different . . . There ain't but one race created on earth, and that's the human race . . . And you can tell them I said so." (Mullen 1992, 33)

She had turned the interview into a sermon by invoking the traditional African American call-and-response pattern, and I had responded in a culturally appropriate way. I thought at the time and still think now that the way we interacted was completely spontaneous. As a folklorist I would call this a performance, but the experience itself made me feel that there was nothing artificial about it.

In my mind Mollie Ford and I had experienced a moment that transcended racial difference through our emotional agreement about racial equality, and we had done so within a cultural frame that was African American. I eventually wrote a paper analyzing our encounter that later became a chapter in *Listening to Old Voices: Folklore, Life Stories, and the Elderly* (Mullen 1992, 25–42). Scholars who responded to the paper or presentations about Mollie Ford sometimes thought I had romanticized the entire event and that Mollie Ford was putting me on, telling me what she thought I wanted to hear. I have romanticized her to a certain extent, but I cannot deny what felt real to me at the time and still does in my memory.

I gave a lecture about Mollie Ford at Western Kentucky University several years later, and the reaction of the audience made me reconsider issues of cultural representation, specifically how a white folklorist depicts a black person in terms of preconceived racial notions. I showed the audience a photograph of Mollie Ford that I took the day of the interview. She is wearing a scarf wrapped around her head and tied in front, a traditional African American head covering that some black women still wear. I also played excerpts from the taped interview, and her high-pitched southern dialect filled the room. About twenty minutes into the lecture, a group of five or six black students stood up in the back of the room and walked out. I immediately thought it was a racial protest against my lecture, and I began to imagine all the things I might have done to offend them. I thought that they might have thought that I was depicting her as the stereotyped "Aunt Jemima" or "Mammy" figure. The history of folklore scholarship is full of such stereotyped images because folklorists have concentrated field research on black people who fit our preconceived ideas about the folk. Until the 1960s, black folk had meant poor, uneducated, rural people, and here I was reinforcing racial stereotypes by focusing on an elderly black woman with a traditional headdress who spoke in dialect.

I worried about this all night and even talked about my concerns with several Western Kentucky folklorists the next day. Then one of them told me that the black students had left to attend a night class. My worry was over nothing, but I continued to think about issues of cultural representation of blacks and realized that even though I was mistaken in this instance, my concerns were real and had profound implications for the study of African American folklore by white folklorists.

European Americans have been interested in African American vernacular traditions since slavery (Jackson 1967, xv–xxiii), and the roots of white perceptions of blacks as a folk group go back just as far. The way whites perceived black people and the way that perception reflects on whites' perceptions of themselves has been an important part of American culture since colonial times (Morrison 1992), and folklore studies have played a significant role in racial dynamics ever since the academic designation of American blacks as a folk in the late nineteenth century (Wiggins 1988, 29). In this book I want to examine the history of folklore scholarship to better understand how African Americans were represented as a folk and how those cultural representations reveal the ways white folklorists imagined themselves. I shall consider several key twentieth-century folklorists as well as include a reflexive dimension in which I critique some of my own fieldwork and publications on African American folklore. Many different groups have been constructed in racial terms throughout American history, and race theories can be applied to all of them—Jewish, Irish, Italian, Chinese, Mexican, and Native Americans to name a few—but I shall concentrate on race as defined between African Americans and European Americans, the way ideas about blackness and whiteness have interacted in determining what it means to be American (Morrison 1992). This book is not meant to be an exhaustive study of race in America; rather my hope is that by examining one area of race relations in some depth and detail this study will make a contribution to overall racial discourse in the United States.

Folklorists and other ethnographers bring certain subjective assumptions to their fieldwork and subsequent interpretations of cultural materials, so knowledge of the personal background of the researcher is a valuable component for understanding their scholarship. I will give a few biographical facts here and a more detailed account at the end of the introduction. I am an Anglo-American folklorist with a strong interest in African American folklore, which has something to do with my birthplace in Beaumont, Texas, and my childhood largely spent in the segregated South in the 1940s and '50s. On the personal level, this book is an attempt to figure out some of the reasons I was attracted to the study of African American culture and to examine some of the ways I have conducted fieldwork in black communities and portrayed African Americans in my teaching and publications. But the personal is only a small part of my overall study of white scholarly representations of black as folk.

The history of folklore scholarship on African Americans has significant implications for the broader study of current racial and cultural politics. Specifically sociologist/folklorist Newbell Niles Puckett, folksong scholars John and Alan Lomax, and folklorist Roger Abrahams were influential in determining how Americans perceive African Americans. The Lomaxes had more widespread influence outside academic circles, but Puckett and Abrahams made important contributions to the scholarship. Many other scholars and writers also made important contributions to African American folklore scholarship—especially Elsie Clews Parsons (1923), Zora Neale Hurston (1935), Sterling Brown, Arthur P. Davis, and Ulysses Lee (1941), Melville Herskovits (1941), Arthur Huff Fauset (1944), Langston Hughes and Arna Bontemps (1958), James Mason Brewer (1968), Harry Middleton Hyatt (1970–78), Bruce Jackson (1974), Gladys-Marie Fry (1975), Daryl Cumber Dance (1978), Gerald Davis (1985), William Wiggins (1987), John Roberts (1989), and John W. Work (2005)—but the four I concentrate on here are representative of the research of white folklorists from the beginning of the twentieth century to the present.

Research on the history of African American folklore scholarship has been spotty at best; we have several important studies of John Lomax (see chapter 3) and Zora Neale Hurston (see chapter 2), but there is a dearth of research on black folklorists. Adrienne Lanier Seward made a good beginning in her article "The Legacy of Early Afro-American Folklore Scholarship" (1983), and John Szwed made an early contribution with an introduction to the work of the neglected black folklorist Arthur Huff Fauset (1971). More recently John Roberts has given us a theoretical frame from which to interpret the history of African American folklore scholarship (2000), Gerald Davis has investigated the important early research of Thomas W. Talley (2000), Cassandra Stancil has done the same for Carter G. Woodson (2000), and Robert Gordon and Robert Nemerov have found and published important lost manuscripts by black scholars John W. Work, Lewis Wade Jones, and Samuel C. Adams, Jr. (Work 2005). As Gerald Davis points out, the "insider" perspective of these black folklorists presents a very different cultural representation of African Americans than that of their white counterparts, "paralleling the development of American folklore as a legitimate academic discipline—including the discovery, articulation, and maintenance of the rather unflattering, and sometimes primitive, notions of African-American expressive performance that American folklorists liberally shared with their social science and humanities brothers and sisters—was a vigorous, dynamic, hermeneutic enterprise of research and interpretation of African-American materials by African-American scholars" (2000, 93).

The research to correct this gap in the historical scholarship is well underway now, and I leave that enterprise to the black folklorists who are currently undertaking the research. They will provide an insider perspective on those original insider scholars while I try to do the same with white folklorists who were cultural outsiders. I do not mean to suggest that black scholars should study only African American cultures or whites European American cultures. In fact, I hope that more black scholars will engage in the examination of whiteness. Because the power differential between white researchers and their black subjects causes problems of cultural representation, self-representation by black scholars becomes a major scholarly goal, but it will take both black and white perspectives on both cultures to accomplish a thorough scholarship.

Although I am concentrating on white folklorists, scholarship by black folklorists and scholars will be an important part of my approach since they provide the other side of the dynamic opposition of racial construction. For instance, in analyzing the African American folk belief research of Newbell Niles Puckett in the 1920s and '30s, I shall compare it to the research on hoodoo beliefs by Zora Neale Hurston during the same period. As a black southerner, Hurston provides a clear contrast to Puckett's white southern assumptions. She was critical of white scholars who were studying African American folklore, and she established an important critical perspective for all folklorists and scholars who followed. Another revealing comparison is between Alan Lomax's research in the Mississippi Delta and that of black scholars John W. Work, Lewis Wade Jones, and Samuel C. Adams, Jr. (Work 2005). In addition to the field researchers, African American theorists such as Toni Morrison (1992), Henry Louis Gates (1985, 1988), bell hooks (1990, 1992), Gerald Davis (1992, 2000), Cornell West (1994), and John Roberts (2000) have provided significant critiques of the scholarship on race. I use their theories throughout this work.

One thing they all agree on is that race relations have to be considered as hegemonic discourse; that is, whites' relations with blacks always take place within a power differential in which whites are dominant. What Bernth Lindfors says about European cultural displays of Africans historically also applies to folklorists' research on African Americans: those displays "tended to replicate and reinforce the dynamics of the unequal relationship that had existed between colonizer and colonized, master and slave. Africans were again denigrated, humiliated, dehumanized, and exploited" (1999, x). Despite the good intentions of many liberal white researchers, the results of their research often misrepresented cultures and functioned to maintain power over black subjects. As John Stewart pointed out in his evaluation of an earlier draft of this book, "The issue turns on power, and the experience of exploitation among the powerless, not on the liberal's penchant for 'accommodation.'" In this study, I always will consider white researchers' thoughts and actions and the responses of their black subjects within the context of that power structure.

A fundamental principle of this study is that race is "socially constructed," that is, race is not scientifically based in biological difference but is culturally determined. When we see a person with different skin color or physical features, our perceptions of that person are grounded in attitudes learned within our own culture. As literary critic Henry Louis Gates, Jr., says: "Race, as a meaningful criterion within the biological sciences, has long been recognized to be a fiction" (1985, 4). Racial difference, once one gets beyond perceived physical difference, is imagined; it is not intrinsic and not biologically based. All too often cultural assumptions about race are stereotypes that reinforce prejudice and influence racist behavior. Even though social constructions of race exist, by definition, in the imagination, they are real in terms of behavior: when a lynching takes place, the "imagined" racial differences have very real and horrific consequences. Folklore studies may be academic, but the implications of racial representations in folklore are significant beyond academic life.

Critical race theory began to develop in the scholarship in the late 1980s and early '90s as a means of focusing on the dynamics of interaction between races (Crenshaw et al.1995; Delgado and Stefancic 2001). It is grounded in the social construction of reality and concentrates on how concepts of blackness and whiteness are inextricably intertwined (Morrison 1992). This social/intellectual process has been going on for hundreds of years and can be seen in journals, diaries, letters, and novels—in fiction and nonfiction. As white scholars wrote about African Americans as folk, they not only created images of blackness, they also constructed whiteness since concepts of the two races were oppositionally determined. Blackness was explicitly described, but whiteness was implicitly imbedded in white descriptions of blacks. Whiteness was the unexamined side of the opposition because it was considered to be the norm (hooks 1992, 30). This is one of the reasons why the present study focuses on white folklorists: their constructions of blackness as folkness have been assumed to be factual and have therefore gone unexamined in folklore scholarship except for a few important recent scholarly works (Roberts 2000).

Critical white studies have arisen in the last fifteen years to more thoroughly examine the white side of the dynamic (Delgado and Stefancic 1997; Fine et al. 1997; Ware and Back 2002). I will use theories from white studies to analyze the way folklorists' representations of black folk implied underlying assumptions about whiteness. Obviously, the study of race includes the study of racism, and it is important to recognize the effects of racism on the victim, "But equally valuable is a serious intellectual effort to see what racial ideology does to the mind, imagination, and behavior of masters" (Morrison 1992, 12). My examination of white folklorists, then, will take racism into account, but this is not primarily a study of racism per se, but a study of the broader issues of racial representation. My major purpose is not to identify instances of racism in the writings of white folklorists, but to better understand the processes whereby racial concepts inform what they write.

Toni Morrison's *Playing in the Dark* (1992) has been especially useful to me in theoretical terms; her critique of the way white concepts of blackness were part of a cultural process of creating whiteness in American literature has application to American folklore studies grounded in ethnographic fieldwork. Morrison's critical focus on whiteness is important because, as bell hooks points out: "Those progressive white intellectuals who are particularly critical of 'essentialist' notions of identity when writing about mass culture, race, and gender have not focused their critiques on white identity and the way essentialism informs representations of whiteness" (1992, 30). Although Morrison is dealing with American fiction, her literary theories have direct relevance to ethnographic and folkloric writing. She coins the term "Africanism" for "the denotative and connotative blackness that African peoples have come to signify, as well as the entire range of views, assumptions, readings, and misreadings that accompany Eurocentric learning about these people" (1992, 6–7). "What Africanism became for, and how it functioned in, the literary imagination is of paramount interest because it may be possible to discover, through a close look at literary 'blackness,' the nature—even the cause—of literary 'whiteness' . . . What parts do the invention and development of whiteness play in the construction of what is loosely described as 'American'?" (1992, 9). Melville Herskovits defined Africanism much earlier in a more general way as "African cultural heritage in the New World" (1941, 3).

I suggest that the "literary imagination" includes the "ethnographic imagination" since literature and ethnography both are imagined constructions of reality. Fiction is more open to the imagination, but ethnography is not simply objective fact; rather, it is a process of interpretation that is at least partially fictionalized (Clifford and Marcus 1986, 98–121). The ethnographer and folklorist are more limited than the novelist in the ways they can represent reality, but their representations of the world they observe are still filtered through their imaginations and culturally learned assumptions. Morrison emphasizes that in order to critique the written construction of blackness and whiteness, the scholar needs to examine language closely—the connotative words, images, metaphors, and other literary devices that are the means whereby writers create the Africanist persona (1992, v–xiii, 67–69). I propose to take, in Morrison's words, a "close look" at the way white folklorists' construction of blackness in their published work on African American folklore, especially their language, reveals the nature and cause of their assumptions about whiteness, and where relevant the way black writers' constructions of racial difference are part of the dynamic. Critical race theory makes it clear that white folklorists' romantic and pathological conceptions of African Americans were part of a larger complex and often contradictory cultural process in which fear and desire toward blackness were maintained simultaneously. By applying this theory, we can determine how American folklore scholars not only helped to create the image of African Americans as folk in the popular imagination but also how folklore studies are implicated in the construction of whiteness in America.

To Morrison and other critical race theorists, race is at the center of American consciousness. Going back to the eighteenth century, "It was this Africanism, deployed as rawness and savagery, that provided the staging ground and arena for the elaboration of the quintessential American identity" (1992, 44). The necessity of race to Americaness continued through the nineteenth and twentieth centuries and remains central to our identity today: "Race, in fact, now functions as a metaphor so necessary to the construction of Americaness that it rivals the old pseudoscientific and class-informed racisms whose dynamics we are more used to deciphering" (47). Morrison does not use ethnographic examples to illustrate this point, but there are plenty at hand: Newbell Niles Puckett and John Lomax were both grounded in the nineteenth-century pseudoscience of cultural evolution, and later twentieth-century folklorists such as Alan Lomax, Roger Abrahams, and I continued to use race as a central metaphor, sometimes unconsciously, for American identity.

Following Morrison's lead, literary critics have done a better job examining literary representations of blackness and whiteness, but not much has been done on how folkness and blackness and whiteness relate together in folklore studies. The scholarship of Puckett, John and Alan Lomax, Abrahams, and my own provides revealing primary material for such a study because we are all to one degree or another examples of what Frantz Fanon called "the [white] man who adores the Negro" (1967 [1952], 8); that is, strongly attracted to African American culture and motivated by good intentions. Fanon was writing in 1952, and "Negro" was the accepted term used by both blacks and whites at the time; it remained so until the late 1960s and early '70s when "black" became the norm. All of the folklorists examined in this study used "Negro" in their writings including the early publications of Roger Abrahams and myself; therefore, "Negro" in the title suggests the historical nature of the book, and I will use it in appropriate historical contexts while using "black" elsewhere. "Adore" still has ongoing significance in describing the way white folklorists romanticize African American culture, and I will explain the nuances of its meaning later in the introduction.

I will examine the historical record and my own research from the perspective of reflexive ethnography which says that the ethnographer must recognize his or her own subjective position as an influence on the fieldwork and subsequent cultural representations of the people being studied (Fabian 1983; Clifford and Marcus 1986; Marcus and Fischer 1986; Hufford 1995). Recognition of subjectivity is especially important in the study of race since the construction of race is by definition a subjective process. The most scientific of social scientists is still subjective in his or her study of others. When folklorists or anthropologists conduct field research, their underlying assumptions influence their perceptions of and behavior toward the people with whom they are working. They select certain kinds of data to collect and ignore other kinds partially based on their own cultural attitudes.

The focus on white subjectivity in the present study could lead to an imbalance of cultural representation and the neglect of black experience. As literature scholar John Hellmann (2006) pointed out to me, "An unrelieved focus on the subjectivity of the folklorist—psychological, theoretical, political—however admirable a quest to increase 'self-awareness' on the part of folklorists, may produce a danger of repeating what it is studying (i.e., a book in which representations of blacks are discussed purely in terms of the projections of folklorists)." I have tried to avoid this possibility by keeping the dynamic model of critical race theory in mind throughout—the two-way process of the construction of race involves not only white imagined blackness but also the reality of black life. For instance, white social scientists studying residents of black inner-city neighborhoods in the 1960s observed and interviewed black informants to provide data for their studies. These were often areas with high crime rates and some social dysfunction. That was a social reality. The problem came when white researchers interpreted the causes of the social problems in racial terms and applied them to black people in general from their narrow research findings (see chapter 6). Stereotypes entered into the scholarship based on both imagined blackness and the reality of behaviors in contexts of poverty and racism.

Finally then, the articles, books, records, films, museum exhibits, and festivals produced by folklorists and other fieldworkers are cultural representations of the groups being studied, not, as some observers assume, the culture itself. Each individual scholar filters his or her observations through a cultural and personal lens. The resulting representation, like the concept of race, is a subjective social construction that will undergo change through time. Newbell Niles Puckett's 1920s and '30s publications about African American folk beliefs reveal the racial attitudes of his time, just as John Lomax's books and records from the 1910s to the 1940s are products of his historical context and my publications are of mine. This is not to say that culture itself entirely determines human behavior; rather, individuals create culture through their behaviors and expressions, whether artistic or scholarly. A dynamic interplay exists between the past and the present, between the group and the individual. Individuals are influenced by past practices and current group attitudes, but they make individual decisions that have moral and ethical implications in the present. My theoretical model is culture as dynamic symbolic process, not as static superorganic determinant of behavior. I am among those ethnographers who followed Ruth Benedict and Victor Turner in insisting "on culture as creative process and on the ways in which performers and performances . . . not only follow but also revise and revitalize accepted rules, acting out and challenging aesthetic conventions and social values . . . More than simply reflecting or expressing social structure and worldview, any significant new form reconstructs cultural reality . . ."(Babcock 1993, 225–26). This is as true of the cultural productions of scholars as it is of the folk performers we study. Within particular cultural contexts, individual folklorists produce cultural representations, and once those products are out there in published or recorded form then they too become part of the cultural context whereby others are influenced in their perceptions of African Americans or other groups deemed to be folk.

The white researcher, then, is trapped in his or her cultural perception of blackness, and white cultural assumptions will remain part of the academic construction of African Americans as folk. One promising solution to this problem is collaborative or reciprocal ethnography (Foley 2001; Lawless 1992), for white folklorists and other social scientists to work closely with black scholars and members of the black community being studied. This involves the sharing of field research findings, the testing of interpretations, and when there is a difference of interpretation, including all sides in published results (Lawless 1992). This is in keeping with Johannes Fabian's (1971) concept of intersubjectivity: since absolute objectivity is impossible, the ideal is to consider various subjective positions to arrive at a consensus of intersubjectivity that in this case would include cross-racial dialogue even before research results are published. I have attempted collaborative research in interviews and writing with Reverend Jesse Truvillion about his life story from 1995 to 2000 and in my fieldwork on black children's rhymes from 2000 to 2002. Those efforts were successful to a certain point, but complications ended the collaboration with Reverend Truvillion. I will explain the complex issues of collaborative research across racial boundaries in more depth and detail in chapters 7 and 8.

Like racial concepts, folkness is itself a cultural construction that is historically connected to the social conceptualization of blackness. The folk were invented during the eighteenth-century Enlightenment by Herder, Vico, and other European intellectuals (Wilson [1989] 1973). There was also a "historical connection between the Enlightenment and the institution of slavery—the rights of man and his enslavement" (Morrison 1992, 42) so that some important notions about race and the concept of folk originated during the same historical period. White Europeans were imagining an Other who was stuck in the past—in other words, traditional—to better define themselves as modern. The folk were originally conceived as rural, isolated, uneducated white Europeans with strong connections to an imagined romantic past that modern educated people had lost. But it did not take long before the folk and the racial primitive became associated as similarly inferior yet romantic classes. Part of the examination of representations of African Americans, then, is also an investigation of the changing concepts of folk and folklore (Roberts 2000).

Race consciousness has drawn a hard and fast line between black and white America, but the reality of cultural history indicates that there have been complex interchanges between European American and African American cultures from the beginning so it is a mistake to see their cultural expressions as separate and monolithic. One of the areas where interaction across racial lines has taken place historically is blackface minstrelsy; a large segment of the scholarship on race has focused on minstrelsy and white mimicry of black style from nineteenth-century minstrelsy to twenty-first century hip-hop (Roediger 1991; Lott 1993; Rogin 1996; Lhamon 1998, Tate 2003). I shall refer to that scholarship throughout this book, but as Susan Gubar reminds us, cross-racial mimicry is not one way: some light-skinned upwardly mobile black people have been attempting to pass for white since the nineteenth century. There are obvious differences between the mockery that is often a part of black-faced minstrelsy and the emulation of whiteness by black people for purposes of escaping racism and achieving upward mobility, but there are similarities in that both involve pretending to be the other race. Role playing across racial lines is what Gubar calls "racechange," and she sees this as evidence of the cultural intertwining of black and white: "The term is meant to suggest the traversing of race boundaries, racial imitation or impersonation, cross-racial mimicry or mutability, white posing as black or black passing as white, pan-racial mutuality" (1997, 5).

Her study concentrates on cross-racial mimicry in the arts, but I propose to apply the concept to folklore scholarship in which white scholars attracted to African American culture use their research and writing as a means to fathom "the inscrutable Negro soul" (Puckett 1926, vii). There is ample evidence in the scholarship to indicate that white folklorists were attempting to become black on symbolic and emotional levels to acquire a greater understanding of African American folk culture and to satisfy their own psychological needs. Newbell Niles Puckett wrote poetry in black dialect, Alan Lomax sang and played blues in a black style, Roger Abrahams modeled his politics after '60s black militancy, and I danced to rhythm and blues music in imitation of African American dance styles even as we all pursued our social scientific research on black folk culture. The current generation of white folklore scholars who study African American culture reflects the same pattern: for instance, Barry Lee Pearson (1984, 1990, 2003), David Evans (1982), and others play blues guitar and conduct research on African American blues music. No doubt this has given them rapport with the musicians they interview and a valuable perspective on the role of music in the culture, but such white scholarly mimicry of black styles has not been thoroughly critiqued. The study of white folklorists who take part in the cultural process of mimicry has implications for the study of white artists who mimic black styles;

the white folklorist who writes black dialect poetry is very different than the white performer who sings blues or hip-hop, but there are some intriguing underlying connections.

The other side of the cross-racial process would be black writers and scholars who feel that through their educational upward mobility they have left their African American folkness behind as they symbolically pass for white in the academic world—at least this would be the perspective of writers who romanticize the black folk past as the source of black identity in the present (Favor 1999, 2–4). Examples of this tendency among black intellectuals would include literary scholars Houston A. Baker, Jr. (1984) and Henry Louis Gates, Jr. (1988) who formulated theories that reified African American folkness as unique (Favor 1999, 4–6). If folkness is the pure source of black authenticity, then upward mobility through education means abandoning one's lower-class folk roots and becoming more white in the process, symbolically passing. Both white mimicry and black passing are based in racial images that fuse race, folk, and class into complex social constructions with profound implications for scholarly research and cultural representation.

In her book Gubar recognizes the problems inherent in black and white scholars trying to cross racial boundaries to conduct research:

> The query "How can white people understand or sympathize with African Americans without distorting or usurping their perspective?" too glibly assumes that there is such a perspective. Indeed, how can one posit a genuine, uncontaminated white cultural identity or a unique black racial autonomy, given the cross-racial entanglements and influences mapped throughout these pages? What the history of racechange teaches is that race and color are not immutable categories but classifications with permeable boundaries. Or, to put it another way, that neither black nor white . . . artistic productions, experiences, groups of people . . . can be understood as unitary, entire, monolithic, coherent" (1997, 247).

This idea not only undermines racist assumptions about difference, it also suggests that scholars on both sides of the color line can justifiably speak about the other since they share many commonalities as well as differences especially in terms of the influence of African American culture on European Americans. Black writer Albert Murray formulated a similar concept some thirty years ago in *The Omni-Americans: New Perspectives on Black Experience and American Culture* (1970) when he said that American culture is "incontestably mulatto." James Baldwin said it more philosophically, "Each of us, helplessly and forever, contains the other—male in female, female in male, white in black and black in white. We are a part of each other. Many of my countrymen appear to find this fact exceedingly inconvenient and even unfair and so, very often, do I. But none of us can do anything about it" (quoted in Ware and Back 2002, 83). Within the community that we designate folk, Mollie Ford expressed the same idea, "We all the same color, it don't mean nothing . . ."

Despite the recognition of a racially hybrid mainstream American culture, social constructions based on race purity continue to be espoused on both sides. For instance, black intellectuals have created a concept of African American cultural authenticity that ironically overlaps with the white folklorists' concept of African American as folk since both depend on an imagined pure community of southern rural uneducated blacks isolated from outside influences. This worked to reinforce white scholars' preconceived romantic notions about black folk and to keep them situated in an inferior position, and it gave black writers and scholars a cultural and historical source for African American uniqueness and authenticity. As J. Martin Favor says, "The definition of blackness is constantly being invented, policed, transgressed, and contested. When hip-hop artists remind themselves and their audiences to 'stay black' or 'keep real,' they are implicitly suggesting that there is a recognizable, repeatable, and agreed upon thing that we might call black authenticity . . ." (1999, 2).

According to Favor, authentic blackness has little to do with skin color—someone can be light-skinned and be considered authentically black or vice versa—but blackness is historically grounded in African American folkness. "The critical discourse of blackness . . . places the 'folk'—southern, rural, and poor—at its forefront." In the construction of the folk "certain utterances . . . are accorded a greater value, a larger measure of 'authenticity,' than others" (1999, 4). This pattern can be found in the writings of black intellectuals from W. E. B. Du Bois' *The Souls of Black Folk* (1903) to Harlem Renaissance novelists and poets such as Zora Neale Hurston (1935, 1937) and Jean Toomer (1923) to recent literary theorists Houston A. Baker, Jr. (1984) and Henry Louis Gates, Jr. (1988). They all reified folkness as part of black authenticity, but they also recognized the complexity of black identity formation in terms of the influence of racism, class, and urban environments. Like white folklorists Newbell Niles Puckett, John Lomax, and Alan Lomax, black writers conceived the folk as lower class; for white folklorists this meant upwardly mobile black people ceased to be folk, and for some black intellectuals, middle-class African Americans were likely to be less authentically black. Not all black intellectuals accepted this view; for instance, Ralph Ellison recognized the power and beauty of African American folk culture while maintaining the possibility of an authentic black identity for middle-class educated blacks. *Invisible Man* (1952) is in many ways the story of a man's search for a black identity that included his rural southern background but was not dependent on it. The invisible man both embraces and rejects folkness in the course of the novel.

The problem with both white and black constructions of the folk as a pure source of blackness is that they can be used to reinforce essentialist racial categories: "Returning ultimately to folk culture, or some derivation of it, may also prove problematic because such a strategy never quite destabilizes notions of 'race' and difference that can be, and have been, used in the service of political and cultural oppression" (Favor 1999, 6). Since authenticity is itself socially constructed and not absolute (Handler and Linnekin 1984; Bendix 1997), we must ask ourselves, "Authentic to whom and for what reasons?" There were political reasons for black and white writers and scholars to define folk in romantic and mythic ways, and I shall examine those reasons more closely in the following chapters.

The tendency to dichotomize based on racial assumptions has been a strong current in cultural history for over two hundred years, and it continues to be a persistent idea and practice. We need new theoretical concepts to help us break the hold of racial separation, and Susan Gubar's racechange offers such a new paradigm: "A consideration of white appropriation of black images ... uncovers the extent to which mainstream American culture, no longer Anglo-American, has moved in the course of this century to becoming not only indebted to black aesthetic forms and traditions but itself profoundly African American. Such a fusion holds out the promise of future reciprocity and respect, in the place of past thievery and scorn. A post-racist society cannot possibly come into being until Americans comprehend how the dualism of 'black' versus 'white' has operated to hide the cross-racial dynamics of our interwoven cultural pasts" (1997, 45).

If we accept that we now live in an American society in which African American cultural influences are pervasive, that American culture is, in fact, "profoundly African American," then perhaps we can undermine divisions based on race and replace them with the recognition of deeply interconnected cultures that have combined to form a hybrid American culture. As I examine white folklorists' concepts of folkness and race in the rest of this book, I will be consciously dismantling racial dualism as it existed throughout the nineteenth and twentieth centuries with the hope of constructing a new theoretical paradigm for the twenty-first century.

The idea that cultural hybridity contradicts the false dichotomy of racial difference is also compatible with certain theories and goals of white studies, especially "the new Abolitionism Project" that seeks "an end of whiteness" (Ware and Back 2002, 2). The idea here is that since whiteness can only be defined as "white supremacism; a set of beliefs, ideologies, and power structures rooted in the notion of natural, inherited, God-given superiority . . ." then whiteness must "eventually [be] rendered obsolete as a system of discriminating among humans" (5, 6). One of the ways of doing this is consistent with Gubar's idea about the "permeable boundaries" of racial categories that lead to hybrid cultures (1997, 247). Whiteness scholar Les Back studies American popular music in terms of how in certain circumstances white and black music have interacted to the point of being indistinguishable in sound. White musicians who backed up black singers in recording studios in Muscle Shoals, Alabama, and Memphis, Tennessee, in the 1960s were thought to be black by white and black listeners alike (Ware and Back 2002, 234–60). Since listeners could not see the musicians, they could not have their racial images reinforced. Visual culture is more significant than aural in constructing race (Wiegman 1995, 42): "If all we had was sound, if sound was the beginning and end of what defined a musician, then there would be no white musicians or black musicians, only the colors of sound" (Ware and Back 2002, 260). A particular sound may have originated in and be part of ongoing black cultural and social experience, but it is not racially based in a biological sense. Back and other scholars have focused on white musicians who are theoretically part of the minstrel tradition to delineate how the permeability of racial boundaries is worked out in specific contexts. Music is an important area of focus in my study as well, and I shall return to it many times throughout the book in terms of the problem of blackface minstrelsy and white mimicry of African American style, especially in the tendency of white folklorists' to mimic black style as part of their field research.

As I studied the lives and work of the early twentieth-century folklorists, I began to identify with them and the problems they encountered in studying cultures they perceived as fundamentally different from their own. At first I was extremely critical of the way Newbell Niles Puckett and John Lomax had dealt with black people; then I began to realize that they had to be studied in terms of their own historical context, not just from the racial perspectives of the 1990s and 2000s. This requires a delicate balance of position and tone: to recognize and condemn racism when it occurs but also to be fair in the portrayals of historical folklorists, to identify misrepresentations of African American culture in their work but also to recognize the contributions they made to scholarly knowledge and cultural understanding.

Similar problems occur in the self-examination dimension of this study: how do I treat an earlier version of myself, the young white folklorist who naively went into black communities to collect folklore in the 1960s and '70s? My intentions were good, and I did have a better understanding of African American culture than many other white scholars at the time, but looking back, I recognize many misunderstandings that were, ironically, a result of the innocence of my intentions (Duneier 1992, 137–55). As I began the self-reflexive part of this project, I had the same impulse to condemn myself as I had with the historical folklorists, but as I proceeded I grew more sympathetic toward my younger self. Again, position and tone had to be worked out. To understand why Frantz Fanon would say, "To us, the man who adores the Negro is as 'sick' as the man who abominates him" (1967 [1952], 8), I also must take into account the harsh criticisms that black intellectuals have made of white scholars who study African American culture. "Adore" is a rhetorical device, but it is hyperbole that powerfully suggests the depth of romantic fascination that some whites have with black culture. I recognize the truth of Fanon's statement: that the white bureaucrats and missionaries in colonial Africa in their attempts to do good did terrible harm, that self-identified innocence is often the basis for white scholars assuming the power to generalize about African American culture in ways that ultimately reinforce negative stereotypes (Duneier 1992, 138–39), and that white lovers of black culture can destroy the very thing they love (Cantwell 1996, 58). A theoretical connection runs between Fanon's rejection of racial adoration and the abolition of whiteness: once the concept of race as biological fact has been abolished, racial adoration will also fade away. As Fanon says, "In the absolute, the black is no more to be loved than the Czech, and truly what is to be done is to set man free" (1967 [1952], 9), free from the shackles of racism that include pathological images of blacks as inferior and romantic images of blacks as natural and exotic. Then African American music and dance can be appreciated for what they are—as different cultural expressions not related to biological difference.

Until that ideal state is reached, the intense white love of black remains part of historical cultural processes, and as one of those white men who "adores the Negro," I cannot fully accept Fanon's categorizing me with white men who abominate blacks. Although I recognize a pathological dimension to white love of African American culture, I do not view it as being as evil as racial hatred but rather as a complex mixture of fear and desire. Also Gubar suggests the possibility of white adoration of black as a potentially positive cultural process. Again, her concept of racechange offers a fresh paradigm by suggesting that white fascination with blackness has been an important factor in the creation of our present day hybrid American culture (1997, 45). I will attempt to examine the "sickness" of the Negrophile from a subjective position that takes into account positive results of racechange, although I realize that in this case foregrounding subjectivity could also be interpreted as self serving and that the use of white subjectivity has the possible negative outcome of reifying whiteness as a racial category.

The recognition of subjectivity that reflexive ethnography requires has other personal and scholarly pitfalls. How much personal information about the ethnographer should be included? Some reflexive ethnographies contain more personal details than are necessary to understand the subjective position; they become self-indulgent. I tell my students in fieldwork classes that they should include only personal information that is relevant to the immediate subject, and I have tried to follow my own advice in this work. I will refer to the personal only as it directly relates to my professional life. For reflexive purposes, then, I want at this point to more firmly establish my subjective position by giving a few details about my own background as it relates to racial concerns in my research.

I was born in 1941 in Beaumont, Texas—at that time a totally segregated city. My family lived there until I was in the second grade when my father went to work for a heavy construction company that built refineries and chemical plants, and we began to move throughout the United States and Canada. For about half my elementary and high school years we lived in Texas and Louisiana. The other half we lived in Alberta, California, Delaware, Ontario, and Indiana, usually for a year and at the most two. Wherever we lived it was racially segregated by law or by custom, or there were no black people at all. When I finished high school in Ontario in 1959, I returned to Beaumont to attend Lamar Tech, a college that had been integrated the previous year.

From the age of thirteen, I was a fan of African American rhythm and blues music and later developed a great interest in blues and jazz. That early fascination with black music led to an academic interest in African American culture in college and graduate school. In college I wrote a paper on "Folk Music in Modern Jazz: The Soul Movement" for a folklore class taught by Francis Abernethy, and he invited me to read it at a Texas Folklore Society meeting. My personal love of African American music turned to the beginning of a professional career. As an English major, I was mainly reading literature by whites in the early '60s, but on my own I started to read more broadly in African American literature. I continued to study literature and folklore in graduate school at the University of Texas in Austin, and my interests in African American culture grew, especially under the influence of Roger Abrahams with whom I had a graduate seminar. Americo Paredes directed my dissertation; his interests in ethnicity and cultural difference broadened the context in which I considered African American folklore. The dissertation was based on fieldwork I had conducted among commercial fishermen on the Gulf Coast of Texas, and it contained a chapter on interviews I had done with black fishermen. During the field research along the Gulf, I recorded a black street performer named Bongo Joe and later wrote an article about him (see chapter 5). By this point, African American culture was firmly established as part of my academic focus.

My interest in black culture continued after I finished my PhD and started teaching at Ohio State. Over the years I have conducted research on African American folklore in Columbus, Cleveland, Cincinnati, and Portsmouth, Ohio, and in rural southern Ohio—documenting storytelling, preaching and church singing, quilting, traditional cooking, performing blues and gospel music, and playing children's games and rhymes. Also I have done research in black communities in the Blue Ridge Mountains of Virginia and North Carolina, concentrating on the telling of courtship stories, religious conversion narratives, and life stories of the elderly.

That lifetime of research began when I was working on my dissertation and recorded a black storyteller in Sabine Pass, Texas. In the interest of reflexive ethnography, I want to return to that fieldwork experience in the first chapter of this book. In the second chapter I go back to an earlier point in the history of folklore scholarship to determine some of the basic attitudes toward race that influenced the folklorists who followed, including me. The rest of the book will go back and forth between my own field research and that of other folklorists and between the past and the present in an attempt to show how individual and professional concerns interact in the scholarly construction of race.

1

Race Relations in Folklore Fieldwork

"The Rabbit, the Lion, and the Man"
—tale told by Junior Carter

In 1967 in Sabine Pass, Texas, I interviewed and recorded two black men about traditions in their lives, and both what we said and how the three of us interacted have implications for race relations in the profession of folklore studies and in society. I was a twenty-six-year-old folklorist, still in graduate school, on one of my first field research trips, interviewing Captain Son Brill and his friend Junior Carter on the bridge of Captain Brill's fishing boat. Captain Brill was sixty-four and had been a commercial pogie fisherman in Jacksonville, Florida since he was twelve. Junior Carter was in his early thirties, originally from South Carolina, and worked in the plant that processed the pogie fish. We talked about occupational traditions and race relations in the fishing business. Junior Carter also told several jokes and tales.

I have written about Son Brill's legends and beliefs elsewhere (Mullen 1978, 84–93), and I have used Junior Carter's stories in folklore classes for years, but in all my previous work on them I had concentrated on the texts within their broader cultural context without considering the immediate context of the interview—specifically how racial and cultural differences influenced what went on. As I indicated in the introduction, this is an exercise in "reflexive ethnography" (Clifford and Marcus 1986), a looking back at an incident in my professional life, trying to see it within the historical context of 1967 from the perspective of the present moment that has been influenced by the intervening years of fieldwork experience and writing folklore. Reflexivity means that I must consider my subjective position both within the fieldwork situation and the contexts in which I interpreted the collected material.

The boat that Son Brill, Junior Carter, and I were on was tied up less than twenty-five miles from where I was born—Beaumont, Texas, a mainly segregated city in 1967. I had been studying African American folklore and culture in graduate school and was still a romantic fan of black music and cultural style (see the introduction). I slowly learned about what was later called "cultural hegemony"—the exercise of power by a dominant culture—but at the time I was barely aware of such things as the exploitation of black musicians by white producers and record companies, and I had no idea that white scholars were also exploiting black folk, that, in fact, I was part of a process of academic exploitation. Even after I became more politically aware, I still had the tendency that white fans have of romanticizing African American culture, a more subtle form of racism than I had grown up with. Out of this background came the young white folklorist interviewing black people for the first time. I had not taken any ethnographic fieldwork courses, and my academic knowledge of the culture had not prepared me for this kind of fieldwork. In some ways, this may have been an advantage since Son Brill, Junior Carter, and I had to work out together the way we would talk about black/white relationships.

As I interviewed Brill and Carter, I made many "communicative blunders," to use Charles Briggs's term for the mistakes ethnographers make when they attempt to force an interview structure on informants who may have their own cultural ways of communicating information that the interviewer is not aware of (1986, 26, 109). As city-dwellers and television watchers, Brill and Carter understood the nature of an interview, and their speech also contained examples of metacommunication—"statements that report, describe, interpret, and evaluate communicative acts and processes" (2)—that I did not understand at the time. As Briggs points out, we can learn how to better understand and interpret discourse across cultural and racial lines by closely examining the communicative blunders in our ethnographic interviews (4). Brill, Carter, and I were coming from different cultural backgrounds with different ways of speaking, but the conversation we had was a mutual process of creating meaning (25).

We did not talk directly about race at first; rather Junior Carter told a series of obscene jokes—a country bumpkin who does not know about modern toilets, a man who complains about the size of his wife's vagina, a man who is worn out from sexual intercourse with an insatiable woman, a boy having intercourse with his grandmother, and a man looking for crabs in a town called My Ass, Florida. The first joke he told established the tone.

"Say that guy left from Georgia, going to New York. He had never used the bathroom on the train before, so he asked the conductor if he could go to take a crap, you know. The bathroom—the conductor told him, 'You can go right back in there and use that room right in there.' He went in there and the lights was off. So he pulled his pants down and sat down, and the bowl was real cold, you know. So he jumped up and reached up and tipped the light on, you know. So he say, 'Damn, my mama ain't never let me shit in her bread pan before.'" Brill chuckled. "So he saw the window heisted, backed up there and sticks his ass out the window, you know, and started shitting. So after awhile, they passed by the street, and there was men scooping up the sidewalk with a shovel; they saw that ass out the window, and they went to whipping him with that shovel, you know. So when he came back, the conductor say, 'How you find the shitting?' He say, 'I find it successful, but that electric asswiper you got gonna kill somebody yet.'" Brill and I laughed.

Junior Carter told this story first, I think, because he assumed that Brill and I shared certain attitudes with him—a modern urban perspective and an awareness of the country bumpkin stereotype. Jokes of this nature are often told among white and black storytellers who are members of groups freshly removed from the country. My parents both grew up in rural environments, and Junior Carter's and Son Brill's probably did too. We could share in our superior status as we laughed at the ignorance of the bumpkin. Race was not mentioned directly in the story, but the assumption might have been made that the man on the train was black. In which case, this could be part of the minstrel stereotype, and Junior Carter was laughing with a white man about the antics of a black bumpkin, thus making the storyteller superior to the racial stereotype.

Another early story Junior Carter told also had an implied racial stereotype in it. "Said, uh, one time a man had a mule, you know, a pretty mule way back there in the olden days with a saddle on him, you know. He had the mule trained, you know, ever time you goose him in the side the mule would break wind, you know, phhht. A woman standing on the corner, says, 'Hey. Give me a ride to town.' He say, 'I don't mind getting you to town, but I got a deal.' She said, 'What is it?' 'Ever time my mule break wind,' said, 'we gotta stop and fuck.'" Brill chuckled at this point. "She says, 'Okay, okay.' So they went on down the road a little bit, and he hit the mule on the side, you know, and the mule say, 'Phhht.' 'Whoa! Fuck time!'" I laughed then. "He stopped and him and her fucked, you know. Goddamn, really giving it good to the woman, you know. They went on up a little further, about another mile or two, he goosed the mule in the damn side, and the mule hauled off and farted again. 'Phoooo.'" Brill chuckled again. "'Whoa, fuck time!' And he gave that woman a good fucking that time. Got on the mule and started on back to town. So she saw what he did. She goosed the mule in the side, and the mule broke wind. Say, 'Hey, your mule done broke wind.' 'Get up, mule, go on into town.' After awhile they got in there by a puddle of water, you know, where it was cool and a lot of trees. Hauled off and goosed the mule in the side. Said, 'Hey, mister, your mule done broke wind. Time for us to fuck.' He said, 'I wouldn't give a goddamn if that mule shit, I'm going to town.'" All three of us laughed.

Roger Abrahams says of this story, "This picture of women as sexual creatures is not simply one projected into expressive lore. To the contrary, the image of the sexually demanding woman arises from real situations which the men themselves see as taxing" (1970b, 115). The story may be culture specific in the gender roles it portrays, but it is also cross-cultural: both black and white men have the insatiable woman stereotype as part of their expressive lore. Junior Carter, Son Brill, and I were interacting on the basis of shared stereotypes and of common experience with women. This was partly based on a sexist stereotype and partly on an admission by men that they sometimes cannot keep up with a woman's sexual desire.

Some of the jokes Carter told were indirectly about race since they projected certain stereotypes about black men and women, but they also established a masculine bond between the three of us that temporarily transcended race. I did not recognize what was happening at the time, that I had brought my own sexist attitudes to the situation. My education in feminism was not to begin for another couple of years, but from the perspective of the first decade of a new century, I now see the irony of momentarily displacing racism with sexism. We were all laughing together at this locker-room humor even though segregation would not allow us to share the same locker room. We came together as men laughing at women as sex objects. This sexist process actually enabled us to establish a rapport that made it easier to talk about race later.

The subject of race came up as a result of talking about the pogie fishing industry that in Sabine Pass was all black, from the crews to the captains. I asked, "How did that come about, that it's all Negro?" Son Brill replied: "Well [six-second pause], most of that is [seven-second pause] from uhh, I would say, getting along, one part, it's hard to mix uhh [Carter agrees "Um umm" at this point as if he knows what Brill is going to say and wants to encourage him to mention race directly] colored captain, white captain." I interjected, "Yeah," also to help him talk about something that was difficult for a black man and white man to talk about. Clearly, Brill was hesitant to talk about race directly; before he did there were long pauses, false starts, and formulaic phrases. A few minutes later in bringing up another aspect of racism, he did it again: "I would say, I'll tell you something else now [four-second pause], believe it or not [five-second pause before he mentions an example of racism]." "I would say" and "I'll tell you something else" are examples of metacommunication, and he used them throughout the interview; they foreground the communication process itself, drawing the listener's attention to what he is saying as communication (Babcock 1984, 66). Using the first person pronoun "I" and the second person "you" emphasizes the interview situation, the speaker and the listener interacting. In this case, Brill's metacommunication functions both to delay and emphasize the importance of what he is about to say. As an elderly southern black man from a segregated society in 1967, Brill may have been talking directly about race with a white person for the first time, and this was certainly the first time I had done so, which helps to explain our hesitance.

Early in our discussion, I revealed my liberal idealism by mentioning the possibility of racial cooperation, "I saw, I met a colored guy working on a boat, shrimp boat out of Port Arthur, and he had a white captain, and they got along alright." Brill seemed to reject my idealism when he responded with an example of a lack of cooperation between blacks and whites. I was probably trying to exercise my power as interviewer by trying to get them to agree with my opinion, but Brill resisted. Later, though, he gave an example of racial cooperation. "Now, you do have some boats have a white crew, colored captain, but those fellas were partly raised together. You understand what I mean?" he asked to again engage me in the dialogue metacommunicatively. I responded, "Yeah, know each other," and Brill went on, "They personally know each other. Now they'll get along alright. Otherwise, they won't." Carter, however, gave a negative example. "Some raised right around together and never get along." Brill's idea reinforced my previous statement about the possibility of racial harmony but circumscribed by a very specific situation. White and black have to be "raised together" for this to happen, and even then, as Carter pointed out, it might not happen. Brill seems to be suggesting the idea that racism can exist more easily on an abstract level, but once individual humans interact, whites are more likely to overcome their prejudices—Twain's Huck and Jim, for example.

Captain Brill also talked hesitantly about racism within the black community, and Carter was in agreement with what he said. Brill told me, "I can take a crew of men and you could take one. I hire a crew of colored men and you hire a crew. They work for you better than they would work for me." Carter agreed, "They would." I asked, "Why is that?" And Brill replied, "Well, I don't know, but they will." Carter again agreed, "They will. They will." I think Brill's point here was about the racism of black against black, the acceptance of the oppressor's racist stereotype of the black man as incompetent for leadership positions. Carter was supportive, encouraging, and in emphatic agreement with Brill when Brill started to talk about race, establishing solidarity between two black men as they explained their attitudes toward race to a white stranger. They were attempting to educate a white person about the intricacies of race within the black community.

Even after several minutes of talking about race, there was still indirection in the discourse. Carter and I talked about "it," whites and blacks working together, without ever saying the words "integration" or "segregation." Instead of segregation, I said "all colored," and they used "mixed up, white and colored" for integration. We kept the discussion personal and occupational, not acknowledging the political implications. I said "Negro" first, then they said "colored," and we settled on "colored" as the agreed-upon term. Folklorist and informants were both feeling their way around what they all realized was a sensitive subject in a racist society. We negotiated the language to be used. On those rare occasions when blacks and whites talked about race in the Old South, perhaps this was the nature of the discourse. My sense of it now is that Son Brill, Junior Carter, and I were engaging in and extending a tradition.

Our discussion of race gradually shifted from deference on Brill's part to a stated recognition of agreement. Brill said, "If I was captain of this boat and was to hire a white chief, why, we wouldn't get along," suggesting that because of white racism, a white chief would not take orders from a black captain. But he never said directly that racism was the cause. When he did seem about to explain this behavior as racism, he hesitated and backed off: "That's everywhere. You see [four-second pause], it's just something, I don't know, it just won't work." I stated it more directly, "Is it that the white man doesn't want to work for the colored man?" Brill responded, "I would say that." Except that he did not say it, he waited for the white man to say it. As a white person, I was in the position of power, and Brill and Carter deferred to that power; they accommodated themselves to the white interviewer and got their points across indirectly.

Finally, Brill did state it. "He [the white man] don't want to take orders, I would say. Captain, when you use that word Captain, he's got to do what you ask him." He then said something that brought us together in agreement: "*You know as good as I do that a lot of mens don't want to do this*" [emphasis added].

"You know as good as I do" was a metacommunicative statement (references to the first person speaker and second person listener) that suggested not only agreement but also an attempt on Brill's part to move the discussion to another more honest and direct level. I then said in agreement, "Yeah, that's bad, but that's the way it is," and Brill said, "He shouldn't, he shouldn't feel thata way, shouldn't feel that way." I agreed, "No," and Brill summed up, "It's just something you can't do anything about." We agreed that racism is bad, but we also took a conservative stand on the possibility of change, implying that this behavior is so entrenched in southern society that the civil rights movement might not change people's hearts. I do not think I really felt this way at the time, and perhaps Son Brill did not feel this way either, but we were trying to reach some kind of agreement about race at this stage of the conversation.

After all this discussion of race, Brill revealed the deeper reasons for pogie fishing boats having all black crews and captains. He explained the mechanisms an oppressed people must use to get some economic advantage. I asked him, "Was it easier for a colored person to get into the fishing business in the South than maybe some other business, or uh . . ." Brill responded, "It was a little too tough for a white man if you want to know the truth about it." Carter agreed. "Too much work." I asked, "So that's why the colored people got a good start in it?" Brill said, "They just couldn't take it. They tried it. It was tested out with the white man; they couldn't take it. That's the reason it's one-sided, all colored people. That's the reason the colored captain got a berth. Otherwise he never would come in here." This was another breakthrough in our conversation; he was openly critical of whites as too weak to handle the physical labor of pogie fishing that at the time involved pulling in the nets by hand—his image of blackness as strong directly related to one of whiteness as weak. This construction could be accepted by both blacks and whites but with different interpretations of its more specific meaning. Black people might see black physical strength very positively in such powerful folk heroes as John Henry, and whites might see it in a primitivist way, black as physically strong but mentally weak. White racial romantics might see it as John and Alan Lomax did—black strength as part of American national character—the physical labor that made a strong nation possible (see chapters 3 and 4). Underlying all these images would be the oppositional image of white as physically weak.

Son Brill's explanation of the actual mechanisms used by black fishermen to take over the industry indicated that mental acuity was as necessary as physical strength. He started with a metacommunicative phrase for emphasis.

"Understand me now, a whole lot easier for a colored man to make a captain in a way than it was for a white man. White man would—the fishermen were all Negro, just about. If you was to come on this boat as a captain, and we's all colored on here, why we say, 'We ain't going to learn him nothing.'" Carter agreed, "Unn uhh." "You couldn't make it." Carter said, "No." "You'd probably be on here a couple of weeks, and man they'd put you off because you couldn't produce. Therefore the colored man had a better chance . . . Otherwise, we never would have had no Negro captains." Carter's interjections indicated that he was aware of these mechanisms and agreed with the need for them. This open discussion of strategies of the oppressed with a representative of the oppressor came only after hesitations, indirections, and careful negotiations about appropriate language, and only after they were sure that I was sympathetic to their position.

After he told me of the in-group mechanisms to get work, I indicated my support by saying, "Sounds fair enough though," and laughed. Brill continued with other incidents of racism in his occupation, "That's right. I know the time right aboard these boats [four-second pause] colored man wasn't allowed on the bridge." Carter asked, "Wasn't?" And Brill said, "No sir. He didn't come up on the bridge." I said, "They carried their prejudices out to sea with them." Brill said, "That's right." I said, "That's bad. But now you're running them." Brill agreed, "Oh yeah. Yeah. The highest position a colored man could get board these boats was dry boat [a much smaller boat that was used to lower the nets]. You see that little boat sitting on the back of the Sandy Hook? That little boat. That was about as high as he could get, in that little boat. That's the highest position he could hold, dry boat." Brill's image of "that little boat," repeated three times, became a visual metaphor for the racist attempts to deny blacks equal opportunity to advance in their chosen occupation. We were sitting on a boat that dwarfed the small dry boat, signifying both white power and Brill's success in overcoming it. This is an example of the speakers creating the context for the verbal interaction (Briggs 1986, 25, 108): we were on a fishing boat surrounded by other boats, but it took Brill's verbal references and his listeners' understanding of his metaphor to give them social and political meaning.

To indicate my support of Brill's point and to make it clear to him that I was not a racist, I told him and Carter about working for and taking orders from a black man who I respected. By talking about my experience working with black men on a construction labor gang in New Jersey, I was attempting to establish my white liberal credentials and to distance myself from southern white racism, and this did seem to open up the discussion to more political concerns. This was also an example of my using liberal "innocence" to gain power in a racial situation (Duneier 1992, 139). Brill then mentioned his own white boss in a way that suggested it was a parallel situation. "I know what you mean. Just like our boss." However, it soon became clear that his boss was a racist, and that the case was entirely different for a black man with a white boss. "Now, uh, I was telling him the other day. He like to raise a lot of hell, you know, when he's talking to you . . . And he talked to me just like he would, you know, to the boys or something. He—this kinda old stuff, off the wall. And I talk to him just like he is the boss." He was critical of his white boss, but again in an indirect way, characterizing his abusive speech as, "He like to raise a lot of hell" and "This kinda old stuff, off the wall."

As a younger man who grew up in the generation of the civil rights movement, Junior Carter was able to express his feelings about race more directly than Son Brill. He made the conversation more explicit when he said, "Now you take just like up in Carolina, they had that thing about discrimination up there. What they thought up there, they wanted, the colored boys wanted to marry the white girls, but that wasn't it. What they wanted was the equal—if you do a job, and you get paid, and if I'm colored if I can do the job, pay up the same money. That's what we wanted up there, but them older heads just couldn't get it in their heads. They thought we wanted to marry each other." I said, "Yeah," and Brill said, "That's the most, uh, most—," and I interrupted him, "And that's crazy." Carter agreed, "That's crazy." Brill added, "That's the most, uh, back—but people just got the wrong idea about the whole thing." Carter echoed, "The whole thing." Like the famous incident in Ralph Ellison's "Battle Royal" where the Invisible Man accidentally says "social equality" to an audience of white southerners (1952, 33), Carter was about to use the politically charged phrase "equal rights," but instead switched to an example to make his point. His reference to "older heads" seems to be code for white men, but it excludes the young white man he is talking to. The young black man, the young white man, and the old black man all agree that these racist ideas are absurd as our overlapping speech indicates.

Carter then called for equality: "Shucks, if I see a place out there that I want to buy me, build me a house and I worked for it, and let me spend my money. If I want to go places, I can go if it's a public place. But they don't figure that way. A lot of people figure it different." He was clearly in favor of integration in housing and public facilities, but he was still careful not to directly criticize whites, referring to them as "some people," and he still was not sure if I was one of those people who "figure it different." By 1967, the civil rights movement and the ideas of Martin Luther King had become widely accepted by southern blacks, and Carter had been involved in the civil rights movement in South Carolina. "No, I told them one day, they had a big meeting up there in Carolina. I told them, 'That's all we want. If I go in there and if I can operate, or if I can fly an airplane, if I got education enough in the world and if I pass that test, let me have it. If you know more than me, you take it.' A lot of people don't see it." Like "older heads," "a lot of people" is code for whites and might have included his white listener; this formulaic phrase was a closing disclaimer, allowing his listener to express a different point of view.

The earlier telling of dirty jokes made it easier to talk about race and sex. Junior Carter brought the subject up directly when he referred to the white stereotype of black men wanting white women, but when Brill talked about race and sex, he was extremely vague: "It's just as many colored people, I would say men, as far as the women, will never change . . . And you couldn't make them change, as far as that part. But it feels, some people just feel like that's all they want, that's all they want, but that ain't it. No, that ain't it." Carter was able to talk about sex more directly because he was younger; Brill represented an older generation that would not feel comfortable talking about sex with a white person.

As with the discussion of race, talking about sex and race became more revealing the more we talked. Carter said, "But you take colored people now, and you take like you say 'white,' you just one color. But you take colored people—" Brill interrupted to finish the sentence for him, "And any color they want." Carter continued, "Any color you want. You can go out there and get a woman that looks just like she's white; you can get a dark, dark woman, or you can get a black woman, or you can even get a high yellow, or a red woman. All the women is out there; all you got to do is pick out one." The repeated use of the second-person pronoun by both men is interesting here; they put the emphasis on their white listener's perception of race and move from a general view of "colored people" to a more specific view of "black, brown, and beige" women, creating a potential sexual encounter between me and a black woman. Their emphasis on the range of colors is part of an older black folk idea and anticipation of the later concepts of Rainbow Coalition and "women of color" although expressed in a sexist way since the women were viewed as sex objects. Still, a definite racial pride came out: the implication was that white is bland and lacks variety. In terms of critical race theory, their representation of blackness as vital constructed a counter image of whiteness as bland.

I shifted the discussion to traditional narrative poems, toasts (Abrahams 1970a, 97–172), which we had talked about earlier. I said, "Well, getting back to some more of this traditional material, you say both of you have heard the toasts that I was talking about a while ago?" Carter asked, "What ones was that?" I said, "Well, any of them." Carter said, "Any of them, yeah I've heard them." Here I was definitely imposing an interview structure on what had been a conversation, exercising my role as folklorist in charge of the proceedings by shifting the focus away from the discussion of race to the collecting of folk tales. I then questioned them about the contexts in which stories were told. "And they tell them around here? How often do you hear them?" Carter said, "Sometimes you get with a bunch of boys." And Brill added, "Anytime just sitting around." Carter said, "Bunch of boys ain't got nothing else to do, sit down shooting the bull." After they described the usual contexts of performance, I said, "I'd like to get together with them . . . I'd like to catch them all sometime. I'd like to get some of those toasts." And Carter began to tell a story.

"You ever, you ever hear that one uh, uh, about that er ah that rabbit and that uh lion got talking about who ruled the heaven and who ruled the earth? Er ah, say the rabbit told the lion one time said, 'Brother Lion,' said, 'God rule the heaven and man rule the earth.' Brother Lion told him, 'That's shit!' He say, 'God rule the heaven and I rule earth.' So the rabbit told the lion, said, 'I'm gonna let you meet man.' So that Sunday morning, they went out. Rabbit went by and picked the lion up, told him, 'Come on, let's go meet man,' you know. So they left going on down the road. And after awhile they met a little boy rolling a hoop along, you know. Lion broke at him, you know. Rabbit told him, 'No, no, Brother Lion,' say, 'That *will be* man.' 'God damn I thought that was man!' They went up the road a little bit further, and there's a old fella, you know, cutting up wood on the woodpile with an axe. He broke at him. The rabbit said, 'No, no,' said, 'that *have been* man!' you know. They went on down the road a little further, say they met a man on a horse, you know, with a Winchester rifle and a forty-five on his side and big bull whip, you know. So the rabbit say, 'Now damn if that ain't man there!' you know. So the old lion squared off and made a pass at him. Say that man went to shooting him in the face with that bullwhip, you know, and when he turnt round he went to shooting him in the ass with that damn Winchester. Say that damn rabbit asked that lion, said, 'Did you meet man?' He says, 'You goddamn right!' He said, 'I ain't never seen the lightnin' so fast in my face and thunder in my ass in all my damn life!'" Brill and I laughed. "Said, 'If you think I'm lying, take a glimpse at my ass when I pass.'" We laughed some more. "He had fucked him up" (Aarne 1964, AT 157 Learning to Fear Men; Dorson 1967, Tale #18 "King Beast of the Forest Meets Man").

Junior Carter took my interest in traditional stories as an invitation to tell one, in this case not a rhyming toast, but a related genre, a prose animal tale. Since there are a number of toasts about animals, "The Signifying Monkey" being the most widespread, the story of the rabbit and the lion was a logical choice to tell. I assume that Junior Carter did not perform the rhymed metrical toasts, but this story was probably the closest to a toast in his repertoire. There was another reason for telling this tale: it fit into the context of the preceding discussion about race. Within the African American tradition, animal tales are often symbolic stories about race relations. Junior Carter was demonstrating his abilities as a storyteller and at the same time continuing our discussion of race.

Unfortunately, I have not had the opportunity to interview Junior Carter again to determine what his interpretation of the story is, but I have worked out a possible interpretation based on the text, the interview context, and knowledge of African American folk culture. Roger Abrahams has influenced my interpretation of the story since he was one of my professors at the University of Texas while I was conducting this field research. His book *Deep Down in the Jungle* (1970a) and a seminar I had with him had a profound influence on my view of African American folklore (see chapter 6). I gave him transcriptions of Junior Carter's stories, and he used several of them in another book *Positively Black* (1970b). He says of the rabbit and lion story, "This is a parable of accommodation, not the sort of story one therefore finds among the young men; but, like the newer stories, it talks in terms of learning to live with fear and of defining one's relations with others in terms of power" (1970b, 50). I must have incorrectly attributed the storyteller's age when I gave Roger the transcriptions since Junior Carter was a young man when he told the story. Roger's point is still valid, I think; a young black man in Texas in 1967 could still be an accommodationist, but the situation was actually more complex when seen in the context of the rest of the interview, including the dynamics of interaction between storyteller and folklorist.

Roger says that the man on the horse is the "white man-boss," and I agree. In terms of the previous discussion with Brill and Carter, the man on the horse is also Brill's racist boss in the pogie fishery and the "old heads" in South Carolina who do not understand Carter's call for equality; "The Man" is also me, the white folklorist in the position of power to collect, transcribe, and present to the public the words of the two black men, to represent them to the outside world. There is potential for oppression in this situation: the fieldworker can become the "schoolteacher" figure of Toni Morrison's *Beloved* (1987), a social scientist who uses his research materials to reinforce racist stereotypes. I like to think that I have not abused the power of that position in my own fieldwork and publication, but I now know that I have exercised that power in ways that were unintentionally harmful. Brill and Carter may not have known the intricacies of the academic process, but they did know that I was a potential interpreter of their culture.

Here, then, is my interpretation of the story, recognizing that meanings are multiple and fluid, that my understanding will not be the same as the storyteller's, and that his may have changed as much as mine over the years. From a historical perspective, the lion during slavery times could be thought of as the young African prince, the slave newly arrived from Africa who does not yet realize the power of the white man and the consequences of confronting him. In that case, the man on the horse has all the characteristics of the patroller, the white overseer on the plantation. In the late 1960s, the lion could be the young militant black who thinks he can win in a confrontation with white authorities—the police, highway patrol, or national guard. The rabbit then becomes the older, more experienced black man, the accommodationist, who uses trickery and indirection in dealing with whites, who always wears "the mask that grins and lies." His job is to teach the lion a lesson by tricking him into a direct confrontation with "The Man," and, of course, the outcome of the story proves the accommodationist point of view.

Is the storyteller, then, himself an accommodationist? Again, the context of the interview, including the story he told next, suggests a more complex role for Junior Carter. He had already established his political stance as an integrationist, not just in word but in deed, having taken part in civil rights meetings in South Carolina. We cannot, then, take the attitude expressed in the story as a direct representation of the storyteller's politics. Throughout our discussion, Junior Carter had directly expressed a more militant attitude than the older Son Brill, but he still recognized the need to disguise his true feelings and to express them indirectly at times, depending on the circumstances. He wore many masks and could be an accommodationist if the situation called for it. (This is similar to Norman E. Whitten's broader idea of "black adaptation," black people adapting to their natural, social, economic, and political environment [1974, 6–10].) The rabbit and lion story more clearly expressed Captain Brill's point of view, and Junior Carter could have been telling it for him, respectfully supporting the older man as he had done throughout the interview. The story, then, is about all three of us: the man on the horse is me, the rabbit is Son Brill, and the lion is Junior Carter, defeated here but ready to fight, in different circumstances, another day. The story has a broader cultural meaning at the same time that it refers to the specific fieldwork situation we were in. Such stories "simultaneously invoke the force of traditional values and comment on features of the ongoing interaction. Such utterances link the normative and contingent, the general and the specific, thus providing valuable exegesis on both spheres (Briggs 1986, 47). In other words, a story told in a particular context is the equivalent of a scholarly article in closely examining cultural and political meanings.

As soon as Carter finished the rabbit and lion story, he launched into another one without a pause, insuring that he would maintain the floor. This story is thematically related to and comments on the previous one.

"Say that colored fella going on down to Georgia going to Baltimore, some way, you know, down that highway down there, said—uh, ain't got no trees, you know, and you can't shit on the highway, you know. So he had to shit, boy! So, he shit, and he had a big old straw hat on, you know. So he covered that shit up. He saw the highway patrolman coming. Throwed the hat on top of that shit, you know, covered it up, you know. He were holding it. So the patrolman come up there and say, 'Hey!' Say, 'What you got underneath that hat?' Says, 'Boys, I've caught one of the fastest son of a bitches you ever seen in your goddamn life!' He said, 'Let me see.' He said, 'No, no, no.' Says, 'He's faster than your eye can see.' He said, 'Damn if I ain't got to see it!' He said, 'No sir!' Say, 'I can't let you get underneath a here,' say, 'he'll get away.' Say 'I just caught him in my hat.'" Brill chuckled here. "So the patrolman said, 'Goddamn if I ain't gonna see.' So he, he reached down there and grabbed his hat up, and stuck his hand underneath, and say he stuck it in that shit. Said, 'Goddamn, look at that!' He say, 'I told you he was a fast son of a bitch! Done shit all over your hand and gone, and you ain't seen him yet!'" Brill and I laughed. "Done shit all over his hand and gone" (Aarne 1964, AT 1528 Holding Down the Hat).

Junior Carter did not say that the highway patrolman was white, but it was understood that in Georgia in the 1960s, he would have to be. By identifying the hero as a "colored fella," Carter established racial confrontation as the theme of the story. The story indicates the complex, multidimensional nature of the label accommodationist. The man who shit on the highway is like the rabbit in that he uses trickery and indirection, but he does not just stand off to the side and watch, he has been pulled into a confrontation because of segregation laws that forbid him to use any public toilet. The highway patrolman is the modern version of the man with the Winchester rifle and bullwhip, the white authority who enforces the racist laws. His defeat extends the political implications of the rabbit and lion story; there is no fight, but through wit and deceit there exists the possibility of overcoming fear in the never-ending struggle for power.

The "colored man" of the story is someone that both Junior Carter and Son Brill can identity with. This is the Son Brill who used deceit to undermine white captains in order to become a captain himself. This is the Junior Carter who wants equal access to public facilities: "If I want to go places, I can go if it's a public place." The accommodationist role includes the indirection and deceit of the trickster and the protest of the bad man; it is a pragmatic role for survival and change. If the last two stories are related and both reflect the immediate circumstances of the interview, then I have to recognize myself in the highway patrolman. Even though I was a supporter of the civil rights movement, I was still part of the white southern power structure that supported the police in their enforcement of racist laws. Junior Carter had talked and told stories until he had me laughing at a fellow white man; he tricked me as surely as the colored man tricked the highway patrolman. But in this case, the manipulation was part of a strategy to get me to agree with his point of view: the three of us laughed together at the predicament of the white man. From our first tentative discussion of race, we moved to an understanding and an agreement expressed through storytelling, recognizing that beyond our momentary little circle racism still prevailed.

When a black folklorist interviews a black storyteller, there is an assumption of agreement on certain issues from the beginning; they do not have to go through the same process of establishing rapport that Son Brill, Junior Carter, and I did. For example, Paulette Cross (1973) was a student at Indiana University when she tape-recorded another black person—Ronald Tylor—telling jokes in 1968, one year after my fieldwork on the Gulf Coast. The political climate was similar in 1967 and '68, but Ronald Tylor and Junior Carter were very different black men, and the relationship of fieldworker and informant was vastly different. Tylor was a twenty-three-year-old graduate student from Milwaukee, and he and Cross appear to have known each other for some time. Their discussion of race was direct from the beginning.

C[Collector]: Why do you usually tell [the jokes] and where?
I[Informant]: I tell jokes about white people cause they're funny. I tell 'em with the fellas . . .
C: Because white people are funny or because the jokes are funny?
I: Well, because number 1, white people are funny and number 2, because the jokes are funny . . . If you can laugh at someone then you don't have to hate 'em so much.
C: Oh I see; I take it that you don't particularly care for them?
I: For whom?
C: White people.

I: Oh I don't mind them. They're negligible you know . . .

C: Why have you gotten so wrapped up in this black nationalist movement? Oh I don't really mean wrapped up—

I: Oh, I'm definitely wrapped up in it. That's a good statement. Well,
because I don't believe we're going to get anything through white
America. I don't believe that we're going to get anything unless we
can address the power structure in America as a group of people,
you know. (Cross 1973, 652–53)

The first joke Tylor told directly expressed his political views, and it is
related to the last two stories that Junior Carter told.

There's this uh—black cat from the north, ya know, he's a bad nigga, and went
down to the south, ya know, driving his uh—white Eldorado Cadillac, and
he drove into this gas station in Southern Indiana. Right in front of him was
another black man in an old beat-up pick-up truck. And the filling station
attendant walked out and he said uh—whatcha want boy? And the black cat
in the pick-up truck said uh—gimmie a dolla wortha regula. And the station
attendant said, gimmie a dolla's worth of regula—what? The black man said,
ah uh, please mista charlie. So mista charlie gave him a dolla's worth of regula
and charged him a dolla fifty and said naw git on out a heah boy. So the black
cat in the pick-up truck left. So then the nigga from the north, he pulls up in
this uh—white Eldorado Cadillac, in his sharkskin suit, silk socks, Stetson
hat, Stacy Adams shoes, just clean, you know. So the nigga reaches over and
pushes a button and the window slides down a little bit and the white cat say,
whaddyah want boy? And the nigga say uh—fill it up. And the white boy say
fill it up, what? He say fill it up man, I ain't got all day, come on, fill it up. The
white boy say, fill it up, what? With gas, fool, come on I ain't got all day. So
the white boy went inside the filling station and he got his rifle and he came
back out with his rifle and he looked dead in the nigga's eye and he pointed
over at a bush about 200 yards away and he said, nigga, see that fly on that
bush 200 yards away? And the nigga say, yea, I see it; so the white boy took
the rifle, aimed and fired and he killed this fly without touching the bush
and he looked back at the nigga waitin for the nigga to respond with uh—if
you please mista charlie but instead the nigga pushed this button and rolled
the window all the way down and leaned over and pushed a button to the
glove compartment, and pulled out a saucer. And he said hold that boy, to
the white cat, and he reached over to his glove compartment and pulled out
an apple and he reached in his inside coat pocket and he pulled out a razor
and he threw the apple in the air and he grabbed the razor and sliced around
in the air with all kinda fast beautiful motions so quick and so fast, that he

peeled the apple, cored the apple, and sliced it so thin in that split second with that razor, that when it hit the saucer it was applesauce. And the white boy said, what uh—what was that uh—regula or ethyl?" (Cross 1973, 650–51; Abrahams 1970b, 72)

This seems to be a retelling and updating of the rabbit and lion story; all the same types are represented in the same confrontational setting. The man on the horse becomes the racist filling station attendant, the accommodating rabbit becomes the timid black man in the pick-up truck, and the lion is now the aggressive "black cat from the north." The difference, of course, is in the ending: the lion defeats the man with the rifle, and the story reinforces the need for militant confrontation and rejects the accommodationist attitude. The militant black man fulfills the white stereotype of the urban black criminal, specifically the pimp with his white Cadillac, expensive clothes, and razor blade as weapon, thus inverting the image from a white negative to a black positive.

Ronald Tylor as an urban, northern, educated black man had been influenced by black intellectual movements of the late 1960s; Junior Carter as a small city, southern, uneducated black man was a product of the civil rights movement of the late '50s and early '60s, and their stories reflect the different political contexts. Paulette Cross as a black folklore student interviewing a black friend was able to deal with the politics of race more directly than I was, and Tylor was able to express his opinions about racism more forcefully than Carter. In their case, race and culture were the common ground that overcame gender difference; whereas, for Carter, Brill, and I, common gender made it easier to talk about racial difference.

Tylor's comments support the symbolic interpretation of the story. Cross asked Tylor, "I take it that you really approved of the actions of that black cat from the north?" And Tylor replied, "Yeah, I really do. For one thing, he's the typical stereotype that whites have about city niggas, you know. They think that all any nigga wants to do is to make a little money and then spend it all on a big car, like that Cadillac. Only in the joke, it shows that that city nigga ain't so dumb after all." And a little later:

C: What does that black man in the pick-up truck mean to you or what makes him important?
I: He typifies the "black sambo" type, you know, the old accommodating "colored" man. He's important because he shows that there are two types of blacks in this country today, the passive "uncle Tom" type and on the other hand you have the type of black man who isn't

going to take any shit from anybody. In a way, this last type sort of fits in with my views on violence.

C: What type of violence?

I: You know, organized to help the black man in this country. To help him get that white monkey off his back. (Cross 1973, 655)

Tylor knew that he had a sympathetic listener in Cross; Carter was not sure about his white listener and had to proceed more carefully even in expressing his less militant views. My interview with Carter and Brill took place about a year before this one, but in some ways it could have been twenty or thirty years earlier. Son Brill, Junior Carter, and I were still saying "colored" and "Negro"; the term "black" never entered our discussion. To Ronald Tylor, Carter and Brill might both be accommodationists: "There are two types of blacks in this country, the so-called colored who would prefer being called colored since it doesn't seem so close to black and more closer to being white. And then there's the black man that's proud of being black and being called black; he doesn't try to assimilate his cultural value within the mainstream of the white society by trying to be something he ain't and by demeaning his own values by attempting to replace them with something that is close to whiteness" (Cross 1973, 655). Son Brill and Junior Carter were to some extent accommodationists, but as I pointed out earlier, this was a more complex stance than Ronald Tylor acknowledged. They did accommodate themselves to me during the interview, but both also condemned racism and called for social equality. The accommodationist role can include protest as well as deceit; wit and guile are used to defeat the white oppressor, a figure who is clearly delineated in both the accommodationist and protest stories, whether he is the overseer, the highway patrolman, or the gas station attendant.

As different as they were, both interview/storytelling situations indicated dynamic change was taking place. As Son Brill, Junior Carter, and I interacted, we were creating new kinds of relationships between the races, and Junior Carter's storytelling was a performance that commented on and extended those relationships. His stories, as traditional expressions, were being used as part of a process of social change, drawing on the past to reshape the present and offer hope for the future. Paulette Cross's interview with Ronald Tylor spoke more directly to the need for political change, but since Cross and Tylor were from the same community and shared certain attitudes, their interaction did not directly involve change in race relations, although Tylor, like Junior Carter, was drawing upon traditional stories to illustrate the need for new relationships between the races.

Looking back on my interview with Son Brill and Junior Carter and the subsequent writing about it, I see it as a missed opportunity to employ a collaborative approach. I should have gone back to talk to them again after I started to analyze the tales. Then I could have asked them what the stories meant and tested my interpretations against theirs. It never occurred to me at the time, and perhaps that effort would have been fruitless if they had not been willing to talk about their own understanding of the stories meanings. The collaborative research that I have conducted more recently has had many positive results but also introduced new complexities into the fieldwork. I have more to say on those issues in chapter 8, at the end of the book.

Reflexive ethnography involves more than stepping back to observe your own field research in the past; it also involves trying to determine the social and cultural influences on the researcher in the present, recognizing subjectivity then and now. When I reread this chapter, I thought that perhaps I was too hard on myself, but that is part of the cultural and psychological baggage white southern liberals can never quite put down. I recognize myself in Andrew Hacker's statement, "Liberals stand in dread of black disfavor, which must be mollified by admitting to oversight or error. Rather than deny the indictment, the liberal tendency is to admit to such bias, and pledge renewed vigilance against future errors" (1992, 56). This chapter has been a catalog of oversights and misunderstandings in my fieldwork of more than thirty years ago, but I think it is a productive endeavor for understanding not only what happened then but also for recognizing the continuing importance of race in fieldwork now.

From the perspective of the early twenty-first century, a time when issues of race are still at the center of American consciousness and racism is still a political reality, we can look back at the late 1960s and see that the idealism about change in race relations of that period has not come to fruition; many racist attitudes remain the same. Just as Son Brill, Junior Carter, and I were tentatively beginning a racial dialog, the need for dialog still exists. Just as Ronald Tylor pointed out the need for radical change in attitudes of both blacks and whites, that need still exists. The folklorist's interview can be a microcosm of larger social issues, bringing forth not only meaningful texts, but also revealing political contexts that can be better understood from a historical perspective. My retrospective examination of the 1960s fieldwork encounter with Son Brill and Junior Carter indicates connections to the cross-racial fieldwork of earlier white folklorists such as Newbell Niles Puckett and John Lomax from the 1920s to the 1940s.

2

Newbell Niles Puckett,
Zora Neale Hurston, and Primitivism

Beneath the crust of culture we all are primitives.
—Newbell Niles Puckett

My interview with Son Brill and Junior Carter in 1967 (chapter 1) was part of a larger fieldwork project on folk beliefs of commercial fishermen on the Texas Gulf Coast. I collected beliefs from African American fishermen that were not found among white fishermen along the coast, and to annotate them, I used a book by white folklorist Newbell Niles Puckett, *Folk Beliefs of the Southern Negro* (1969 [1926]). It was my first use of Puckett's scholarship, but years later I worked with folklorists Wayland Hand and Jack Shortlidge on Puckett's collection of Ohio folk beliefs that were published as *Popular Beliefs and Superstitions: A Compendium of American Folklore* (Hand, Casetta, and Thiederman 1981). My research on Puckett's papers at the Cleveland Public Library eventually led me to a consideration of his cultural representations of African Americans, and later I realized that it would be useful to compare his perspective with that of a black folklorist doing fieldwork at about the same time. For years, I had been teaching Zora Neale Hurston's *Mules and Men* (1978 [1935]), an ethnographic account of her fieldwork in the South during the 1920s and '30s, and since she is widely recognized as the most important black folklorist of her generation, I decided to use her ethnography and her novel *Their Eyes Were Watching God* (1978 [1937]) to compare the insider and outsider perspectives (Mullen 2000c, 122–25).

Both Puckett and Hurston conducted folklore field research among rural African Americans in the South in the 1920s and '30s, with Puckett concentrating his collecting on folk belief, custom, religion, folk art, folksong, and folk speech. *Folk Beliefs of the Southern Negro* was the first extensive collection of African American beliefs and remains an important source of information for scholars. Puckett was born and reared in Mississippi; he received his PhD in sociology from Yale University, and his dissertation was based on fieldwork among southern blacks. His background and education had a direct influence on his representations of southern rural black folk culture. His book and articles reveal a great deal about his racial attitudes, but his published studies are cloaked in the language of scientific objectivity typical of his day. A more direct expression of his emotional attitude toward blacks can be found in his poetry (most of which was not published but can be found in the Puckett papers at the Cleveland Public Library).

Many of his poems were written in black dialect; by assuming the voice of the people he was studying, he was in some ways trying to become black but at the same time implying a subtext of his white assumptions about African Americans. Puckett was aware of the potential conflict between his scholarship and his poetry; he knew that his scholarly writing had to remain objective, but he had a strong desire to express himself subjectively. In 1933, he gave a reading of his poetry to the Cleveland branch of the American Association of University Women, and he made the following statement by way of introduction:

> But the problem to the sociologist is how to incorporate both emotional re-
> actions and accurate observations in the same account. Usually he ends up
> by giving the facts and keeping the emotions to himself or else he gives the
> emotions with fewer of the facts and does not call the result sociology. My
> own feeling has been that these emotional reactions were better expressed
> through poetry than through prose. The American Sociological Society would
> scarcely stand for a sociologist breaking suddenly from careful description
> and analysis into rotten doggerel, so that in my study of Negro plantation life
> I have kept the facts for public consumption and the attempted poetry for
> private enjoyment. I am still undecided whether my verse really made the
> characters more alive or whether it killed them deader than ever. All I can
> say is that some of the verses seem to have the power of recalling in my own
> mind some [of] the emotions which were present when the observation was
> first made. I think on the whole that the poetry has helped (Puckett n.d.).

Puckett did not keep his poetry entirely private; he submitted some of it to southern newspapers for publication. He thought that sociology was too restrictive in excluding the personal and emotional, and that his poetry was a way of communicating a fuller picture of a folk culture.

Hurston also presented her views on southern black folk culture in both ethnographic and literary forms. Besides her major field collection of African American folklore, *Mules and Men,* she also published novels that drew upon her ethnographic fieldwork, including her most famous one, *Their Eyes Were Watching God.* In some ways, both Puckett and Hurston anticipated the possibilities available today for folklorists and anthropologists to combine the personal and the scholarly in reflexive ethnography, but a white folklorist today would not think of reading black dialect poetry in public as Puckett did (although many white singers perform in African American musical styles). Puckett was still in an age influenced by nineteenth-century minstrelsy, an age of white actors playing Amos and Andy on the radio. This is not to excuse any racist interpretations that Puckett made, but rather to place him in the context of his time and his culture to better understand the dynamics of race relations in folklore research. It would be easy to condemn him from the perspective of the early twenty-first century, but this would oversimplify the complexities of race in the social sciences and overlook his real accomplishments as a scholar.

As I pointed out in the introduction, race in the present study is not defined as biological fact, but rather as social construct. Henry Louis Gates says that "Race, as a meaningful criterion within the biological sciences, has long been recognized to be a fiction . . . Nevertheless, our conversations are replete with usages of race which have their sources in the dubious pseudoscience of the eighteenth and nineteenth centuries" (1985, 4). One way of defining racism, then, is "the reduction of the cultural to the biological, the attempt to make the first dependent on the second" (Delacampagne 1990, 85). Throughout the present study I shall make clear distinctions between culture and race. Race as a culturally constructed concept suggests many different and changing historical contexts in which racism exists. Because there are shifting concepts of race, there are many different kinds of racism (Goldberg 1990, xiv). We should also recognize that racism does not always exist as a "set of irrational prejudices," but can take on "the mantle of scientific theory, philosophical rationality, and [even] 'morality'" (xiv). American racism against blacks had various forms in the 1920s and was not the same as forms of racism in the twenty-first century. For instance, some of the racist ideas that Puckett held in the 1920s and '30s were widely accepted by social scientists and intellectuals, both white and black.

Puckett has been criticized as racist by such current African American writers as Alice Walker: "How was I to believe anything they [white folklorists] wrote, since at least one of them, Puckett, was capable of wondering, in his book, if 'the Negro' had a large enough brain" (1983, 11). There was no citation for this statement, and I have been unable to find a reference to brain size in *Folk Beliefs of the Southern Negro.* Moreover, Puckett's writings emphasize cultural and social, rather than biological, causes for supposed black inferiority. His belief in racial inferiority theoretically connects Puckett with southern segregation, but Puckett's ideas about race were of a different and more complex kind. He was a white southern paternalist in ways similar to another folklorist of his generation, John Lomax (Hirsch 1992), who I shall treat in detail in the next chapter. Puckett wanted to uplift Negroes through education from what he and others saw as their barbaric state of superstitious ignorance so that they could join civilized white society. For instance, he referred to folk beliefs about pregnancy and childbirth as "the murderous lore of mid-wifery . . . and the sooner this is recognized the sooner will such superstitions be replaced by modern scientific knowledge" (1973 [1926], 6). This view of folk belief is far from the current nonpejorative folkloric concept as stated by Beverly Robinson, "African-American beliefs are metaphysical traditions belonging to an African world view adapted to an American milieu" (1990, 218), or by Lawrence Levine, "in the cultures from which the slaves came, phenomena and activities that we might be tempted to dismiss as 'superstitious' were legitimate and important modes of comprehending and operating within a universe perceived of in sacred terms. To distinguish these activities and beliefs from religion is a meaningless exercise" (1977, 56). Zora Neale Hurston's concept of folk belief as functioning like religion anticipated the later views of Robinson and Levine.

Puckett, on the other hand, viewed folk belief from the nineteenth-century perspective of cultural evolution and primitivism. He thought "that folk-beliefs and superstitions are *normal* stages of development through which *all* peoples have passed and are passing in their societal evolution" (1973 [1926], 4). He conceived the magic folk beliefs of black people as evidence that African Americans were stuck in an earlier primitive stage of evolution, but that through education they could be pulled out of this stage and become civilized. Puckett was a student of A. G. Keller at Yale and was educated "in the tradition of William Graham Sumner" (Hand 1967, 341), the author of *Folkways: A Study of the Sociological Importance of Usages, Manners, Customs, Mores and Morals* (1906). Sumner, in turn, was influenced by the English writer Herbert Spencer who "adapted Darwin's 'survival of the fittest' to industry and economics" (Bronner 1986, 26). Puckett was part of a long line of scholars who espoused the concept of cultural evolution, and implicit in the evolutionary view was the concept of primitivism, which was such a strong force in intellectual thought that it continued to exist after cultural evolution had been superseded by cultural relativism and functionalism in

anthropology and folklore studies. "Many [relativist] ethnographers, including Boas and Malinowski himself, intended their work to be antievolutionist
in thrust. But they could not always control the way their ideas would be used
by other scholars or received by the general public" (Torgovnick 1990, 8).
Puckett's scholarship offers proof of this tendency since he combined ideas
from cultural evolution and functionalism in his approach.

Despite his acceptance of the cultural evolution model and his corresponding association of superstition with the primitive, Puckett also saw important
functions for folk belief. In an article originally published in 1926, he stated,
"Every single folk-belief is thoroughly justifiable in the light of its times and
meets a definite need on the part of the individual or group, whether it be
illiterate Negro farmers or students at our most advanced universities" (1973
[1926], 6). To his credit, Puckett recognized that superstitious behavior went
beyond race and class boundaries. He added that "the conscientious objector
to folk-lore should also realize that not all of folk-knowledge is pure chaff.
For instance, the Negro farmer says that when the smoke falls towards the
ground . . . it is a sign of rain. Careful scientific investigation has brought to
light natural laws behind these observations which establish them as scientific
facts" (7). On the other hand, he thought there were magic beliefs that had
no basis in science but that might still work on a psychological level. He said
that although the educated person may scoff at hoodoo magic practices, "no
careful observer in the field can deny the fact that these various conjures in
many cases *actually work*. In this sense they represent means of faith-healing
or faith-harming admirably adapted to the temperament of an uneducated
folk" (6). He recognized the psychological efficacy of magic beliefs while
denying any empirical scientific validity. In this, he was more like the functionalists while continuing to hold on to the outdated nineteenth-century
concept of cultural evolution.

Zora Neale Hurston completely rejected cultural evolution and the superior stance over the folk/primitive that it implied. She was very much a
product of the newer American schools of cultural relativism and functionalism, having studied with Franz Boas and Ruth Benedict at Columbia from
1925 to 1927. Her anthropological training enabled her to view folk beliefs
and practices in less judgmental ways than Puckett, although such 1920s
anthropological models as functionalism had their own implicit condescension (B. O'Connor 1995, 41–44). By the time Hurston wrote *Mules and
Men,* which included her description of African American hoodoo beliefs
and rituals, "she was in the process of rejecting scientific conceptualization"
and viewing belief as a subjective insider (Hemenway 1977, 215). The combi-

nation of cultural relativism and her own subjectivity allowed her to avoid the pathological models of Puckett and others. As her biographer Robert Hemenway has pointed out, "*Mules and Men* refutes the pathological view of uneducated rural black people," (1978, xx).

As a black person who grew up in a small community in Florida and who was academically trained in cultural relativism, Hurston had a positive view of African American folk belief. She thought of African American folk belief as part of a system that was comparable to any religion. In a letter to Langston Hughes in 1929, she wrote:

> I am convinced that Christianity as practised [sic] is an attenuated form of nature worship. Let me explain. The essentials are a belief in the Trinity, baptism, sacrament. Baptism is nothing more than water worship as has been done in one form or the other down thru the ages ... I find fire worship in Christianity too. What was the original purpose of the altar in all churches? For sacred fire and sacrifices BY FIRE. . . . Symbols my opponents are going to say. But they cannot deny that both water and fire are purely material things and that they symbolize man's tendency to worship those things which benefit him to a great extent. . . . You know of course that the sacrament is a relic of cannibalism when men ate men not so much for food as to gain certain qualities the eaten man had. Sympathetic magic pure and simple. *They have a nerve to laugh at conjure* (Hemenway 1978, xix–xx).

The "they" she referred to probably included Puckett since his condescension toward conjure is clear in *Folk Beliefs of the Southern Negro*. But Puckett's approach was more complex than his clinging to cultural evolution would suggest. He was ahead of his time in recognizing folklore as part of a creative cultural process.

> Indeed the friendly eye cannot but see many general aspects of folk-thought which might greatly bolster up the racial self-esteem. The countless unique methods employed in conjuration, for instance, speak with convincing eloquence of a wealth of originality. I have collected from the Negroes some twenty-three or more separate and distinct methods of avoiding death when an owl hoots near one's house. These beliefs do not mutter to me of a sterility of folk-thought—could the same mental torrent in some way be turned from avoiding death to avoiding debt the visible increase in material prosperity would leave no question as to its power (1973 [1926], 8).

His ideas here seem to be a mixture of cultural evolution and functionalism; he saw the creativity and originality of conjuring in its cultural context, but he regretted the goals of that creative effort. The assumption was that as blacks moved up the evolutionary ladder, they would redirect this cultural creativity toward more civilized goals—in this case the capitalist, and by implication white, goal of making more money.

Puckett's cultural evolutionary model was not entirely based on racial distinctions, though; he was aware of a class dimension that crossed racial boundaries. He began one essay with this statement: Folk beliefs "are found mainly with the uncultured and backward classes of society, white or colored; and it is to such retarded classes rather than to either racial group as a whole that reference is made throughout this paper" (1931, 9). As a sociologist he thought that along with race, environmental factors were important: "Various elements of the problem may be referred to environmental rather than to racial antecedents and are to be found with isolated rural white folk as well" (ibid.). The class dimension of his theory was within the overall framework of the evolutionary model; most white people had moved up the scale while most black people had lagged behind. Despite his emphasis on cultural factors such as class and lack of education in explaining African American superstitious behavior, his theoretical model still implied racial distinctions; after all, it was the white social scientist who was in a superior position in judging the "backwardness" of black behavior. The notion of blacks as primitive and irrational suggested an oppositional image of whiteness as civilized and rational.

The theory of cultural evolution had supposedly been discredited by the 1920s (Bronner 1986, 64), but the concept was still widely held by many scholars and had become part of popular knowledge. The primitive-to-civilized model of the nineteenth century has become the underdeveloped-to-advanced model of the twentieth century, and race is often a factor in determining where a group belongs on this path of linear development (Outlaw 1990, 67). Puckett thought of his ideas on race as scientific and enlightened; he was not aware of the political implication that the concept of cultural evolution was used to maintain power over already subjugated people. His use of cultural evolution assumed the widespread scholarly definition of folk in contrast to elite, which also implied other dichotomies—illiterate/literate, static/progressive, and rural/urban (Roberts 2000, 76). Puckett's research among African Americans was part of the whole history of folklore as a discipline that, in John Roberts's words, "emerged as a hegemonic discourse on European Otherness for the empowerment of elite classes and the disempowerment of peasant classes and so-called primitives" (77). Puckett was one of the American scholars who "maintained continuity with the European tradition by literally creating peasant classes whose folkness was defined by social marginality and cultural difference" (80), in Puckett's case identifying southern rural Negroes as a folk.

A group of black intellectuals in the 1920s, which included members of the National Urban League and the editor of its publication *Opportunity: A Journal of Negro Life*, agreed with Puckett about the need for cultural uplift and the assimilation of Negroes into mainstream society. Another group of black writers opposed assimilation and included the artists and writers of the New Negro movement and of the Harlem Renaissance; these writers, including Zora Neale Hurston, promoted the cultural distinctiveness of the race in their poetry, fiction, music, and other artistic expressions. According to Harold Cruse, the assimilationists were middle-class blacks who did not support the Harlem Renaissance "morally, aesthetically, or financially" (1967, 38). Charles S. Johnson, the assimilationist editor of *Opportunity* and a leading black sociologist of his day, indicated his agreement with the cultural evolutionary model in his glowing review of Puckett's *Folk Beliefs of the Southern Negro:* "What these beliefs reveal of the fascinating interplay of advanced and *backward cultures,* of the absolute qualities of *ignorance,* of the strangle-hold of superstitions on *untutored minds,* white and black, of the intellectual and spiritual isolation they reflect, of the *warped lives* and *strange psychology* and characteristics of peoples quick to be misunderstood, are the contribution of the book through page on page of living folk lore" (emphasis added; 1926b, 324).

Johnson wrote two editorials in subsequent issues in which he drew on Puckett's research to blame superstition for health problems among southern rural blacks (1926a, 1926c). Many upwardly mobile, newly educated black people were trying to distance themselves from rural African American folk culture—in one sense to become more white—and Puckett's book was seen as evidence of the need to do so; at the same time, Zora Neale Hurston and other artists of the Harlem Renaissance were attracted to and celebrated black folklore in the south. The conflict between assimilation into whiteness versus celebration of blackness continues among African American intellectuals to this day (see chapter 8). African American writers and intellectuals were not monolithic in their opinions, and neither were European American folklorists and anthropologists.

White reviewers of *Folk Beliefs of the Southern Negro* were mainly favorable in their judgments although two reviews in the *Journal of American Folklore* differed in their assessment of the work. Louise Pound seemed to accept the cultural evolution model and its racial implications when she commented, "The pages abound with references to witches, ghosts, devils, goblins, snakes,

black cats, headless horses, and other phenomena of superstition from which
the white race has now pretty well worked itself free" (1927, 102). Melville J.
Herskovits, on the other hand, questioned some of Puckett's cultural generalizations, especially about West Africa.

> Although he refers to a large amount of literature, some of the more important
> sources on West Africa are missing, and it is to be feared that his presentation
> of the cultural situation in West Africa is thereby made less effective. Thus, we
> find that the Negro manifests "shortsightedness, indifference, and disregard
> for the future . . . traits common not only to Africans and many Negroes,
> but to almost all undisciplined primitive peoples." That the West Africans,
> further, are "mostly in a confused state of transition from the state of purely
> nomadic savagery to that of settled agriculture" is, as a statement of the case,
> unfortunate, to say the least. (1927, 310)

Herskovits was one of the functionalists who questioned the automatic primitivism of such scholars as Puckett. He avoided harsh criticism of the book,
but he questioned Puckett's lack of contextual information, "One might only
wish . . . that any continuation of his efforts might be directed toward a fuller
presentation of the entire cultural setting of some of the beliefs with which
he is dealing, a method, one feels, which cannot but clarify the significance
which they hold for those to whom they are of the greatest importance, the
people who believe in them" (1927, 312). Herskovits was part of the anthropological school of Franz Boas, Bronislaw Malinowski, Ruth Benedict, and
others who emphasized the need for examining folk expressions in cultural
context. Puckett, however, was still oriented toward the nineteenth-century
emphasis on texts although in his recognition of the creative functions of
folklore, he was closer to the contextualists.

Puckett may have had mixed feelings toward folk belief, but he saw artistic
genres such as folksong as positive cultural expressions worth preserving.
In this, some of Puckett's ambivalence toward race can be seen. His ideas
about race were an interesting blend of science and romance; he proposed to
objectively study Negro folk culture, but the rhetoric of his scholarly writing
and even more so of his poetry reveals a romantic vision of the Exotic Other.
In talking about folksong, his romantic rhetoric took over: "The white man
most of the time sings from the song book, but the illiterate Negro sings from
the soul . . . Much of the happiness of the uneducated Negro is based upon
his unrestrained surrender to this spirit of song" (1969 [1926], 60–61). His
use of terms such as "soul" and "spirit," although metaphorical, indicate his
essentialist concept of blacks as a race. Here again is an implied whiteness in

his conceptualization of blackness: if blacks sang from the soul in an illiterate oral tradition and whites from song books in a literate tradition, then civilization had cut whites off from the spiritual dimension of life. Blackness is about freedom from restraint and whiteness is about repression of that freedom—certainly an ironic implication given the lack of civil rights for black people at the time. This particular oppositional construction of race continued well into the twentieth century in the scholarship of John Lomax, Alan Lomax, and others, and is still found in popular conceptions of racial difference in the present. Since black folksong came from the soul and was the kind of folklore Puckett wanted to preserve, he appealed "for the preservation of the beauty-things of folk-life—those priceless pearls of folk-thought which daily are being crushed beneath the feet of the unthinking" (1973 [1926], 8).

His attitude toward the beauty of folklore was entwined with his romantic nostalgia for the old plantation South: "The quavering whispers of the old 'songster' can no longer be heard above the uncouth blare of modern music—daily, almost hourly, these superb rhythmic masterpieces die down to golden echoes and pass unwritten to the Land of Forgotten Things" (8). Puckett's attitude toward jazz as a corruption of the purity of African American folk music was very similar to John Lomax's (Hirsch 1992, 194) as was his nostalgia about the Old South that rejected modern changes in music (see chapter 3). Puckett's nostalgia created a central dilemma for him that is a source of his ambivalence about folklore and race: education is necessary to rise above ignorance and superstition, but education will also destroy the positive traditions; progress up the evolutionary scale will cause the loss of a beautiful folk art. His nostalgia is suspect, of course, because it is a white man's imagined past of the plantation Negro that leaves out the everyday horrors of slavery. In this respect, Puckett is part of a long, and still ongoing, tradition of the white southern romance.

Hurston was like Puckett in that there is an underlying romanticism in her representations of rural African American folk culture although her romanticism was of an entirely different political nature than Puckett's; his was based on an ideal of the southern plantation with slaves singing happily in the background; hers was of the independent rural black community in the past and present, existing separately from white middle-class culture and in many ways superior to it. Literary critic Hazel Carby sees Hurston's romanticism in *Mules and Men* and *Their Eyes Were Watching God* as an attempt to construct an essentialist rural/pastoral African American identity based on Hurston's own idealization of the folk (Carby 1994, 28–44). Puckett's romanticizing idealized the past to justify the status quo in the present. Hurston also romanticized the past, but she did so to establish a political basis for change in the present.

Hurston's romanticizing can also be seen as an element in her attempts to make her fieldwork materials available to a wider audience. Hurston had published the material on hoodoo earlier in the *Journal of American Folklore* (JAF), and the version in *Mules and Men* is essentially the same. She was disappointed in the JAF publication because "all the flaming glory" was "buried" on the "shelves of scientific societies" (Hemenway 1978, xxiv), and she was intent on reaching a wider popular reading public (Hemenway 1977, 162–64). In emphasizing the "flaming glory" of the hoodoo rituals, she revealed her insider's view of African American belief and at the same time reinforced her intended popular audience's exotic and romantic expectations. Rosemary Hathaway points out how Hurston's technique subtly undermines romantic expectations as well (2004, 186), but nevertheless Hurston's insider's description has more "glory" than the cold critical language of an outsider scholar and is also more appealing to the general reader.

Hurston left out some negative details that might have undermined her positive romantic portrayal of her subjects. In a 1936 review, black writer Sterling Brown criticized *Mules and Men* for its pastoral romanticism: he said, "harsher folktales await the collector," and concluded "*Mules and Men* should be more bitter, it would be nearer the total truth" (quoted in Hemenway 1978, xxv–xxvi). I believe there is a political dimension to *Mules and Men* that comments indirectly on the harsh realities of racism, as Hemenway (1978, xxvi–xxvii), Susan Meisenhelder (1996), bell hooks (1990, 138), and others have pointed out. Hurston used traditional African American rhetorical strategies such as the trickster and signifying to make indirect political statements about race. She also used examples of hoodoo to illustrate racism and make moral points. For instance, one of her hoodoo narratives is about a racist white man who kills one of his black female servants; her father uses his knowledge of hoodoo to put a spell on the white planter and exact his revenge—the planter's own family turns on him (1978 [1935], 240–42). She did not feel the need to make direct polemic statements as Richard Wright does in *Native Son* (1940) when he uses Bigger Thomas's lawyer as a mouthpiece for his own political views; rather she let the narrative about racism speak for itself. However, the omission of direct statements of condemnation of the horrors of racism does suggest a more romantic view of rural black southern folk culture.

This romantic view can also be seen in her novel *Their Eyes Were Watching God* which has elements of primitivism in it although the opposite of

Puckett's and the cultural evolutionists' version of primitivism. As Torgov-nick points out, primitivism suggests an implicit comparison of the past and the present, of traditionality and modernity: "Is the present too mate-rialistic? Primitive life is not—it is a precapitalist utopia in which only use value, never exchange value, prevails. Is the present sexually repressed? Not primitive life—primitives live life whole, without fear of the body" (1990, 8–9). In one late episode in *Their Eyes Were Watching God*, Hurston's folk characters exist in an anticapitalist and sexually free utopia, indicating how closely aligned the constructions of folk and primitive are. She describes the setting in terms of a wilder African American version of the pastoral ideal: "Ground so rich that everything went wild. Volunteer cane just taking the place. Dirt roads so rich and black that a half mile of it would have fertilized a Kansas wheat field. Wild cane on either side of the road hiding the rest of the world. People wild too" (1978 [1937], 193). Later she describes the char-acters as being one with their natural surroundings: "Blues made and used right on the spot. Dancing, fighting, singing, crying, laughing, winning and losing love every hour. Work all day for money, fight all night for love. The rich black earth clinging to bodies and biting the skin like ants" (197). In this description, Hurston seems to suggest that folk performances of blues and dancing, sexuality, and nature are all one, ironically creating an image of black folkness that is similar to that of white folklorist Alan Lomax (see chapter 4).

Her descriptions of African American cultural and class attitudes toward work and finances in this environment are similar to Puckett's, but instead of his capitalist condemnation of them, she celebrates this attitude: "They made good money. Next month and next year were other times. No need to mix them up with the present" (197). In this anticapitalist, sexually free, close-to-nature setting, Janie, the major character in the novel, and her lover, Tea Cake, live the most idyllic part of their lives together: he plays his guitar and enjoys his friends; she works along side of him in the fields and becomes more fully defined as a woman. In the novel, Hurston draws upon some of her fieldwork experiences and knowledge of folk culture gained as an ethnographer, but she uses them in the creative ways of a novelist with the result that *Their Eyes Were Watching God* is finally more romantic than her ethnographic account of similar material. As what we might call "creative ethnography," *Mules and Men* stands as a detailed and dynamic representation of a complex and creative culture, an effective antidote to the pathological views of other folkloric and literary representations of African American culture. Hurston's positive view of African American belief and practice was probably impossible for Puckett as a white folklorist to have; he brought too many ethnocentric assumptions about superstition to his fieldwork to be able to see any of it as sacred ritual and too many capitalist assumptions about work to view a carefree attitude about money as a positive trait.

Because of Hurston's and Puckett's different insider/outsider perspectives and the corresponding differences in assumptions about race and folk belief, their fieldwork methods were diametrically opposed. Puckett recognized that as an outsider, he could never have a complete knowledge of African American culture, but he also thought he had more insights than most whites. In the introduction to *Folk Beliefs of the Southern Negro,* he said, "After twenty years or more of close association with the Negro, an honorary membership in "de Mount Zion Missionary Baptist Church," and several years' experience as an amateur "hoodoo-doctor," I am convinced that "de signs an' wonders" disclosed here are but outward manifestations of a well-nigh inscrutable Negro soul. My peep behind the curtains has destroyed for me the fable that "the Southern white man *thoroughly* understands the Negro . . ." (1969 [1926], vii). An honorary membership in a black church and acceptance as a hoodoo doctor are evidence that Puckett had some success in winning his informants' trust, but he was not above the use of deceit to get information he needed. In his book, Puckett explained how he became a hoodoo doctor: "After being asked to pay $20 for some trifling information by Negroes, whom I had good reason to believe, were hoodoos, I finally adopted the role of conjure-doctor myself, in order to be able to discuss the tricks of the trade as hoodoo to hoodoo without having to live the rest of my life on 'half-rations'" (206). He also used trickery to gain information from a New Orleans hoodoo-doctor.

> When the conversation lulled, unknown to him I changed the notebook upon which I had been writing, for the [identical] unused one which I had concealed in my inner coat pocket. Then I told him I possessed the power of keeping him from seeing things I did not want him to see. "You have seen me writing in this book," I said, "now read what I have written." Making a pass at the Negro, I handed him the unused book. He opened it and saw only the blank pages. His jaw dropped, his eyes nearly popped out of his head—in fact I thought he was going to fall backward into the "Father of Waters." "My Gawd, white man, you's wonderful!" (213–14)

He later comments on his deception, "Perhaps such practices are not exactly ethical, but I won my man's respect and obtained information, besides testing out the extreme credulity of even the conjure-doctors themselves" (214).

Puckett tried to justify his subterfuges by always keeping his distance from the beliefs. If the beliefs were simply ignorant superstitions, then he could deceive the practitioners in the name of more effective fieldwork. His behavior also suggests the blackness/whiteness racial dichotomy: black ignorance and credulity construct white rationality and control.

Zora Neale Hurston could not have been more different in her approach to fieldwork: throughout *Mules and Men* she becomes part of the community in which she was conducting field research. She got to know the people she was working with to the point of being attacked by women jealous of her relationships with their men. Because she was of the same race and culture as her informants, she was able to conduct participant-observer fieldwork in ways that were impossible for Puckett as a white person. Her fieldwork on hoodoo and conjuration was not done from a distant ethnographic stance but by actually joining hoodoo cults and studying with hoodoo priests, learning their practices firsthand, and being initiated into the groups. From her descriptions in *Mules and Men,* she seems to have become emotionally immersed in her study of New Orleans hoodoo; in many ways she crossed the line between ethnographer and informant, letting subjectivity overcome any pretense of objectivity (Camitta 1990, 25; Jordan 1992, 122). She described one initiation in *Mules and Men* in which she fasted for three days, had five psychic experiences, was carried naked by five men, and had a lightning bolt painted across her body (1978 [1935], 208–9). Her participation in hoodoo rituals gave her a perspective that Puckett's condescending distance did not allow:

> Comparing Hurston's collecting technique with that of Newbell Niles Puckett reveals why she was so much more successful. Puckett had masqueraded as a conjure man himself, trading remedies and rituals with the doctors who would talk with him. He was a white man challenging the black man's power. Hurston was a black woman of great sympathy offering herself as an apprentice to the experienced sorcerer. She wished to learn, beginning with the simple and advancing to the complex. As a result, she not only gained a holistic view of the hoodoo process, but also experienced a series of impressive initiation ceremonies marking her acceptance into the occult world. (Hemenway 1977, 118)

She said that she came to believe in the efficacy of many hoodoo rituals, an attitude that was the exact opposite of Puckett's rejection and condescension. Hurston describes the initiation rituals respectfully and matter-of-factly, though her descriptions are certainly what outsiders would perceive as exotic.

Some scholars have called into question the ethics of Hurston's fieldwork methods because she did not reveal to her informants her scholarly reasons for wanting to be initiated into hoodoo cults and she subsequently revealed their secrets in her publications. She implies that she did not reveal secrets: "in this book all of the works of any [hoodoo] doctor cannot be given" (1978 [1935], 121), but her descriptions are full of details that suggest they were not meant for outsiders. John Dorst says that in part I of *Mules and Men* Hurston based her fieldwork on "a bogus identity, a story that is a real lie, a deception" (1987, 311). For instance, she once pretended to be a bootlegger to win the confidence of a local community (Hurston 1978 [1935], 66). Other scholars defend her use of deception as part of her implicit reflexive critique of white ethnographic studies of black people; she was "signifying" both on her informants and her white readers (Staub 1994, 101–2). Her ultimate goal of educating white people about the true nature of African American culture might justify her lying to get inside the culture. Hurston may have been guilty of some of the same unethical practices as Puckett but for totally different political reasons. They both used deception, but Puckett's practices were based on his dismissal of the beliefs; Hurston's were based on a respect for them and a need to see the inner workings of belief and practice as a religion. Does this justify her fieldwork practices any more than it does Puckett's? From the perspective of present day fieldwork ethics, neither of their methods could be justified, but in their day, such practices were more widespread.

Pretending to be a hoodoo-doctor meant that Puckett continued seeing his informants from a white middle-class perspective, but he also seemed to recognize his own ethnocentrism. "Case studies [of the Negro] etch in the minute details, but are apt unconsciously to reflect the prejudices and interests of the observer rather than those of the observed. Difficulties of location and racial barriers make participant observation of Negro folk culture on a classwide scale practically impossible. In spite of such complications the masses remain the real bearers of the mores of Negro society and direct or indirect contact with them is essential" (1934, 12–13). His grasp of the concept of ethnocentrism in fieldwork did not always translate into a recognition of his own "prejudices and interests" as an observer, just as it does not for folklorists today.

His success in fieldwork with black informants, as defined by a white perspective, was the basis for Puckett's reputation for being at home with "common people." His friend George Kummer wrote of Puckett:

His ability to establish rapport with common people was due in part to his upbringing. He was born July 8, 1897 in Columbus, Mississippi. His father, Willis Niles Puckett, a self-made man, who had parlayed his skill as a brick-layer into a brick factory, the town's principal industry, saw to it that Newbell from the age of ten worked in the factory after school and in summer. There the lad learned to lay bricks and to enjoy the companionship of his father's employees, most of whom were Negroes. Of course, this intimacy with work and workers, especially with Black workers, was decidedly advantageous to him in his future career as a folklorist. (1981, 1534)

Kummer also described Puckett "singing gospel hymns with illiterate Blacks in the South," and added, "There was no condescension in his makeup; he genuinely liked grassroots people and was eager to share his own folk heritage with them" (ibid.). This denial of condescension sounds condescending from the perspective of the reflexive postmodern present, but in Puckett's Old South, his relationship with blacks would have been seen as a model of progressive race relations. His dealings with blacks depended on the tradition of white paternalism, but his methods were effective in fulfilling his need to "peep behind the curtain" of racial difference.

Puckett dealt with the outward manifestations of black culture in his scholarship, but he attempted to penetrate the "inscrutable Negro soul" in his poetry by assuming the character and the voice of a black person, an example of racial mimicry and part of the process of "racechange" (Gubar 1997, 5). Unfortunately, his use of black dialect reinforced many cultural stereotypes. In using black dialect, he was following a tradition established by Joel Chandler Harris and other white writers that in turn influenced black poet Paul Lawrence Dunbar; all these writers presented a sentimental view of plantation slavery. Dunbar, who wrote both dialect and nondialect poetry, was popular in the late nineteenth and early twentieth century, and he was widely imitated by both black and white poets (Gates 1988, 174). I did not find any references to Dunbar in Puckett's personal papers, but it is likely that Dunbar influenced him in both style and subject matter.

The popularity of Dunbar's dialect poetry indicated how widespread stereotypes of black speech were. By the late nineteenth century, according to Henry Louis Gates, "dialect had come to connote black innate mental inferiority, the linguistic sign both of human bondage (as origin) and of the continued failure of 'improvability' or 'progress,' two turn-of the-century keywords. Dialect signified both 'black difference' and that the figure of the black in literature existed primarily as object, not subject; and even sympathetic characterizations of the black . . . were far more related to a racist textual tradition that stemmed from minstrelsy, the plantation novel, and vaudeville than to representations of spoken language" (1988, 176). With his use of black dialect in his poetry, Puckett unknowingly undermined his own goal of cultural uplift for African Americans.

By the 1920s, African American writers recognized the problems inherent in using black dialect in literature, but they were not ready to give it up. James Weldon Johnson thought that the problem was not in the use of dialect itself but in the limited way it was used within literary convention: "It is an instrument with but two full stops, humor and pathos" (1922, xi). Harlem Renaissance writers such as Sterling Brown, Langston Hughes, and Zora Neale Hurston were able to employ dialect to expand the scope of black experience represented in literature, but Puckett was still stuck in the nineteenth century, limited to humor and pathos in his representations of black speech in his poetry.

Puckett's attitude toward folk speech in his scholarly writing prefigured his comic use of black dialect in poetry. He referred to, "the barbaric mangling of healthy English words by the tongue of the would-be Negro savant. The Negro meets with the 'Christian and Deviled Egg Society' (Christian Endeavor and Aid Society) and dwells upon 'dem curious *Cadillacs* (Catholics) what woan' eat no meat on Friday.' . . . leaving the puzzled folklorist at a 'conclusive standstill,' as the Negro would say, as to whether to run for an African dictionary or a Negro interpreter" (1969 [1926], 13). Later in the same work, he says, "But not always is the work a mutilation. At times the creative impulse comes in . . ." (29). He saw some creativity in black folk speech, but he failed to recognize the possibility that what he thought of as "mutilation" could also be creative expression.

Puckett's poem "Fawty-Fo Dave" contains a good example of his comic use of dialect; he has a character say, "I done tole him dat-ah fawty-fo gun / Gwineter funeralize his name." Perhaps Puckett thought of "funeralize" as an instance of the creative impulse, but the comic purpose is clear. The narrator of the prose poem "Reas'nin's of Rastus: On Being Black" says, "A good-taste cullah black are—sign of cultivator-folks, lak rich widder-mo'ners or feet-washin' preacher-people." Using "cultivator" for "cultivated" projects an inferior agrarian image on the black speaker, reinforcing a negative stereotype. Puckett seems unaware of the possibility that these linguistic coinages could be deliberate plays on white standard English, examples of African American signifying (Abrahams 1985, 6–7; Gates 1988, 44–88). The manuscripts of Puckett's poems show that he worked at honing the dialect. In the first line of

"My Hoodoo Charm," he scratched out several of the typewritten words and substituted others in his own handwriting. "Dat Hoodoo-man takes some bristles frum a cat" becomes "Ol' Hoodoo-man git de whiskers frum a cat." Replacing standard English words with dialect suggests he had to overcome his own tendency to write in standard English in order to achieve what he perceived as the appropriate Negro voice.

Puckett's tendency toward pathos can be seen in "Camp-Meetin' Time," which begins "Hit's de time fur fun en frolic caze de cotton crop is made; / Caze de gold'n-rod is bloomin' en Ah sees de 'vitin' shade." Another couplet later in the poem states, "Well jes' look et Sistah Johns'n in her Sunday calico, / She'll be wearin' dat ol' garmint when de Gabr'l trump'll blow." And finally, "Oh de pattin' en de shoutin' en de high-connipshun fits, / En de mo'ners cryin' sighin' whin de Holy Sperit hits." This portrait of African American religion was in keeping with Puckett's scholarly view that Negro and white Christianity were basically different: "Negro Christianity is often Christianity in convulsions, and this religious frenzy of the rural Negro offers much interesting material [for study]" (1973 [1926], 7). Elsewhere he pointed out that blacks were influenced by the emotionalism of nineteenth-century white Christian camp meetings suggesting that he was aware that white and black Christianity were not so different (1931, 20). "Camp-Meetin' Time" and other poems like it are similar to Dunbar's "overdrawn, idealized, and sentimentalized" portraits of the old Plantation South (Barksdale and Kinnamon 1972, 350).

Because of their opposite political positions, Hurston's use of black dialect is a totally different story. She renders black speech with dialect spellings in both *Mules and Men* and *Their Eyes Were Watching God* in such sentences as "Take dem frowns out yo' face and go right on back to Heben and ast God to give you dat bunch of keys hangin' on de mantel-piece" (1978 [1935], 35–36). The dilemma for black writers at this time was to give some sense of the richness of black oral dialect on the printed page without evoking the stereotyped plantation view of Joel Chandler Harris and Paul Lawrence Dunbar. Hurston tried to solve the problem by providing a much more detailed performance context for the speech than previous writers had. As Michael Staub has pointed out:

> Hurston aims in her text to represent black speech as an ongoing process, embedded in various historical situations and relations of power, not a dead, isolatable specimen.
>
> In order to accomplish her goal of presenting black oral traditions as vital and legitimate, Hurston had to do more than document the telling of tales;

she had to address the entire complex of problems surrounding ethnography as a scholarly and a political enterprise evolving in the thirties. (1994, 89)

She places dialogue and the telling of folk tales into speech and performance situations to indicate the complexity and creativity of the language, unlike Puckett who used dialect spellings in conversations with the white ethnographer to make fun of the black speaker. Puckett and other white folklorists such as John Lomax used dialect spellings only to represent black speech, never their own; they speak in standard English. At the beginning of *Mules and Men,* Hurston quotes herself using black dialect: "Ah come to collect some old stories and tales and Ah know y'all know a plenty of 'em and that's why Ah headed straight for home," but she addresses the reader in standard English, "As I crossed the Maitland-Eatonville township line I could see a group on the store porch" (1978 [1935], 9), thus drawing attention to her two roles and to the complexities of speech in social and literary contexts (Staub 1994, 92–93).

Hurston also used dialect to gain acceptance into the community when she takes part in traditional African American discourses such as "woofing," indicating that she is becoming a part of the community (1978 [1935], 68–69). She is at a social gathering when one of the men approaches her.

> "Ma'am, whut might be yo' entrimmins?" he asked with what was supposed to be a killing bow.
> "My whut?"
> "Yo entrimmins? Yo entitlum?"
> The "entitlum" gave me the cue, "Oh, my name is Zora Hurston. And whut may be yours?"
> "Mah name is Pitts and Ah'm sho glad to meet yuh. Ah asted Cliffert tuh knock me down tuh yuh be he wouldn't make me 'quainted. So Ah'm makin' mahseff 'quainted."
> "Ah'm glad you did, Mr. Pitts."
> "Sho nuff?" archly.
> "Yeah. Ah wouldn't be sayin' it if Ah didn't mean it."
> He looked me over shrewdly. "Ah see dar las' crap you shot, Miss, and Ah fade yuh."
> I laughed heartily. The whole fire laughed at his quick comeback and more people came out to listen. (68)

This repartee continues for several pages demonstrating the quick wit of both Mr. Pitts and Hurston. This was a means for her to be accepted by the group, but it also shows the reader that the dialect can be clever, creative, and effective—that the people using the dialect are indeed intelligent, not the ignorant Negroes of Puckett's portrayal. Hurston breaks down the distance between ethnographer and subject thereby at least partially wiping out the superiority of the ethnographer. Hurston's use of dialect is a far cry from the southern plantation tradition of Puckett and Dunbar.

Puckett was like Dunbar in that each wrote both black dialect poems and poetry in conventional nineteenth-century romantic diction. The most striking feature of Puckett's nondialect poetry is the romantic nostalgia for the Old South. The last stanza of "That Old Plantation Bell" and the first stanza of "Dixie" provide telling examples.

> How often in the city with its restless throb and flow
> Have I longed to hear that music that I loved so long ago—
> I am sick of all the shamming, and the fake—also the steak—Just think
>   of all those waffles that Aunt Lucy used to make.
> But a better day is coming—if in Heaven I ever dwell,
> I want the Lord to call me with that old plantation bell.
>
> 'Tis Dixie that the band is playing,
> With Dixie-thoughts my soul is swaying,
> To Dixie-land my heart is straying—
> . . . . To Dixie." (Puckett n.d.)

Both these poems reflect the point of view of a white southerner living in the urban north and yearning for the rural south, but again the nostalgia ignores the economic hardships, social prejudices, and violence that blacks in the South had to face.

Puckett's use of two poetic modes—dialect and conventional poetic diction—suggest the split within himself, his contradictory feelings toward African American culture. On the one hand, he tried to be black by assuming the voice of the Negro, and on the other hand, he distanced himself from African Americans by speaking in his own voice, one based in British poetic tradition. He was both attracted and repulsed by blackness, and this is clearly seen in his poem "Reversion."

> Beneath the Crust of Culture
> We all are primitives.
> And often times an uncouth hand
> Breaks through the Crust, and wakes
> Subconscious chords
> To vague uncanny melody—
> The shapeless songs of yester-years.

The dance begins—the maddening muse
Of grotesque "Jazz" sets in to ooze—
The boom! the clash! the accents blunt,
The saxophone with swinish grunt!
The drone! the screech! the clack! the growl!
The squawk! the snarl! the bark! the howl!
The untamed roar of rugged noise!
Tears Culture down—destroys my poise!

Wierd [sic] musings lash my spirit fast—
Primeval yearnings of the past—
The muggy ghosts of vandal days
Destroy my soul! My spirit sways—
And falls—and dies! And in its stead
A hulking SOMETHING, leering red—
Sneaks in my heart—and turns back time
To ages past—to beasts and slime!

Once more I hear the tom-toms beat,
The muffled stamp of barefoot feet,
The fiendish din of jungle night;
I see the grisly warriors fight
For female love—a fight to death—
Hyenic gasps—volcanic breath!
Again the "Jazz"—the brutal roar—
I am a primitive once more!! (Puckett n.d.)

The concept of cultural evolution underlies the ideas presented in "Reversion": from the poet's civilized perspective in the present, he imagines going back in time to a primitive stage of "beasts and slime." Incorporated into this is a sense that the primitive exists in the present within all individuals at a subconscious level "Beneath the Crust of Culture." The poem is based on Freudian concepts of the unconscious and repression of sexual desire; Puckett seems aware of how his own white repression provoked a need for a representation of the Other as a symbolic release of these primitive impulses. He not only associated blacks with primitive sexuality in his poetry, he also stated it directly in his book: "Due . . . in part, perhaps, to the natural sexuality of the Negro, many less advanced members of that race today are, to say the least, careless in their sexual life" (1969 [1926], 24). Significantly for Puckett's view of racial difference, the descriptions of the primitive in "Reversion" are drawn from images associated with African American culture—jazz, jungle drums, dance, sexuality. These same images were used by Harlem Renaissance poets, composers, and novelists such as Hurston, Langston Hughes, and Duke Ellington to suggest the positive vitality of African American culture; but Puckett used them as something to be feared. Symbolically in the poem, blacks represent the primitive instinct in civilized white people, and that both attracts and repels him. The repulsion is explicit in the language ("grotesque," "fiendish," "brutal") but the attraction is implicit in the poet's inability to resist the pull ("I am a primitive once more!!"). In terms of the social construction of race, black primitive urges have won out over white restraint.

By assuming a black voice in his dialect poems, Puckett was becoming "a primitive once more"; he became the hoodoo-man working on his charm and the deacon carried away in religious frenzy. But in poems such as "Reversion," he could express his fear of the primitive. The poetry and the scholarship are of a piece, both express some of the same underlying concepts about African Americans and race relations, but the poetry reveals Puckett's emotions about race more directly.

The sociologist objectively describing a culture had some deeply subjective ideas that he brought to his work. Puckett's objective research was suffused with culturally learned concepts from his youth in Mississippi and from his graduate work at Yale. Puckett was a product of his own culture and can be seen in retrospect as projecting a basic white image about race—the Exotic Other as closer to a primitive state of development, as a symbol of instinctual impulses that have been covered up by civilization in white people. Zora Neale Hurston was also a product of her culture, and from her insider perspective as a black person, she was able to represent African Americans in a much more positive, nonpathological light. But ironically both Hurston and Puckett share a tendency toward romanticism and primitivism with quite different political motives. Racial politics have become more complex since Puckett's and Hurston's time; there is more awareness of the construction of racial identity and condemnation of essentialist primitivism. However, many of the cultural patterns concerning race that we see in Puckett and Hurston continued to be a part of the representation of race throughout the twentieth century and into the twenty-first. In order to understand the racial scholarship of Alan Lomax, Roger Abrahams, and folklorists writing today, we need to examine closely the careers of other earlier scholars such as John Lomax.

3

The Racial Relationship of
John Lomax and Henry Truvillion

As I have traveled up and down the South
these recent years, I find myself always looking
for Nat, the dear friend and companion of long ago.

—John Lomax

John Lomax was born in Mississippi only ninety miles from where Newbell Niles Puckett was born, and even though Lomax was born thirty years earlier, they shared many of the same cultural attitudes and scholarly concepts. Both were grounded in nineteenth-century Southern culture, and both believed in the theory of cultural evolution. They shared a fascination with African American culture and a desire to know more about it. Their careers were quite different, though: Puckett worked in a relatively obscure academic environment, while Lomax conducted his research on a much more public stage. Lomax's association with the Library of Congress, his widely read collections of folksongs, and his "discovery" of such important folksingers as Leadbelly made him one of the best-known folklorists of his day.

When John Lomax was recording African American singers for the Library of Congress in the 1930s and '40s, he brought his assumptions about race to the field research and to his subsequent writing about the artists and their cultures. His attitudes toward race have been explored by David Evans (1982), James McNutt (1982), Jeff Titon (1987), Jerrold Hirsch (1992), Charles Wolfe and Kip Lornell (1992), and Nolan Porterfield (1996). In turn, these authors have created various representations of Lomax in their publications. Collectively, these scholars have described the abstract cultural beliefs and values that influenced the way Lomax perceived African Americans; not enough, however, has been written about his specific relationships with black people and how they helped create, maintain, and alter his worldview. The abstract "-isms"—romanticism, pastoralism, paternalism—that undoubtedly influenced his assumptions have been identified; I want to examine in some depth and detail his relationship with a major black informant, Henry Truvillion. My investigation into this relationship has been greatly enhanced by the recollections of Henry Truvillion's son, Reverend Jesse Truvillion, whose own memories of Lomax give new details on the processes of folklore fieldwork and representations of the folk.

Jesse Truvillion's recollections about his father and his childhood in the Big Thicket of East Texas provide a unique perspective. Ethnographic scholarship usually provides only one view: that of the ethnographer. Jesse Truvillion gives us the family's view of Henry Truvillion not only as singer, but also as father, husband, minister, worker, and community member. This is the insider's view and an example of cultural self-representation. We can see beyond John Lomax's limited representation of an African American folksinger and instead view a fuller portrait of a human being. This portrait is itself a cultural representation based on memory and emotional attachment, but it has incalculable value in helping us understand Lomax's representation as it contrasts with Jesse's perspective on his father. Before we get to a consideration of the relationship of John Lomax and Henry Truvillion, we need to examine the cultural context and racial assumptions that Lomax brought to his fieldwork and resulting publications.

John Lomax portrayed Henry Truvillion in ways that fit white views of black people at the time; in examining their relationship and Lomax's publications and recordings about Truvillion, I join with Hirsch, Porterfield, and other scholars in constructing an image of John Lomax as a folklorist that is, at least partially, based on my understanding of Lomax as a person. The dilemma here is the tendency to view white folklorists of the past from the perspective of early twenty-first century attitudes toward race. As Nolan Porterfield points out in his biography of Lomax, "Those [racist] attitudes, although indefensible from an enlightened point of view, were nevertheless commingled with a sensibility which complicates any effort to dismiss him as a simple racist" (1996, 169). Lomax's attitudes toward race were complex; they were based on nineteenth-century cultural assumptions about blacks, his emotional early childhood experiences, his formal education, and social and fieldwork contacts with blacks from a different socioeconomic milieu. A constant in his life was the conviction that his interest in African American folklore and culture was based on sound moral and ethical principles, that he was interested in the well being of his black informants and of African Americans in general.

·

Despite perceptual gaps between today's folklorists and those of Lomax's generation, there are cross-generational similarities in the concern for the well-being of people from minority cultures. In the past, in particular, these concerns were too often expressed in hierarchical and condescending ways; but many, perhaps most, folklorists from the 1930s to the 1990s have tried to understand and communicate respect for other cultures to each other and the general public. Even that well-intentioned perspective, though, led to cultural misrepresentations (Duneier 1992, 137–55). Lomax's generation made mistakes, and mistakes continue to be made today, but growing scholarly self-awareness is a positive development in solving the dilemmas of representation.

Born in Mississippi and raised in Texas, John Lomax was a product of white southern culture, and his ideas about race were grounded in the pastoral romanticism of the plantation (Hirsch 1992, 184–85). Like other white southern scholars, Lomax thought that industrialization, urbanization, and technological change were destroying the southern agrarian way of life, including folk traditions of African Americans. Like Puckett, Lomax admired certain kinds of African American folklore as art—especially folksong—but he followed prevailing scholarly theory in seeing the singers he recorded in the field in evolutionary terms as expressing a more primitive culture. Porterfield quotes Lomax as writing that the Negro was "a simple, emotional, imitative, human being" with "a child's eager and willing adaptableness to his environment." Porterfield then comments, "That sweeping and tragic misconception was his earliest, most deeply held notion of blacks, and it would always prevent him from seeing the basic contradiction: if they were inferior, how could they create the exalted art that he so cherished and respected?" (1996, 170). I think the answer to Porterfield's question lies in Lomax's perception that black inferiority was the source of their great art, that there was a primitive source to African American folksong (Torgovnick 1990).

Lomax's view of blacks as inferior was combined with a real compassion for their plight; unfortunately, this caused him to treat black informants in a paternalistic way. His paternalism toward blacks reinforced his sense of whiteness as magnanimous, part of a larger cultural dynamic in the Old South (Morrison 1992, 17). There is evidence of paternalism in his relationship with Henry Truvillion, but this pattern is most clearly reflected in his relationship with his most famous informant, the black singer Huddie Ledbetter. In their biography of Leadbelly, Charles Wolfe and Kip Lornell paint a sympathetic picture of Lomax, but they question the way he assumed a parental authority over Leadbelly (1992, 143–85). For instance, they document the financial control that Lomax tried to maintain. Lomax's paternalism suggests a pattern of white "innocence" as a basis for power over the recipients of his paternalism. Mitchell Duneier identifies this in white liberal social scientists in the 1960s and later (Duneier 1992, 137–55), but it also applies to the politically conservative Lomax. He too assumed that his good intentions always led to beneficial results for black people, not recognizing how his negative stereotypes functioned to keep black people "in their place."

Lomax both accepted and reinforced traditional generalizations about race. David Evans quotes a 1917 essay by Lomax as evidence of Lomax's "grossly stereotyped view" of blacks:

> There surely exists no merrier-hearted race than the negro, especially in his natural home, the warm climate of the South. The negro's loud laugh may sometimes speak the empty mind, but at the same time it reveals a nature upon which trouble and want sit but lightly. . . . It is credible, at least, that the negro's self-pity is based on his feeling of race inferiority—a feeling of which he may well be only sub-consciously aware. . . . And it seems further credible that he has come to lump the troubles for which he himself is largely to blame along with the inevitable hardships of his situation until he has grown to regard himself as the victim of hard luck, generally abused by everybody; and, at least in many instances, he seems not averse to nursing his gloom a little. (1982, 38)

While Evans recognizes that retrospective judgments about historical figures are problematic, he also sees the need to identify racial assumptions that influenced Lomax and other early blues scholars (32–105).

There are certainly racist assumptions in Lomax's statement—he seems to be "blaming the victim" in current terms—but some of his ideas are still found today among social critics, both black and white, who condemn what they see as a tendency for blacks on welfare to self-identify as "victims" (Sykes 1992; Sowell 1997). In addition, like Lomax, two black psychologists during the 1960s posited a black self-hatred based on a perceived sense of racial inferiority (Grier and Cobbs 1968). John Szwed pointed out how earlier pathological models of African American culture persisted into the 1960s: "These 'culturally different' behaviors (i.e., different from white middle-class culture) continued to be treated as evidence of deviance, as social pathology, as failures on the part of individual black people in the face of oppression; and if these behaviors became recognized as patterned and normative, they were nonetheless treated as part of a deficit culture, a kind of negative culture existing in the absence of a real one" (1969, 160).

Pointing out the persistence of these ideas into the 1960s and later does not excuse Lomax's racist assumptions; rather my aim is to demonstrate an unfortunate continuity in the perceptual framework. Lomax identified some real social problems based on racial and class difference, but the flaw in his thinking—like that of some writers today—was in considering them linked to biology rather than to social factors. Lomax's attitudes were widespread in his generation, and he had moral and ethical intentions in his study of African Americans. I agree with Jerrold Hirsch that we must go beyond the limited goal of identification and condemnation of racism to gain an understanding of race relations in historical context (1992, 185)—Lomax's and our own.

Both Hirsch (1992, 196–97) and Porterfield (1996, 20–21) mention a black friend from Lomax's childhood as an important influence on his attitudes toward race: Nat Blythe came to work on the Lomax farm when he was eighteen, and nine-year-old John Lomax taught him to read and write (J. Lomax 1947, 9–12). They played together, and according to Lomax, he learned his sense of rhythm from Nat, another example of white mimicry of black style among folklorists. "I came to love Nat with the fierce strength and loyalty of youth" (11). When Nat turned twenty-one, he was given his savings and he left. Lomax writes, "I have never since seen or heard of him . . . As I have traveled up and down the South these recent years, I find myself always looking for Nat, the dear friend and companion of long ago. I loved him as I have loved few people" (12). His love of Nat continued to reinforce his sense of white magnanimity for the rest of his life. Hirsch interprets this quest as Lomax's "search for a lost world" of the nostalgic pastoral South (1992, 196), and I do not think it is too farfetched to imagine that Lomax symbolically found Nat in the black informants with whom he developed friendships. His childhood friendship with Nat could be continued on an emotional level with someone like Henry Truvillion.

Lomax's emotional bond to black people can also be seen in some of his fieldwork encounters. At a southern prison camp, Lomax asked for the names of members of a singing quartet. One of the men responded:

> "My name's John Lomax."
> "That's my name, too. Why are you bringing our name to such a place?" I demanded.
> "Jes' got inter a little trouble." He looked embarrassed. "The jedge jes' give me two years."
> "Where did you come from?"
> "Holmes County, Mississippi, near Durant."

Holmes County was also my birthplace. That boy's mother may once have rocked me to sleep. (1947, 141–42)

The emotional closeness is clear in Lomax imagining a common mother figure, the traditional stereotype of the black "mammy," but the southern paternalism is equally apparent (Hirsch 1992, 196–97, Titon 1987). Henry Truvillion was also born in Mississippi, and Lomax may have felt some of this same kinship toward him.

John Lomax and his son Alan first recorded Henry Truvillion singing work songs in 1933, and they mentioned him in print the next year in *American Ballads and Folk Songs,* spelling his name "Trevelyan" (1934, 14). The book included the texts of three songs attributed to Henry Truvillion: "Tie-Shuffling Chant," "Nachul-Born Easman" ("Casey Jones"), and "Shack Bully Holler" (14–17, 34–36, 45–46). Later, John Lomax included descriptions of Truvillion and excerpts of his songs in a recorded lecture, "Adventures of a Ballad Hunter" (J. Lomax n.d.). Several of Henry Truvillion's chants and songs—"Unloading Rails," "Tamping Ties," "Possum Was an Evil Thing," and "Come On, Boys, Let's Go to Huntin'"—are included on a Library of Congress recording (Botkin n.d.). More extensive descriptions of Truvillion came out in Lomax's 1947 autobiography, *Adventures of a Ballad Hunter,* which includes a ten-page section about one of his later visits—in either 1939 or 1940—to Truvillion's house (253–62). Since Lomax's 1933 visit, Henry Truvillion had become a preacher and was interested only in singing spirituals, not secular songs, but gradually Lomax was able to talk him into singing work songs and allowing his children to sing their play songs.

Lomax considered Henry Truvillion one of his most important discoveries: "Deep in the piney woods of Texas, I had found another great singer . . . equally interesting and productive of songs and rich tales" (253). He wrote of Truvillion's "authentic and artistic mastery of [the] medium" of Negro work songs (262). He went on to describe his collecting from Truvillion: "In 1934 Alan and I had followed Henry into the East Texas timber lands where the Wier Brothers were cutting lumber. He was the boss of the track-lining gang, and his calls and songs had made interesting and beautiful records. I was still eager to save for the Folksong Archive all that Henry Truvillion had stored away in his 'rememberance'" (253).

His descriptions of the place and the work indicate some of Lomax's romantic notions about African Americans as folk:

Originally Wiergate, on the Sabine River, was a Texas sawmill community in the midst of a great dark forest of pine that stretched through what was No-man's Land between Texas and Louisiana. There Henry Truvillion, as foreman of the railroad gang, followed the lumberjack crew through the forest with new spurs of track, laid and moved by his crew as needed. Out along these spurs thundered cars loaded with yellow pine logs. The cars rolled on Henry Truvillion's rails. He was the boss, and all day long—the year round—he kept the men moving by his songs and calls. Railways must be built to drag the big logs to sawmills miles away; the work must go on. (255)

The "No-man's Land" of the Big Thicket was once an impenetrable forest and swamp, but logging and other developments since have reduced it to a much smaller area now designated the Big Thicket National Preserve. At the time of John Lomax's fieldwork it was still a "great dark forest of pine," which qualified it as an appropriate setting for the folk who for Lomax's generation of folklorists had to be isolated from civilization (Filene 1991, 605; Hirsch 1992, 188, 193). Lomax clearly had set out to find isolated groups to fulfill his scholarly conceptions: "Our purpose was to find the Negro who had had the least contact with jazz, the radio, and with the white man" (Lomax and Lomax 1934, xxx). The social constructions of race and folk come together here: the isolation of black folk reinforced them as primitives out of touch with civilization. Through his collecting and publishing of cowboy songs and African American work songs, Lomax was one of the first American folklorists to romanticize masculine outdoor occupations as an appropriate context for folklore (Hirsch 1992, 199). This was part of his larger concern with American romantic nationalism: he recognized that the United States could not have become the prosperous and powerful nation it was without the work of millions of African Americans. And though this perspective may be part of his romanticizing, it is also a historical fact.

Some of Lomax's romanticism can be seen in a positive light, but his use of dialect spelling in *Adventures of a Ballad Hunter* reveals a more negative underlying assumption about race just as it did in Puckett's use of dialect. In one instance, Reverend Truvillion begins a story by mentioning that he had collected seven dollars after preaching the previous Sunday. Lomax quotes the rest of the dialogue, "How much went to you and how much to the Lord," I asked irreverently. "I takes it all. The Lawd done had plenty; he don't need it." "What kind of sermon do you preach?" "That depends. Sometimes my congregation's paralyzed, then I has to revise 'em." (1947, 254)

Just as in Puckett's case, "dialect had come to connote black innate mental inferiority, the linguistic sign both of human bondage (as origin) and of the continued failure of 'improvability' or 'progress,' two turn-of-the-century keywords" (Gates 1988, 176). Representations of dialect in literature and scholarship, derived largely from the minstrel and plantation novel traditions, underlined negative valuations. Lomax's use of dialect creates a definite distance between him and Henry Truvillion because there are no dialect spellings in Lomax's speech. In addition, this particular description does not suggest that Lomax thought of Truvillion's coinages as linguistically creative. His use of "revise" for "revive" here, as well as his earlier transcription of "rememberance" for "remembrance" is condescending and chosen for comic effect. In another taped interview, Truvillion demonstrates his verbal creativity when he says, "[I have] met all kind of folks, studied humanology a little bit," but Lomax does not include this quote in his autobiography, and might have represented it as comic if he had.

Lomax also puts this bit of speech in Henry Truvillion's mouth: "Yes sir, Boss, I got your letter all right . . ." (1947, 253), underlining Lomax's own sense of entitlement. Jesse Truvillion says that he never heard his father call Lomax or any other white man "Boss." There is the possibility that Jesse's memory is faulty in this because it does not fit his present image of his father, but the evidence in *Adventures of a Ballad Hunter* suggests that Lomax used "Boss" indiscriminately when rendering black speech addressed to him. According to Lomax, most black men he encountered in his fieldwork, especially prisoners, call him and other white men "Boss" (for example, 144, 150, 151, 172, 176, 178, 179, 180, 190). This usage reflects a common form of address, but was likely not universal. As Lomax generalizes all black men to this position, he implicitly underscores their position in a racial hierarchy.

Another element of racial hierarchy comes in Lomax's attitude toward the art of African American folksong. Lomax clearly appreciated Truvillion's songs as art, but he felt the need to compare them to elite art to justify his evaluation (Hirsch 1992, 191). For instance, Lomax wrote, "His voice ringing like steel, never repeating himself, his collected calls would make a grand opera" (1947, 260). A few pages later, he observes, "That this music, part of it touchingly tender, has been the product of this labor, should inspire some poet to create a mighty epic as a tribute to the men of toil who helped to build America" (262). Some folklorists today would be more likely to see the singing of Henry Truvillion and other folk performers as magnificent art in itself not needing a literary poet to turn it into another form. In the last quote we again see an example of American romantic nationalism, in which male workers were represented as embodying the best in our national character. This pattern was prevalent in the 1930s—not only among southern scholars, but also among such national figures as Benjamin Botkin (Hirsch 1987). The tendency to compare folksong to western elite art to legitimize it did not end in the 1930s and '40s; blues scholars of the 1960s and '70s often spoke of black blues singers as existential poets (Titon 1993, 229), and some positive evaluations of contemporary folk music still depend on comparisons with "elite" music (for example, Texas traditional country singer Don Walser has been referred to as "the Pavarotti of the Plains").

Lomax's insistence on justifying folk music in elite terms was related to his view of blacks as more savage than civilized (Hirsch 1992, 187–88). He thought that the power and beauty of African American music sprang from a primitive source. In the introduction to *American Ballads and Folk Songs,* he describes a group of black singers: "Eager, black, excited faces, swaying bodies, the ring of metal to mark the beat of the songs, tones such as came only from untrained voices—free, wild, resonant—joined in singing some semibarbaric tune in words rough and crude, sometimes direct and forceful, the total effect often thrillingly beautiful" (Lomax and Lomax 1934, xxxiii). In terms of critical race theory, his characterization of blacks as "semibarbaric," "wild," and "free" reflects back on his own whiteness as civilized, tame, and emotionally repressed. I shall explore these reflexive dimensions of racial construction in more depth in the next chapter. The influence of primitivism is another connection between Lomax and Puckett, but unfortunately belief in cultural evolution and primitivism did not die out with their generation: writers during the blues revival of the 1950s and '60s also envisioned African American art springing from primitive sources (Titon 1993, 225; Mullen 1997, 16–19; also see chapter 5).

At times, Lomax's representations of African Americans were influenced by his need to make his books more entertaining for a general audience. Part of Lomax's literary technique in *Adventures of a Ballad Hunter* was based on his awareness of commercial potential in his writing: throughout his adult life, he wanted to sell books to add to his income (Porterfield 1996, 183, 226, 238). To make his autobiography entertaining, he dramatized field-work encounters with dialogue in a way reminiscent of Zora Neale Hurston's technique in *Mules and Men* (1978 [1935]). For instance, in *Adventures of a Ballad Hunter* he gave snatches of conversation between Henry Truvillion and himself: "'Are those your children?' I asked as several pairs of bright eyes peeped around the corner of the house. 'Yes sir, five head; at least my wife says they're mine'" (253). But part of the dilemma of representation is that the author cannot control an audience's reaction; this passage could be taken in a number of different ways depending on a reader's assumptions. The passage seems to me, however, to offer readers humor at the expense of Henry Truvillion and his family.

In addition, Lomax—like all folklorists—was selective in what he presented in published versions of his fieldwork encounters. What he left out is significant. In his description of the context in which the work songs were performed, Lomax quotes Henry Truvillion: "I holler an' call some of my best men by name. Chances are I'll call Hank Stevens, Sonny Watkins, Sam Justice, Jim Williams, to git their linin' bars an' go down there. I have to tell 'em where to git it" (257). Lomax then describes the rest of the action and gives the words to the song, but he does not comment on Henry Truvillion's use of his men's full names. Why not call them by just their first names? Jesse Truvillion told me that this was done to show respect for the personal dignity of each man. When analyzed within the context of an oppressed minority culture, the use of full names could also be seen as a means of "signifying," indirectly commenting on the white boss's practice of calling the workers "boys" or only using their first names. But it would be asking too much of a white scholar of Lomax's generation to do the kind of analysis of signifying that Roger Abrahams (1985, 5–9) and Henry Lewis Gates, Jr. (1988, 64–88) have done; surely Lomax's lack of commentary reflects the kind of cultural blindness white scholars of the time brought to their understanding of African American rhetorical strategies.

Not that Lomax was completely unaware of the complexity of race relations in fieldwork; for instance, he was interested in how he was perceived by black informants. On the Library of Congress field recordings from his 1940 visit with Henry Truvillion, Lomax asks:

> JL: Henry, going back, what did you think of Alan Lomax and me when
>   we first came to see you?
> HT: (slowly) Well, I, I formed it up to be just about what it is. You see,
>   take a fella traveling as much as I have, met all kind of folks, studied
>   humanology a little bit, and I can pretty near tell a man from a bur-
>   glar for some reason (laughs)—if you're a skunk [or not]. I can size
>   up and come pretty near telling if he's a businessman or a burglar.
> JL: Businessman or a wha—, a buzzard?
> HT: A burglar.
> JL: A burglar, oh. (J. Lomax 1940)

I am not sure this is the answer that Lomax expected or that he understood how cleverly Henry Truvillion avoided answering him directly. He never tells Lomax exactly what he thought of him; rather, he comments on his own skills at observing and judging human character based on his wide travels and extensive experience. Perhaps Truvillion was suggesting that Lomax could have been a burglar out to steal his songs. If Truvillion had any reservations about Lomax at first, the racial politics of the day would not have allowed him to express them directly.

Immediately following this exchange, Lomax asks what Mrs. Truvillion thought of the visiting folklorists, and again Truvillion avoids answering. Then Lomax says, "I got the impression that she didn't like us, our looks very much."

> HT: (after a pause) She's very, very kind-hearted along there. Anybody's nice to her, be kind to her. . . . You and madam [perhaps a reference to Ruby Terrill Lomax] can just come in, just take charge, go right ahead, she's all right with it.
>
> JL: Of course, I know that now, but I'm talking about way back when you lived up in the quarters of the Wiergate. I remember, I remember you had to shut the door before you could sing about even Zachariah up there. (Ibid.)

Henry Truvillion explains that he shut the door in an attempt to keep from being interrupted by drunken men walking through the quarters, not as a result of his wife's concerns about his singing. Truvillion seems to be defending his wife's hospitality and perhaps being critical that the Lomaxes "took charge" when they came into his home. In *Adventures of a Ballad Hunter*, although Lomax mentions Mrs. Truvillion's reluctance about having her husband sing secular songs, he does not give Henry Truvillion's explanation.

Lomax left another significant part of the 1930s and '40s fieldwork experience out of his published materials. In an essay about his father and Lomax, Jesse Truvillion writes that the two men told stories, sang songs, asked and answered questions, and discussed issues "with raw frankness, as only two friends would" (1996, 24). Jesse told me that his father and Lomax often engaged in heated theological discussions, and I listened to several that are preserved on Library of Congress field recordings. But these discussions are not found in Lomax's autobiography. Instead, we get the kind of dialogue quoted above when Reverend Truvillion says, "Sometimes my congregation's paralyzed, then I has to revise 'em"—dialogue that reinforces racial stereotypes.

Although not formally educated, Henry Truvillion, like most lay preachers, knew the Bible well and had given much thought to religious issues. For instance, several discussions between Truvillion and Lomax on the Library of Congress field recordings indicate a more profound awareness of theology on Truvillion's part than Lomax's portrayal of him suggests.

> JL: Henry, how long, how long since you've been ordained as a minister?

HT: About fourteen months.

JL: About fourteen months.

HT: Yeah.

JL: Did that cost you anything, to be ordained?

HT: No sir, about fifty cents for gas money.

JL: [Laughs] How many preachers to ordain you?

HT: About eight.

JL: What did they do, Henry? What was the ceremony? Tell me what the ceremony was.

HT: Well, they wanted to know from me what was the church, the Baptist church. How many churches was there. About the Lord's Supper—you know, in the Lord's Supper, how would I give it? Would I give it to the members of the particular church where I was pastor, or who would I give it—who would I give it to? And all like that. Finally, I told them fellas just like Daniel, Shadrach, Meshach, and Abednego, told them they would never catch me. I wasn't particular about how I answered them because *they* hadn't called me to preach. They asked me, would I give the Lord's Supper to just the members of the particular church where I was pastor? I told them I'd give it to everybody present, I'd pass it around to everybody present. They told me that wasn't right; I told them, yes it is, that's the Bible. . . .

JL: Would you give it to the Methodist if he happened to be there?

HT: If everybody present, pass it to him. The Lord's Supper protects itself.

JL: Whites as well as colored?

HT: Yes sir. No respect for a person's color. Pass it around, if he's, if he's, he knows himself. I told them because I read the scriptures pertaining to this here, and explain it to them what it means, then I pass it around. That'll be between just him and his God so that I ain't got a thing in the world to do with it. Jesus passed it to everybody present . . . he passed it to everybody present. Told them, "Take and eat ye all of it. This is my broken body." Told them as he passed the cup, "Take the cup, drink ye all of it. This is my blood I shed for man . . ."

JL: They passed you on that, did they?

HT: Yes, they passed me.

JL: Unanimous vote?

HT: Yes sir.

JL: Nobody voted against you?

HT: No sir. (J. Lomax 1940)

Truvillion's grasp of biblical concepts is clear in this dialogue—as is Lomax's condescension toward the entire process of ordination in the black church when he asks if the committee passed Truvillion on a unanimous vote. The new reverend compares himself to Daniel in the lions' den and Shadrach, Meshach, and Abednego in the fiery furnace, explaining through metaphor that he trusts in God rather than in men—even in the preachers testing him—and he applies this same concept to his future administration of the Lord's Supper.

Jesse Truvillion remembers details that also suggest more than was included in Lomax's edited account: "I heard my dad enlarge on this 'protects itself' declaration many times, and always with Biblical quotes. Church divisions in churches were, according to him, 'man-made and not God-intended.' Those who serve the Lord's Supper are only servants, he contended. Jesus serves the real Supper, and it is all spiritual" (55). From the recordings and from Jesse's memories, Henry Truvillion's biblical knowledge and thoughtful consideration of religious issues are apparent.

But Lomax did not reproduce the recorded discussions about religion in his autobiography. The intelligent black minister did not fit the stereotype of the laughing Negro with a sometimes "empty mind" (Evans 1982, 38), but the preacher who said he had to "revise" his congregation when they became "paralyzed" did. The intelligent black minister did not stay in his place in the southern paternalistic scheme of things. Here again, Lomax's portrayal of Truvillion may have had more to do with his attempts to entertain readers in order to sell books than with his personal opinions of the man. Lomax had a great deal of personal respect for Henry Truvillion, but his representation of him was limited by his culturally learned assumptions about blacks, just as our perspectives are limited today.

How did the Truvillion family react to what we now perceive as Lomax's condescension toward their father? From everything Jesse Truvillion and his sister Dora Nisby have told me, their father and mother liked and trusted John Lomax and his family. The children never heard any criticisms of John, Ruby Terrill, or Alan Lomax, and they had good relations with the Lomax family during the years when there was contact between them. However, one area of potential strain in the relationship was that for many years the Truvillion family did not know what became of the recordings of their father and the children.

According to his autobiography, Lomax usually told informants about working for the Library of Congress; perhaps this was one way of impressing them and inducing their cooperation. For instance, he recounts his remarks to a southern prison preacher as follows: "I hope you will preach your favorite sermon to the boys tonight. The Captain has agreed for me to record it, and I plan to deposit the records in the Folksong Archive of the Library of Congress. A thousand years from now people can listen to the words you will preach" (1947, 221). It would seem that Henry Truvillion was aware that the recordings would be housed at the Library of Congress because there is a contract signed by Henry Truvillion and dated June 11, 1943, in the Archive of Folk Culture, which grants permission to the Library of Congress to publish several songs on a record for the sum of twenty-five dollars. Perhaps there has been a misunderstanding about this information in the family, or the knowledge was lost after Henry Truvillion's death in 1948. Whatever the case, the Truvillion family was not aware of their father's place in the history of American folksong until Jesse Truvillion's accidental discovery of a Library of Congress recording in 1963. In a 1996 essay, he describes the family's response to this "unbelievable discovery" at a friend's home in Upper Ridgewood, New Jersey (1996, 23–24). He writes, "Never did we know the role of the Library of Congress. The discovery in the music room in Upper Ridgewood surprised me, and when I called my mother in Texas that night, she, too, was quite surprised" (24).

Even though they did not know the recordings were in the Library of Congress, the Truvillions had heard Henry Truvillion's songs on record before. Lomax gave a field recording to Truvillion that, as Jesse Truvillion recalled, became a source of excitement for the family and the community:

> Mr. Lomax gave Daddy a copy of one of the recordings. It was a twelve-inch disk, and it was recorded in the woods on the job site, with my dad directing his men in unloading rails and tamping ties.
>
>   On several occasions hands who had worked with Daddy came to visit, requesting the playing of the record so they could hear my daddy call out their names. This was a big thing in those years. (24)

Lomax routinely gave copies of recordings to his informants at a time when most folklorists did not share field-recorded material with performers. He knew that playing recordings back to the singers made them feel good about themselves. He quotes the singer Willie George's response: "'I'se important,' she said after she heard her records played" (1947, 289). Henry Truvillion must have felt a similar pride when John Lomax recorded him.

Jesse Truvillion has nothing but kind words to say about the Lomaxes when he described his memories of them during taped interviews:

> So what you had here was seventy men under the leadership of Henry Truvillion whose field hollers, whose stories, whose worksongs and so forth have been preserved by John Lomax and his family under a contract with the

Library of Congress. All of this good information I knew nothing about as a child when I was watching all these recordings take place. I witnessed two kinds of recordings take place: one was the stories that Lomax recorded my father's telling at home in the evening with the whole family in what we called the living room. This was a hardwood floor room, and there were space rugs and so forth around, but the floors were important to the process because this recording machine, [with] which he is really directly recording a record, created hair, looked like human hair; long black strands of hair came off this—what would have been a smooth disk to start with, great big fifteen-inch kind of a thing, with the picture of the dog listening to his master's voice, all of this very fascinating.

In this rural Texas piney woods area, this was a fascinating, very unique kind of entertainment for family to go in and hear the old man tell stories, number one. Number two, to have a quote "white man" in the house, in the living room with all this special arrangements, and with the idea that my Dad is going to tell stories, sing songs, and so forth. And for some unknown reason to the family this John Lomax wants to record it. Well do I remember Mrs. Lomax [Ruby Terrill Lomax] on two or three different occasions; a son of John Lomax [Alan Lomax], I think I remember probably only once. He remembers me much more.

We were very young; there are five of us in the family, two boys, three girls. The oldest girl is named Ruby, and she's on one of the recordings singing "Mary Wore a Red Dress" with her dad. In a real way, this was all we knew; the Lomaxes were quote what we call "good white people" in real segregated Texas. (Truvillion 1995)

The Lomaxes must have stood out as racially progressive because they came into the Truvillion home expressing a strong interest in the family and their culture. There were undoubtedly other "good white people" in the area, but few white people in East Texas at that time would have thought to record the traditions of African Americans.

Jesse remembers other details about the shavings from the recording machine: "Mr. Lomax, as we all called him, gave me a buffalo nickel to 'clean up the hair' the machine left on the floor. The amount of black hair was considerable, but I think my mother was the one who actually swept it up when the sessions were over. The nickel was a gift to me" (1996, 24). In a short story set in the 1950s, Flannery O'Connor has a black woman lash out at a white woman for giving her son a penny, rejecting the white paternalism she perceives in this Old South custom (1971); the Truvillion family perceived this action in the 1930s as an acceptable kindness. In many ways, the Truvillion and Lomax families operated within the restrictions of racial social institutions of their times.

In all of his reminiscences, Jesse Truvillion paints a positive picture of Lomax. "John Lomax was likeable. He liked Daddy, and he, on several occasions, gave gifts to our entire family. I particularly remember some Christmas gifts from Mrs. Lomax, although I don't remember the years. They were people we liked and they liked us" (1996, 24). Nolan Porterfield writes that the Lomaxes sent Christmas gifts to many of John Lomax's favorite informants (1996, 480). Although the Truvillions were the most prosperous black family in the area because of the father's position as foreman on the track laying crew, the Lomaxes sent old clothing to them on occasion, a common white practice in the 1930s, and one that continued at least into the '40s and '50s when I was growing up in segregated southeast Texas. This custom fits the paternalistic white southern view of blacks, but it also suggests the caring attitude of John Lomax and his family toward those they perceived as less fortunate.

There are letters from informants in the Lomax papers at the Archive of Folk Culture in which they ask for money or gifts from Lomax, and on one occasion Henry Truvillion asked the Lomaxes for a specific item. In his 1939 fieldnotes, Lomax says, "When we bade him goodbye at the end of the week he requested us to send him a 'Breeze-case, to carry my Bible in to church and to Conference,'" and in his 1940 fieldnotes, Lomax adds, "When we gave him a handsome solid leather portfolio to carry his Bible in, he said proudly: 'The district superintendent's don't look no better.'" Also in the 1940s fieldwork file is a letter from Henry Truvillion written after he received the briefcase—a letter that belies Lomax's stereotypical view of the simple Negro proud of his "breeze-case."

> Dear Mr. Lomax
>
> I received your letter was glad to hear from you glad to hear from you at any time, found family and I well. When I got your first letter I was so busy that I haven't had the time to write you, getting the children ready for school, trying to preach too. I have four children going to school now. So when you come you may bring plenty paper and pencils also I have just about wore my Brief Case out so you come or I will be too glad to see you, and will try my best to get some one to sing for you. I will see my boss when you come it may be that you can come out on the job.
>
>   looking to hear from you soon
>   Your friend   Family sends love
>   Henry Truvillion

Since his family was prosperous by its own community's standards at the time, why did Reverend Truvillion ask for the briefcase? Perhaps he was concerned about buying such an article at a local white store, sensing that he would be perceived as "uppity," or perhaps he felt he was owed something for all the help he had given Lomax. In any case, the letter does not project any of the obsequiousness of the stereotyped "Uncle Tom" behavior toward whites.

The Truvillion family's positive view of John Lomax is based on a number of factors: the kindness and compassion of the Lomax family, the personal friendship of the two men, the acceptance on both sides of the reality of race relations at the time, and the subsequent honor brought to their father by the Library of Congress recordings and Lomax's references to him in his publications. Until a recent rift between Jesse Truvillion and me (see chapter 8), that positive reaction to folklorists continued in the Truvillion family's relationship with me. Jesse often told me how pleased he is with the honor brought to his father's memory by our collaborative publications and presentations at professional meetings. His sister Dora Nisby wrote to me after I presented a paper on Henry Truvillion at the Beaumont History Conference in January 1997, "Thank you for the honor that you bring to our family by sharing publicly my father's contribution to American Folklore" (Mullen 2000a, 172).

John Lomax's legacy to American folklore studies was enormous and complex—a mix of invaluable contributions, mistakes in judgment, and images of African Americans tinged by his culturally learned attitudes about race. One of the most positive aspects of his legacy was his influence on his son Alan to be a folksong collector. Alan Lomax went on to become one of the most important folksong scholars of the twentieth century.

4

Alan Lomax and the Romantic Politics of Race

> These people, confined to their shacks
> and their slums, really possessed America;
> they alone, of the pioneers who cleared the
> land, had learned how to enjoy themselves
> in the big, lonesome continent; they were
> the only full-blown Americans.
> —Alan Lomax

In 1933 John Lomax set out from Dallas on a folksong collecting trip with his seventeen-year-old son Alan.

> At Terrell, Texas, thirty miles from Dallas, Alan and I made our first recording. A Negro washerwoman, as she rested from her work, sang a baptizing song:
>
> Wade in de water, wade in de water,
> Wade in de water, chilluns;
> Gawd goin' to trouble de water.
>
> Though her voice was high-pitched, it had a liquid softness that made the effect beautiful and moving. Alan blinked his eyes as he bent over the machine. Long afterward he told me that from that moment he felt no further doubts about enjoying ballad-collecting. He suspended his college career and worked with me steadily for the next two years. Alan also became my equal partner in three books of folk songs (J. Lomax 1947: 114–15).

This moment of emotional bonding between father and son and American folk music was to have enormous consequences for the future of American folklore scholarship. Alan took up the mantle of his father's love of and dedication to collecting folksongs, especially those of African Americans.

American and world folk music became the central concern of Alan Lomax's life, both professionally and personally, and his professional life always had at its core an emotional attachment to the music and the people who made it.

In his own autobiographical work *The Land Where the Blues Began* (1993), Alan Lomax describes another personal emotional response to a song he heard while with his father on a field trip, but he adds the distinctive political dimension that so separated him from his father. He first quotes a song he heard on that trip.

> When I get back home, I'm gonna walk and tell
> That Brazos River is a burning hell.

"I was seventeen when I first heard this song. I stared into the dusty black faces of the convicts who were singing—shame and anger spilled over me. These are my brothers, these are my brothers, I kept repeating to myself. Out of their pain they have made a river of song. How can I repay them for this hard-won beauty" (283). The response is as emotional as the one in his father's account, but it is also political with a sense of both the beauty of the song and the injustice that produced it, combining emotion and political intent, guilt and action.

Yet another example of his youthful emotional response to folk music came on an earlier lecture tour with his father and brother John Jr. when Alan heard Native American music. "The music was old and stirred one to fight, to make love violently" (Filene 2000, 48). Whether he was stirred to cry by a Negro spiritual, stirred to fight or make love by an Indian song, or stirred to take political action by a protest song, Alan Lomax's emotional responses to folk music became a part of his research and writing for the rest of his life. Even after he received formal training in anthropology and took a scientific approach to the study of music, his emotions were fused with his scholarship. Looking back on his professional life from the 1990s, he admitted, "There is an impulsive and romantic streak in my nature that I find difficult to control when I go song hunting" (1993, 3). During his career he expanded his interests from folk music of the United States to the music of Europe and Africa, but he always maintained a love of African American music and culture, and his cultural representations of black Americans continued to be influenced by his emotional assumptions about black people as well as his intellectual and political training.

Despite following in his father's footsteps, from the beginning he also had major differences with the senior Lomax, especially over politics. The scholarship on John and Alan Lomax has tended to consider them together, blurring some of the important distinctions between them (Bluestein 1972, 105–13; Filene 1991; Carby 1998, 101–9). One often reads about "the Lomaxes'" influence on American folksong scholarship, but especially for purposes of examining their attitudes toward race, they have to be treated separately. It may be appropriate to talk about them as one entity in the early days of their fieldwork together, but as Alan grew older, he grew further away from many of his father's beliefs. As I pointed out in chapter 3, John Lomax was in many ways still a nineteenth-century Southern conservative on race issues, but Alan Lomax was a twentieth century leftist liberal on race. They were connected by their romanticizing of African Americans, but it was a very different kind of romanticizing because of their different ideologies. The father was a segregationist, the son a committed supporter of civil rights. Their political differences went beyond race: on their 1932 lecture trip, father and son argued about "Alan's Communist friends" and his "communistic activities" (Filene 2000, 48). Despite these great political differences, both men were emotionally attached to black people and committed to convincing the American public of the artistic achievement of African American folksong.

Toni Morrison's concept of "Africanism" is very relevant to Alan Lomax's cultural representations of African Americans, especially how his image of blackness reflected back on his sense of his own whiteness. As I pointed out in the introduction, "Africanism" means "the denotative and connotative blackness that African peoples have come to signify, as well as the entire range of views, assumptions, readings, and misreadings that accompany Eurocentric learning about these people" (Morrison 1992, 6–7). To determine the nature of Lomax's Africanisms and how they reveal whiteness, I will follow Morrison in looking closely at the connotative words, images, metaphors, and other literary devices that are the means whereby Lomax created the Africanist perspective (1992, v–xiii, 67–69). Perhaps of all the folklorists I examine in this book, he is the best example of how Africanist constructions lead to larger concepts of American identity.

In writing about the black singers and musicians he recorded—Leadbelly, Jelly Roll Morton, Muddy Waters, Son House, Fred McDowell, Ed Young, Sid Hemphill, Napoleon Strickland, Sam Chatmon, Forest City Joe Pugh, and others—Alan Lomax was using actual people as a basis for characters in an ethnographic narrative. This is not to deny the reality of these men as individual people, but to recognize that their representations in print, photograph, and film were based on the way one researcher and author perceived them. Postmodern theory in both literature and ethnography recognizes that all writing, even the most "factual" and "objective," offers a subjectively constructed picture of reality (Fabian 1983; Clifford and Marcus 1986). For instance, in Lomax's memoir about his field research with blues singers in the Mississippi Delta, *The Land Where the Blues Began*, he "fictionalized" his experiences in the same way all people do in telling their life stories by being selective and using connotative language, metaphors, and images (Titon 1980). An obvious example of fictionalizing in Lomax's memoir is that he conflated two fieldtrips into one (Work 2005, xvi). He also created characters out of the people he described much as a fiction writer does. The ethnographic creation of these black characters by a white writer is also reflexive; that is, in describing and interpreting black musicians Lomax was revealing himself and his own fears and desires as a white man. He formulated an "Africanist persona" that "is an astonishing revelation of longing, of terror, of perplexity, of shame, of magnanimity" (Morrison 1992, 17)—all qualities found in Lomax's writings about African Americans and in his father's writings about him.

The seeds of Alan Lomax's creation of an Africanist persona can be discerned in his father's autobiography *Adventures of a Ballad Hunter* (1947). At Angola prison in Louisiana, they encountered nearly a hundred black women prisoners. While the elder Lomax talked to the Captain, seventeen-year-old Alan went into the dormitory.

> Later I found him seated in the dining room, a bunch of comely colored girls grouped around. . . . The girls swayed as they sang, their young and supple bodies moving in perfect unison to the rhythm of the song. . . . To me it was a strange, strange picture, for the manager had told me that nearly all these girls were from New Orleans or Shreveport, life-termers for murder. One young amazon, shiny black, handsome, eighteen, vibrant with vitality, was doing her best to attract Alan's attention. They crowded around us both until the time came for us to go, like eager children starved for the outside world (120–21).

This "strange, strange" scene clearly is charged with sexual desire for both the describer and the described; given the racial context of the South in the 1930s, the language here—"comely colored girls," "young and supple bodies," "shiny black amazon,"—suggests the taboo nature of white male desire for black women, and the young woman's attempts to "attract Alan's attention" make the sexuality explicit. The "longing," "terror," and "perplexity" Morrison refers to in the relationship of white author and Africanist persona (1992, 17) are found in both father and son. John Lomax attempts to hide the sexual nature of desire by picturing the young women as children attracted to him and his son because they represented the outside world. The longing is complexly mixed with "terror" and "perplexity": Lomax's use of "strange, strange" suggests his perplexity, and his mention that these "comely colored girls" were also murderers indicates the underlying unspoken terror.

Terror was at the heart of Alan's response to a black male convict a few pages later, at least according to his father.

> As Alan told him good-bye, Iron Head playfully dropped the red inside rim of each eye entirely over the eyeball. The shocking horror of the sight terrified Alan. "Dat's de way I looks when I'se a bad nigger," chuckled Iron Head. This little interlude probably was to please Alan or to cover up his own emotion in saying goodbye (J. Lomax 1947, 122).

As with the attempt to gloss over the sexual desire in the episode with the black women prisoners, Lomax attempts to explain away the terror here, but Iron Head's depiction of himself as a "bad nigger," though offered humorously, seems to be a reminder to the white men that there is something to fear in him. *Adventures of a Ballad Hunter* is full of such episodes where a black person was probably "signifying" with Lomax, playing with white expectations about blacks.

Both father and son were drawn to southern prisons as sites for collecting African American folksongs. Their stated reasons were that these were the places where black isolation from whites had created circumstances conducive to the purest expression of black tradition, part of their criteria for folk authenticity. The elder Lomax wrote, "Our purpose was to find the Negro who had had the least contact with jazz, the radio, and with the white man" (Lomax and Lomax 1934, xxx). Because of their isolation from white influence, black convicts "slough off the white idiom they may have once employed in their speech and revert more and more to the idiom of the Negro common people." Work songs, whether sung in prisons or in the prisonlike levee camps and plantations, were not sung for whites but for the expression of the black man's own deepest concerns: "In them the Negro workman is likely to speak his free mind" (J. Lomax 1947, 113). For John Lomax, the convict becomes culturally blacker in prison, speaks in the black idiom and expresses his concerns more directly in his songs. Alan Lomax agreed with this concept of authenticity as is indicated by his judgments about the commercial recordings of Leadbelly after his release from prison: "Not complete authenticity, but . . . the nearest thing to it that could be achieved away from the prison farms themselves" (quoted in Filene 2000, 73).

John Lomax implies that conditions in prisons were like those during slavery and that by going into prisons the folklorist can in a sense go back in time to a more authentic source of African American music and culture. This suggests that in their attraction to blacks in prisons, John and Alan Lomax were part of a broader cultural process whereby whites used slavery to deal with issues of "historical, moral, metaphysical, and social fears, problems, and dichotomies . . . The slave population, it could be and was assumed, offered itself up as surrogate selves for meditation on problems of human freedom, its lure and elusiveness" (Morrison 1992, 37). I think that the incarceration of black people in America has served that same function, replacing slavery in the American imagination as a way of meditating on problems of freedom. The writings of John and Alan Lomax about their fieldwork experiences with black convicts offer rich material for analyzing the complex cultural process of imagining freedom in America.

From the beginning of their fieldwork among blacks in southern prisons, issues of freedom arose. "Our best field was the southern penitentiaries. We went to all eleven of them and presented our plan to possibly 25,000 Negro convicts. Most of these men and women saw in us hope that once more they might get out into the 'free world.' At every opportunity they told Alan and me their pitiful stories. Alan seemed to want to set them all free. Perhaps they sang for us in the hope that we could help them. They did sing in every instance that we asked them" (J. Lomax 1947, 112–13). The idea that the white man was the hope of freedom for the black convict was based in John Lomax's southern paternalism, but his son brought a new dimension to it; his later political activism can be traced back to this moment of pity and desire to help. Both father and son were paternalistic, but Alan's concern took a more liberal and activist direction. The racially reflexive dimension of dealing with the lack of freedom can be seen in John Lomax's representation of white magnanimity in Alan's wanting "to set them all free." At the same time that they felt sorry for the black men who were denied freedom, they must have felt their own sense of freedom more intensely. They would remain free while the prisoners would remain in prison, just as in a larger sense whites would be free while blacks were enslaved. As Morrison points out, "For in that construction of blackness *and* enslavement could be found not only the not-free but also, with the dramatic polarity created by skin color, the projection of the not-me" (1992, 38). John and Alan Lomax had their whiteness reinforced by contact with blackness and their own sense of freedom intensified by the lack of freedom of the prisoners they were recording. "Nothing highlighted freedom—if it did not in fact create it—like slavery" (ibid.), and in the Lomaxes' research and writing slavery took the form of black imprisonment.

In doing research among and writing about black prisoners, John and Alan Lomax could also deal with white fears of "the bad nigger," both creating and controlling the imagined primitive criminality associated with African Americans. That was going on in their encounter with Iron Head and also can be seen in their attempt to sell singer and former convicted murderer Leadbelly to the American public. As Benjamin Filene states: "At the same time [that] the Lomaxes ennobled Lead Belly as an authentic folk forefather, they thoroughly exoticized him. Their publicity campaign depicted him as a savage, untamed animal and focused endlessly on this convict past." For instance, on occasion they had him perform in convict clothes and depicted him in overalls and bare feet in a publicity photo. In a letter to newspapers to publicize concerts, John Lomax wrote: "Leadbelly is a nigger to the core of his being. In addition he is a killer. He tells the truth only accidentally. . . . He is as sensual as a goat, and when he sings to me my spine tingles and sometimes tears come," and added that he was taking his life in his hands by traveling with him (Filene 2000, 59). He told reporters that Leadbelly "was a 'natural,' who had no idea of money, law, or ethics and who was possessed of virtually no restraint" (60). I think that this represents only one side of John Lomax's view of Leadbelly and that even though both he and Alan used hyperbole to promote Leadbelly as a bad man, his son had a different view of him.

Hazel Carby is one of those scholars who lumps the Lomaxes together, not recognizing the radical differences between them, especially in their representations of Leadbelly. She says that in their public relations campaign on behalf of Leadbelly, the Lomaxes created an image of black masculinity as benign on the surface and violent underneath and in doing so helped create an aesthetics of black folk culture. "Such an aesthetics is particularly significant, not only because it reveals [John] Lomax's own desires and fears, but because these desires and fears are then reproduced as commercially marketable qualities, as desires and fears that the public will be eager to consume" (1998, 104). To counter the image of Leadbelly as a violent black male outlaw, they made sure that it was clear he could be controlled by respectable white men (105–9). Carby has some valid criticisms of John and Alan Lomax, but her representation of them is one-sided to fit her overall argument; for example, based on John Lomax's use of a metaphor comparing blacks in their natural singing habitat to birds in theirs, she claims that both men viewed prisons "as part of the natural habitat of black people" (103), ignoring the extensive folksong fieldwork both conducted outside prisons with lawful black citizens and the radical differences between the two when it came to race. (For a more balanced view of the relationship between the Lomaxes and Leadbelly see Porterfield 1996 and Wolfe and Lornell 1992.)

In fact, the way each symbolically constructed Leadbelly represents a crucial turning point in their political/racial views. "Leadbelly was a living representative of . . . a collective curse and a collective guilt as well as a potential power, one that John Lomax could exhibit but not confront in its total meaning because, unlike Alan, in whom Marx had awakened a class consciousness and Freud the sexual subtext, his personal project . . . demanded a strict policing of class, racial, and gender boundaries" (Cantwell 1996, 75). Father and son shared the fascination with African American culture, but the older man was still of the nineteenth century and incapable of examining his own attraction to black music in the way the younger was. John was always looking at southern black culture from the outside, but Alan wanted to cross the barriers of race and assimilate the black experience. "This required a deeper identification, a poetic sublimation if not a frank acknowledgment, of the racial fascination that had driven John Lomax, and that Alan Lomax would consummate by unmasking in American folk music the African spirit in which, for Alan, all its musical, sexual, and political power lay" (ibid.). Alan Lomax's desire to assimilate blackness was not new though; he was part of a cultural tradition of white men imitating black style that goes back to black-faced minstrelsy of the nineteenth century (Lott 1993; 52, Cantwell 1996, 54–55).

Alan Lomax's political differences with his father went beyond their representations of Leadbelly and resulted in different concepts about black prisoners in general, but they did share some of the same basic assumptions as is revealed in Alan's memoir. *The Land Where the Blues Began* contains a long chapter on his fieldwork in southern prisons, as well as other references to prisons including a comparison of the conditions in prisons to those in levee camps. Like his father, he saw the prison system as being like slavery: "Conditions in these state pens perpetuated the worst aspects of plantation slavery and of the 'free penitentiaries'—the levee and forced-labor camps." As in slavery, "In the burning hell of the penitentiaries the old comforting, healing, communal spirit of African singing cooled the souls of the toiling, sweating prisoners and made them, as long as the singing lasted, consolingly and powerfully one. This habit of group singing throughout all activities is the very core of African tradition" (258).

There is an implicit comparison with slavery here since group singing functioned the same way for prisoners as it did for slaves, but even more important is an underlying assumption in this statement that places the

African American group singing tradition outside history, connecting the African past, the period of slavery, and twentieth-century black life—a timeless and mythic dimension of African American experience. This is, I think, an example of what Morrison calls "dehistoricizing allegory" that "produces foreclosure rather than disclosure. If difference is made so vast that the civilizing process becomes indefinite—taking place across an unspecified infinite amount of time—history, as a process of becoming, is excluded from the literary encounter" (1992, 68). Morrison limits this trope to literature, but as I indicated earlier, the same kinds of racial devices can be found in ethnographic writing. Lomax seems to be excluding the possibility of change by placing black folksinging outside of time on a functional level; however, his thinking is more complex than this.

After setting up this timeless mythic view of African American singing, Lomax contradicts it a few pages later: "Although this tradition of communal song began to decline under the individualizing sharecropping farm system, it continued to flourish in the penitentiaries of the South until they were desegregated and reformed in the sixties" (1993, 261). Here he suggests that historical change in the form of desegregation caused the demise of communal singing thereby undermining the "dehistoricizing allegory" that he implied earlier. The argument becomes even more contradictory though because he feels that the core African cultural trait of communal cooperation continued to manifest itself in different forms after communal singing in prison declined. Using the approach he developed to study the relationship of folksong style and culture, "cantometrics" (1968), Lomax sees certain functions of folklore related to certain performance styles:

> This intertwined, unified, overlapping style is peculiar to black Africa and African America. It is one manifestation of a group-involving approach to communication that allows everyone present to have an input in everything that is happening. Dance, ritual, work, even conversation, are all performed in this overlapping, participatory way. It animates the basketball court as it does the dance floor. Multileveled conversational style, each level understood and reacted to, is the rule in black folk society (1993, 261).

His functionalist approach makes for sweeping statements about an entire folk culture encompassing all genres of folk expression across time and space. We are back to the "dehistoricizing allegory" that seems to foreclose the possibility of change by placing basic functions of folklore outside history, but evidence throughout the rest of *The Land Where the Blues Began* and his other writing indicates that Alan Lomax did not believe this.

The contradiction between the historical and the ahistorical is implicit in functionalism, and Lomax was merely following the principles he learned in his reading of the anthropological functionalists who influenced his thought. Functions could be both universal and culture specific, both timeless and bound to a specific historical time. For instance, Malinowski posited functions that existed in cultures across time and space: he saw magic beliefs and rituals as serving the psychological function of relieving anxiety for primitive people as well as for modern, urban, advanced people (1979 [1931], 40). Malinowski, along with Havelock Ellis and Sigmund Freud "shared the same goal, even when they disagreed on details: they sought the universal truth about human nature and conceived of primitive societies as the testing ground, the laboratory, the key to that universal truth" (Torgovnick 1990, 7). Lomax's function for group singing "to make them consolingly and powerfully one" (1993, 258) and the function of the overlapping performance style "that allows everyone present to have an input in everything that is happening" (261) fit the functionalist principle of maintaining cultural stability (Bascom 1965 [1954], 297). One facet of functionalism, then, is basically ahistorical since it posits certain elemental functions that are true across all cultures and all times; this led Lomax to make sweeping functional statements that imply an idealized African American culture that was outside time and resistant if not impervious to change. On the other hand, functionalism could be used to explain behaviors within very specific social and historical contexts, such as Lomax's explanation of African American promiscuity based on close living quarters and enforced breeding during slavery (1993, 84).

Functionalism and cultural relativism provided an academic basis for the 1930s and '40s leftist political activism of folklorists and other social scientists (Hirsch 1988; Filene 2000, 137–38); these approaches were the source of a major theoretical and political split between Alan and his father that had implications for their concepts of race. The senior Lomax was a survivalist of the cultural evolutionary school while Alan's functionalist training caused him to reject cultural evolution and to see cultures in a relativistic way. These theoretical approaches were widespread among public folklorists such as Benjamin Botkin in the 1930s, as Jerrold Hirsch pointed out (1988, 51).

The new generation of folklorists who came of age in the '30s learned from such functionalists as Malinowski who studied primitives to understand how their cultural expressions functioned. They applied this same method of close observation of cultural behaviors to the American folk, such as lower-class African Americans, to determine how folksongs and tales functioned closer to home. The problem, of course, was in the underlying and unexamined link between primitives and the folk: despite the liberating effect of functional-ism and cultural pluralism, the new theories maintained the old elite/folk hierarchy and continued the influence of primitivism on folklore studies. The dichotomy of the civilized and the Exotic Other was maintained in the shift from cultural evolution to cultural relativism. Commenting on a passage in Malinowki's *The Sexual Life of Savages,* Marianna Torgovnick says, "We are pulled through this passage until we come up against a magically powerful 'I,' the I of the ethnographer, the privileged part of us. That I is an observing eye, a scientific eye, but also an I who likes being powerful, who exults in having all of them under ethnographic observation" (1990, 4). So too, folk-lorists doing ethnographic fieldwork in the United States maintained their power over the folk despite their commitment to cultural equity—a term Lomax used later in his career.

Despite this hegemonic relationship, the positive political effect of func-tionalism and cultural relativism was great. Benjamin Filene points out how this worked for the New Deal folklorists of the 1930s and '40s including Benjamin Botkin, Charles Seeger, and Alan Lomax: "Folk song [from the perspective of cultural evolution] was a delicate remnant from a bygone era, and the folklorist's job was to preserve it from being trampled by the pernicious forces of change. Functionalism, in contrast, encouraged New Deal folklorists to see vitality in folk forms" (2000, 138). Benjamin Botkin was especially important in making the political use of functionalism more widespread; he "worked out an approach that rather than regarding American folklore as disappearing saw it as something still being created—in the city as well as in the country, in the factory as well as in the fields" (Hirsch 1988, 55). "Influenced by functionalism . . . the New Deal folklorists shifted the profession's mission from preserving cultural relics to exploring the processes by which culture was created and transmitted" (Filene 2000, 139). (Filene is not entirely accurate in suggesting that interest in transmission was new to the functionalists because for years the prevailing literary historic geographic approach had focused on transmission although with an emphasis on text and not context.) Functionalism became more than an academic theory, though; it became the basis for political action (143) including addressing the needs of black people for civil rights and equality. This was the social and political context in which Alan Lomax developed his academic and political ideas.

The influence of functionalism on Alan Lomax can be seen in an article he wrote in the *Journal of American Folklore* (1946) and in remarks he made at the "Four Symposia on Folklore" (Thompson 1953)—statements indicat-ing how functionalism became politicized and was related to his concept of race. In the article, Lomax was critical of the prevailing historic-geographic comparative approach to folklore because it "regards the folk as ignorant and simple-minded receptacles for traditions and ideas which they themselves do not understand." "The idea which I wish to develop here takes issue with this approach, regards folklore as having a function within the context of its social environment, believes that the best interpretations of folklore may be obtained in the end from the folk themselves, and holds that the objective of the folklorist is not only an historical one, but one of recording and interpreting a living human tradition" (1946, 507). He not only directly rejected the textual approach of the historic-geographic method but also implicitly the cultural evolutionary approach, so "old-hat" by this point in the history of the scholarship that he did not see a need to mention it. He thought that with the functionalist approach "it would be possible to make recommendations to various agencies and individuals engaged in active social work in the community . . ." (508). In other words, he was espousing what later came to be termed applied folklore.

A few years later, he stood up at an international symposium on folklore held at Indiana University and stated his theoretical and political beliefs in front of a group of historic-geographic comparativist folklorists:

> We, who speak for the folk in the market place here, have obligations to the people whom we represent. If our activity is solely to enrich a city, urban, middle-class culture, the suspicion that some of the folk have of us might actually be justified, that we are folklorists basically because we are enriching ourselves, either with prestige or actual money. So, I think, that we have to work in behalf of the folk, the people. We have to defend them, to interpret them, to interpret to them what is going on in the world which they do not make, but which begins to move in upon them and to crush their culture. (Thompson 1953, 159)

There is certainly magnanimity here, but there is also condescension toward the folk who it is assumed cannot interpret or represent themselves. Still, this had sweeping political implications for folklorists in the late 1940s. From the apolitical and at times ahistorical tenets of academic functionalism, Alan Lomax along with Benjamin Botkin, Charles Seeger, and other New Deal folklorists built a leftist and very historical political creed influenced by Marxist concepts of class for folklorists and other ethnographers who worked directly with disenfranchised people. He applied this to any minority group he perceived as disenfranchised, but because of his background and emotional attachment to black people, African Americans became the main group he concentrated on in his fieldwork and political activism. Lomax seemed not to recognize the implicit contradiction in functionalism's ahistoricism and his Marxist historical adaptation of functionalism so that even in the 1990s when he wrote *The Land Where the Blues Began,* he made no attempt to explain how his mythic timeless view of African culture (Africanist in Toni Morrison's terms) could fit with his demands for political change for black people. There was no contradiction in his mind because the romantic mythic view was based on a deeper emotional concern for black people that was, in turn, part of the complex and contradictory desire and fear at the center of the cultural processes that constructed whiteness and blackness.

To understand the relationship between folklore, race, and politics in Alan Lomax's career, we must also consider the Popular Front movement of the 1930s and '40s and the folk revivals of the 1940s, '50s, and '60s because he was an active figure in both movements.

> The Popular Front was the insurgent social movement forged from the labor militancy of the fledgling CIO, the anti-fascist solidarity with Spain, Ethiopia, China, and the refugees from Hitler, and the political struggles on the left wing of the New Deal. Born out of the social upheavals of 1934 and coinciding with the Communist Party's period of greatest influence in US society, the Popular Front became a radical historical bloc uniting industrial unionists, Communists, independent socialists, community activists, and émigré anti-fascists around laborist social democracy, anti-fascism, and anti-lynching. (Denning 1997, 4)

The Popular Front came into being and grew into a powerful movement just as Alan Lomax was coming of age; it was a movement that viewed the folksongs he was collecting and beginning to devote his life to as an important tool for social change. As Robbie Lieberman points out, "folk song, more than any other cultural form, expressed and reaffirmed the Popular Front spirit. It was simple and direct; it invited mass participation; it expressed the concerns of the common person" (1989, 49). For Alan Lomax, this ideology was rooted in his fieldwork with African Americans. In a 1960 article he cited an example of a black singer he recorded who sang a song against the sharecropping system while the white farm owner was listening. Lomax emphasized that the singer took a chance on punishment to get the song on record and then made the general point that his recording machine was "a voice for the voiceless" (1997 [1960], 44). Lomax set himself up as the mediator between the folk and the rest of the country to bring the political protest message in their songs to a wider public audience; he could be involved in the process of cultural commodification while maintaining his leftist ideals.

Within the American folksong tradition, the African American folksong took on added political importance for the Popular Front and especially for Alan Lomax who developed "a democratic ideology which stressed the virtues of the common man and the dignity of oppressed groups such as the Negro . . ." (Bluestein 1972, 105). This ideology recognized cultural difference between African American and Anglo-American, but it emphasized commonality and the development of cultural hybrids: "Although Alan Lomax recognized the profound prejudice against the Negro in America, the merging of white and black folk traditions revealed a unity that undercut surface tensions . . ." (110). Alan's awareness of the process of hybridization of white and black cultural traditions had profound political implications for his Popular Front beliefs and activities.

I cannot go into all of Alan Lomax's leftist folksong activities of the 1940s here, but certain details indicate the importance of race in his political ideology. He featured African American singers and Anglo-American singers who emulated black styles in the concerts he promoted and the records he produced; for instance, he worked to include black singers Leadbelly and Josh White in Popular Front concerts and recordings, and he promoted white singers such as Woody Guthrie who exemplified the hybridization of black and white styles. As Robert Cantwell says, Alan Lomax "staked out" an "ideological field of a racial and racialized 'folk'" (1996, 113) by recognizing class similarities of disenfranchisement among different cultural groups. The folk were defined as disenfranchised, and black people came to represent all of the folk through their extreme marginalized position. The problem in unifying these groups for political purposes was in overcoming the seemingly huge cultural differences between African Americans and European Americans, and Lomax found the solution in his fieldwork.

Through his study and field research, he came to recognize how the folk music of blacks and whites had been influencing each other from slavery to the present and that these cultural exchanges did not end with music. "White and black southern folk culture, within many regional variations, shared a wide range of kinesic styles, musical forms, linguistic elements, culinary practices, religious observances, and the like . . ." (65). Cultural interaction could be a metaphor for the ability of different groups to come together for political purposes, later expressed as a cultural "patchwork" in Lomax's films. This recognition of black/white cultural syncretism was the basis for a political ideology that could argue for social equality and civil rights; a sense of a shared culture based on class and cultural interactions led to shared political goals for Alan Lomax and other activists in both the

Popular Front and the folk revivals. Lomax anticipated later cross-racial cultural theories such as Albert Murray's "Omni-Americans" (1970) and Susan Gubar's "racechange" (1997).

No single folk revival occurred in the United States but a series of revivals were connected by certain figures who transcended their own generation, including Alan Lomax (Cantwell 1996; Filene 2000; Cohen 2002). One of the earliest indications of a twentieth-century folk revival was the popularity of folk festivals. These took place in the Appalachian Mountains (Whisnant 1983) and sprang up in other parts of the country including the historically and culturally important National Folk Festival that began in 1934 (Lloyd 1997). What came to be known as the urban folk revival was part of the Popular Front in the 1930s and '40s, and its political ideas were carried over into the revival of the '50s after the Popular Front had faded. Robert Cantwell sees similarities between these folk revivals and nineteenth-century minstrelsy, a connection that has implications for Alan Lomax's construction of whiteness and blackness. "Like blackface minstrelsy, folk revivalism is a form of social theater in which we develop the protocols for negotiating relations among groups and classes, as well as our own transition from one state, condition, or membership to another, discovering ourselves contrastively as we invent the 'folk,' experiencing ourselves reflexively as we emulate them' (1996, 54–55).

Cantwell's concept of the invention of the folk as an interactive reflexive cultural process is similar to Morrison's theory about the interdependent construction of whiteness and blackness and can help us better understand how Alan Lomax racialized and politicized the folk. "In its very invented-ness [folk revivalism] embodies a structure of knowledge and an incipient system of affirmative values in which a critical historical perspective, an alternative or oppositional cultural politics, and even a prescriptive social-political program all become possible" (55). Alan Lomax was in many ways the prototypical folk revivalist: he helped invent the folk in America with an emphasis on black folk who became emblematic of political ideas that were contrasted to entrenched white European-American politics. The folk revival of the 1950s took some of the political ideals of the Popular Front and merged them with the burgeoning civil rights movement, and by the early 1960s revival singers such as Bob Dylan, Joan Baez, and Odetta came to be seen as spokespersons for African Americans and other disenfranchised groups. Alan Lomax, Pete Seeger, Woody Guthrie, and many other folk singers and folksong enthusiasts of the Popular Front of the 1930s and '40s laid the foundation for the folk revival of the '50s and '60s, and some also became active participants in the later revival.

Here again, Robert Cantwell's critique of the folk revival is useful in analyzing the role that Alan Lomax played in the cultural politics of race. "It is
particularly significant that America's deepest social division, the one between black and white, should be the site of folk revivalism's most visible
early efflorescence and its most persistent theme. Here the invention of a
folk is historically allied to the larger collective project of inventing the black
Other and of assigning the cultural indicators within which the black social
being remains circumscribed and controlled" (1996, 55). Alan Lomax helped
to invent the concept of folkness as related to lower-class African Americans
that has prevailed in American culture since the 1940s. As a participant in the
Popular Front and later folk revivals, he was a key figure in creating popular
images of African Americans as folk from the 1930s to the present. I have
tried to provide a sense of the general social and political context that helped
produce him and that he helped create. We must now turn to his writings
to see specifically how he constructed blackness and whiteness, focusing on
the central question: Why was he so attracted to African American culture
in the first place?

I think that at the core of his being Alan Lomax wanted to be black; he was
in some ways the epitome of Fanon's "man who adores the Negro." Ample
evidence in his writing suggests that he knew this about himself; but before
he could be fully black in his imagination, he had to go through a long and
complex process of assimilation into black culture. In many ways, his 1993
memoir, *The Land Where the Blues Began,* is the story of that process of assimilation. He was attracted to black people through their music even before
he started going on fieldtrips with his father. The very first paragraph of the
preface to his memoir offers an anecdote illustrating the taboo nature of that
attraction: "In order to hear the blues, when I was very young, my girlfriend
and I slipped into the black ghetto of my Southern hometown under the
cover of darkness. If we'd been caught there, we would probably have been
expelled from the university" (xiii). One reason the black world was forbid-
den to white youth was the sexuality associated with it, as is implicit here
and as Lomax makes explicit later in the book. The taboo made blackness
even more attractive, and Lomax was determined to "penetrate the Southern
facade and learn something about what life was like on the other side of the
Jim Crow line" (xviii). Alan Lomax, whose functionalism was influenced by
Freud, might agree that his use of "penetrate" twice to describe his desire to
learn about black life (xv, xviii) has underlying sexual connotations. Later, I
shall take up the sexual theme in his memoir in more depth.

Many incidents throughout the book illustrate Lomax's desire to be accepted by black people as one of their own. When first starting his fieldwork in Mississippi in the 1940s, he was both elated by his successes in crossing over and disappointed by not being able to be completely accepted.

> I was a white stranger, but my experiences with Willie B. and Son House made me feel somewhat at home here. I was filled with deep excitement that at last I had slipped under the barbed wire that had always separated me from blacks, and could now begin to see something of the lives that lay back of the music that I was devoted to. I knew I was cut off from these people by a chasm that I could not bridge alone, but now I had black comrades who would vouch for me. Where were my friends from Nashville? As I hurried through the laughing, chattering multitude, no one looked at me, but everyone was aware of me, for they stepped aside as I approached, especially the older people, and so I moved through a path of empty air that enclosed me and isolated me as effectively as if I had been in a glass bubble. (29–30)

The metaphors here give a sense of the contradictory processes of imagining whiteness and blackness early in Lomax's career. At the same time that he as a white person could "feel somewhat at home here," he was also aware of being "in a glass bubble." I think that not only his successes recording Willie B. and Son House made him feel at home but also his background as a southerner who had grown up in close proximity to black people; this was part of his awareness of the cultural hybridization between black and white. Despite that proximity, he also felt the isolation caused by racial and cultural differences: the "empty air" of the glass bubble suggests the sterility of the white environment he carries with him as contrasted to the liveliness of the black community around him. In terms of his narrative as ethnographic allegory (Clifford and Marcus 1986), his quest to be black had just begun.

One of the major ways Lomax sought entry to the black world was through identifying with their oppression. The first fieldwork experience he recounts finds him in conflict with white southern authority figures because of his association with blacks. One night in Memphis he was listening to a blues singer in a vacant lot when two white policemen shone their flashlight in his eyes and pointed their guns at them. Lomax explains that he came from Washington to record blues, and one policeman responds with, "Washin'ton. Jis what I thought," and the other, "'Sociatin with niggers." "Whyn't you take all this nigger crap back where you came from?" A little later the policemen roust them out with, "'Git movin, you damn niggers,' punching my friends with his nightstick." "'And you, you nigger lover,' said B., not touching me, 'you walk ahead and mind you walk straight.'" (1993, 6). This incident functions as a framing device for the overall narrative of the book by setting Lomax up as empathetic with black people, on their side against the white oppressors. The white southern insult "nigger lover" becomes a badge of honor to be worn proudly because it places him closer to the black men although Lomax is careful to include the detail that the policemen punched the black men but did not touch him. He is empathetically close but because of skin color not subject to the same harsh physical treatment. Also significant, it seems to me, is the setting: Beale Street is the legendary home of the blues, a place associated with the essential core of southern black folk culture, and here is Alan Lomax partaking of that culture on a face-to-face basis. This kind of black and white encounter continues throughout the book, usually with the white people presented as oppressors.

Lomax seems to be consciously constructing whiteness from what he thinks is a black perspective to more fully identify with blacks himself, as his next encounter with the law indicates. A suspicious plantation manager took him to the local sheriff's office where the sheriff threatened to throw him in jail for associating with blacks. He was eventually released, but the experience had a profound effect on him: "I had a taste of the humiliation every Southern black experienced every day of his life, and it was hard to swallow. I felt I had been bluffed into an apology, but as a member of the first interracial team to work in the delta, I felt I had to be careful" (24). Here again is the strong identification with blackness, momentarily becoming black through the experience of oppression.

Yet another such episode is given later in which a powerful policeman is angry with him because he is recording in a black barbershop (128–29). Lomax conveys the idea that the danger of recording blacks in the south increased as his fieldwork continued. After he had made several recordings in Mississippi, a liberal white journalist told him to get out of the state: "Don't stop till you cross the Mississippi line, because if they catch you with those tapes in this state, I won't be able to help you. You'll be a goner" (152). I do not doubt the reality of danger to whites who were sympathetic to the black condition in the south; one need only look at the deaths of white civil rights workers a few years later to see the reality of that danger. The point I wish to make is about Alan Lomax's rhetorical use of that real danger in his memoir: he uses these episodes to project his empathy with black people, to become more like them by sharing their experiences of oppression.

Interestingly, in some of these encounters between blacks and white authority figures, Lomax pictures the white men as weak. He meets an unfriendly white plantation manager right after hearing an emotionally powerful blues performance by Son House. "A white man in khaki work clothes was sitting at the wheel of a pickup truck, his face pale with fear and anger. He looked so small, so shrunken after what I had just seen and heard that I almost burst out laughing" (20). Lomax sets up a contrast between powerful blackness and weak and ineffectual whiteness, a pattern he repeats several times in the book. For instance, on one occasion, he is in a black church listening to an oratorically effective black preacher whose "introduction of the rather ordinary-looking little white mayor would have made the angel Gabriel retire behind his wings" (44). In both cases it is the magnificence of African American traditional cultural expression that makes the white men seem weak. As with the earlier examples of black and white contact, Alan Lomax's representation suggests that he is looking at whiteness from what he imagines to be a black perspective, but, in fact, he is still very much the white liberal southerner looking at the black experience from outside. He can perceive of white weakness only because he is white himself and ultimately not subject to the same degree of oppression.

In *The Land Where the Blues Began,* his direct construction of whiteness, as opposed to implied contrasts with blackness, is almost entirely negative: the white policemen are oppressive, the white plantation managers are mean-spirited, and the white prison guards are brutal. Undoubtedly this was the reality of what he observed, but I think we can still see it as a literary construction because in his fieldwork with white folk performers and the resulting publications and films, he presents a much more positive picture of whiteness. For instance, in his "American Patchwork" films, Lomax shows white Appalachian musicians, singers, and storytellers Tommy Jarrell, Nimrod Workman, Phyllis Boyens, and Ray Hicks as kind, thoughtful, family-oriented people (1998a, 1998b). In *The Land Where the Blues Began* he selects only negative encounters with whites because this reinforces his attempt to assume a black perspective. Even in this book, though, there are a couple of positive views of southern whites although neither of them is specific. "All through our Delta research we met blacks who had benefited from their association with the white planter aristocracy" (1993, 163). He mentions mixed-blood or house servants being given land, jobs, education, or help in starting businesses but gives no specific examples. These middle-class blacks are also, by Lomax's class definition, not the folk; the kindness of whites toward them results in upward mobility that removes them from the oppressed category necessary to be folk. This creates an unstated paradox: Lomax is against oppression but oppression is a necessary component of folkness; as oppression is eliminated, so are the folk. Even in this positive representation of whiteness, there is an implied negative.

One other example of a positive image of whites appears in the book, but it too springs from a negative. Lomax is critical of William Faulkner's portrayal of Mississippi "poor white trash" as dishonest conniving variations on Flem Snopes, forgetting Faulkner's positive poor whites such as Lena Grove and Byron Bunch (1932). "My years of song collecting among the backwoods folk of the South had convinced me that they [poor whites] were among the gentlest, most charming and amusing people on this earth." But Lomax does not include any of these "charming" whites as characters in *The Land Where the Blues Began,* only the brutal and mean-spirited ones. This is indicative, I think, of his personal ambivalence about his own whiteness. At the same time that he yearned to be black, he clearly identified with his own "peckerwood" background. Part of his resentment toward Faulkner's depiction of lower class whites was that "We Lomaxes had been Mississippi poor white trash" (1993, 327).

His ambivalence also can be seen in a discussion he had with a blues singer about white "yahoos." Lomax was recording Houston Bacon at a tourist camp when the white owner came in and told Houston to get off the bed. Alan turned off the recorder and he and Houston continued to sip whiskey. Bacon said, "That's a yahoo. A yahoo come to town. Otherwise known as a peckerwood. Did you get her down on record?" In response Alan mimicked the woman's voice, and the men had a good laugh. "But we couldn't get the ball rolling again. Everything had gone flat" (185). Whiteness has interfered with communication between a black man and a "white Negro" to use Norman Mailer's term (1957). In the same scene, Lomax admits to the reader, "My father's people were 'peckerwoods' from Meridian, Mississippi, 'from the upper crust of the poor white trash,' he used to say." Bacon continued his assessment of the type: "These yahoos—it's just a certain class of folks. If you sing this song [that made fun of them] around them, you better run. You can't fool with songs like this if you want to stay in this part of the country," and he then sang the song (186). Lomax comments, "Delta blacks saw this apparently innocuous ditty as a highly charged satire on poor white behavior, too offensive, indeed, too dangerous to render in their presence" (187), *except* in Alan's presence seems to be the implication. Lomax is manipulating whiteness, blackness, and class here; he identifies himself as a yahoo, but then distances himself from it because by singing the song in his presence, the singer was showing his trust in the white man. This is the Alan Lomax who had gone north, been educated, and returned to the south having transcended his peckerwood roots. As a southerner, he knew the racial dynamics of the south, but as an educated man he saw himself as above the racism of white southerners. He has the best of both worlds because of his dual consciousness.

His attempts to be empathetic and accepted by blacks finally led to epiphanies in which he imagines that he is black. Three of these episodes occur in the book, each one more intense than the last. All of these experiences are examples of what Susan Gubar calls "racechange": "The term is meant to suggest the traversing of race boundaries, racial imitation or impersonation, cross-racial mimicry or mutability, white posing as black or black passing as white, pan-racial mutuality" (1997, 5). As I said in the introduction, this cultural process is crucial to understanding the role of mimicry in the attraction of white folklorists to African American culture: Puckett writing dialect poetry, John Lomax acquiring his sense of rhythm from a black man, Roger Abrahams adapting 1960s black political style, and my own dancing to rhythm and blues. The first example in *The Land Where the Blues Began* comes early in Lomax's Mississippi fieldwork when a blind black man mistakes him for a black minister. He goes along with the misconception to "slip under the barbed wire" and gain knowledge of black culture he could not obtain as a white man (1993, 33–37). Lomax tried to act the part: "'But you know you're doin' wrong,' I said in the most ministerial tones I could assume," but Lomax had to hide his laughter at the situation, "'That's right, son,' I said, choking" (33). He thought he succeeded in fooling the blind man and collected information that the man would not have told him had he known he was white, including a story about the hanging of "three or four hundred colored folks" by white people in Tupelo (36). As they parted, the blind man asked "the revrun" to pray for him, and Lomax placed "another half dollar" in his hand. Lomax makes no further comments on this incident, but it takes on more significance when compared with the other two episodes.

The first attempt at being black was based on a mistaken assumption by another person, the second came about through Lomax's own spontaneous volition and had to do with singing in a black style. He makes the point that Delta hollers "are impossible to notate and very difficult to sing," and then adds, "As a youngster, I tried to sing whatever we recorded, with varying success, of course, but I never could do a 'holler' to my own satisfaction. I tried for years and finally gave up. Then came a moment when a holler spontaneously burst out of *me*" (273). After he was inducted into the army, he was subjected to humiliating and exhausting treatment and then put on KP duty. He came to the last hours of a sixteen-hour shift with his hands in boiling dishwater and feeling more miserable than he had felt in his life. "At that moment, without thinking, I let loose with a Mississippi holler. Loud and clear, my levee-camp complaint rang through that hellish army kitchen . . . I went on hollering and the sound got better. I got to feeling *good*. All those years and finally those Delta blue notes were coming out of me." A black sergeant overheard him, and Alan was afraid that he would get extra KP duty. "But all the black sergeant did before he walked off was to say in a kind of nice way, 'Hey, man, you sound like you from down home.'" (274). It was years later before Lomax formulated his cantometric approach to analyzing folk music, but cantometrics suggests that this was a very significant experience for him. An important principle in cantometrics is that performance style and cultural identity are connected. By being able to sing authentically in a difficult black style and by receiving the approval of a black man, Alan Lomax was becoming black. He sees himself as living something close to the black experience, but more significantly, I think, he is reliving the experiences of the black-faced minstrels of the nineteenth century and all of the white singers who imitated black style in the twentieth, from Jimmie Rodgers and Elvis Presley to Mick Jagger and Eminem.

Lomax must have seen his own assimilation of black style as going beyond that of other white performers because of his sense of shared experience: "I could sing them that day on KP because my situation resembled that of the black muleskinners and convicts of the Deep South . . . Submerged in feelings of anguish and despair, at last I sort of had the blues, and so could sort of holler, at least well enough to pass muster with a Deep South drill sergeant" (ibid.). (I wonder if Elvis Presley felt humiliation and despair and sang the blues while he was on KP duty in the army.) "Sort of" provides a crucial qualification: "Of course, my black friends, doing time in the levee camps and the prison farms, lived their whole lives in far more painful situations than the one that had reduced me to despair on KP" (1993, 274–75). Gubar points out that whites sometimes attempt to become black "so they will understand and sympathize with" black oppression (1997, 25), and this seems to be the case with Lomax. However, the ramifications of white mimicry are more complex: "We need to understand white masquerades as a mockery of and menace to the Other, as an assertion of difference, but also a form of competition, as an admission of resemblance, a gesture of identification or solidarity, even a mode of self-mockery" (44). All of these factors figure into Lomax's field holler, and although he recognizes the limitations of racial mimicry, he did not seem to be aware of the menace. As deeply as he had felt the black experience, he knew that the identification can never be complete and that the yearning to be black will continue for the rest of his life. The impossibility of fulfilling the desire to be black is an important component in the dynamic interplay of whiteness and blackness. Lomax will remain free while his black friends will remain enslaved by oppression.

Alan Lomax not only spontaneously sang hollers in the Army, he also sang blues songs on an LP (1958) and in the film *The Land Where the Blues Began*

(1998c). His attempt to absorb black singing styles places him in a long-standing tradition going back at least to nineteenth-century minstrelsy. Eric Lott interprets the meaning of "white Negroes"—blackface performers who learned black performance styles from direct contact with black men—who were the antecedents for Lomax and others in the twentieth century: "What appears in fact to have been appropriated were certain kinds of masculinity. To put on the cultural forms of 'blackness' was to engage in a complex affair of manly mimicry . . . to wear or even enjoy blackface was literally, for a time, to become black, to inherit the cool, virility, humility, abandon, or *gaite' de Coeur* that were the prime components of black manhood" (Lott 1993, 52). Although Lomax himself does not reflect on his singing in black styles as an attempt to appropriate black masculinity, the white tradition of doing so was so firmly ingrained in American white masculine behavior by the mid twentieth century that it would be difficult to deny this, especially when one considers the importance of sexuality in the cultural construction of blackness.

By singing in a black style and therefore becoming black in his own mind, Lomax was in danger of erasing the very blackness that he loved.

> But actual or symbolic identification with a marginalized group can also make one equally contemptible, in danger not only of the same subjection but of contamination by the Other. Hence, with one's own worthiness and power called into question, the minstrel or revivalist, actually or imaginatively squeezed into the same space as the Other, his own body inhabited by the Other's, recovers his power by first appropriating, and then mastering, the expressive forms and performances of the despised group . . . and in effect doing away with the Other out of love. (Cantwell 1996, 58)

If whites can sing the blues in a totally authentic way, then black blues singers are no longer needed, but the psychological implications are more complex. Gubar posits a connection between white mimicry of black style and lynching in terms of what Patricia J. Williams calls "spirit-murder": "What the murderer was trying to kill was a part of his own mind's image, a part of himself and not a real other" (Williams 1991, 72). Both racial mimicry and lynching arise ironically out of subconscious white guilt over past crimes against blacks—in the case of lynching a direct erasure of the body that represents the image of guilt, and in the case of minstrelsy a symbolic erasure through imitation.

On a conscious level Alan Lomax identified with the black Other and welcomed the contempt he received from whites for being contaminated, thereby reinforcing his sense of magnanimity and separation from whiteness. On this more surface level, he did not use mastery of the music as a means of maintaining his own power because he recognized his limitations in this regard by often denigrating his own musical abilities (1958; 1993, 274). His field holler could then be seen as containing elements of self-mockery, but his self-awareness ended there. On the subconscious symbolic level, he was engaged in "spirit-murder," doing away with the Other by taking his place (Williams 1991, 72). Gubar quotes Diana Fuss (1995) on this point, "'*every* identification involves a degree of symbolic violence' . . . because identification—like representation—entails the 'process of killing off the other in fantasy in order to usurp the other's place'" (Gubar 1997, 75).

The third example of Lomax's mimicry of black style leads to a racial epiphany in which his identification with blacks reaches a new level of intensity. It comes at the very end of the book and functions as a closing frame for the narrative. Alan Lomax was drinking and talking one night with three well-known blues musicians, Big Bill Broonzy, Memphis Slim, and Sonny Boy Williamson. "I surprised them by singing some snatches of Arkansas prison work songs that I knew. Memphis looked at me quizzically and then began to chuckle. Big Bill winked, and although I never asked, I believe they thought that perhaps I had served time in the Arkansas pen, as apparently they had" (1993, 459). This is another incident in which Alan Lomax convincingly communicates to black men how culturally black he is, or so he thought. Did they really think that this educated white man had spent time in an Arkansas pen, or were they chuckling and winking at the absurdity of his pale imitation of their singing? Is this another of Lomax's fantasies of blackness being fulfilled? There are many places in the book where he has enough distance from himself and his desires to recognize that he is fantasizing, but here I think he wanted to be accepted so badly that he convinced himself that it happened.

This incident led to a black and white epiphany with the same three musicians a short time later. During the recording session, Memphis Slim talked of conditions in the segregated South:

> "You know, if you go in a store, you didn't say 'Gimme a can of Prince Albert.' Not with that white man on the can."
>
> "What would you say then?"
>
> "Gimme a can of *Mister* Prince Albert."
>
> We were caught up in gales of squalling laughter that racked Sonny Boy. We were howling down the absurdity, the perversity, and the madness that gripped the land of the levee, a beautiful and fecund land, rich in food and genius and good living, and song, yet turned into a sort of purgatory by fear.

> Now for an instant we understood each other. Now in this moment of laughter, the thongs and the chains, the harsh customs of dominance, the stupid and brutalizing lies of race, had lost their fallacious dignity, but only for an instant. The blues would begin again their eternal rhythm, their eternal ironic comment . . ." (472).

Finally here in the last chapter of the book, Alan Lomax becomes one with a group of black men, something he had yearned for all his life. In all of the previous descriptions like this, he had indicated his whiteness in one way or another. Here there is no reference to his race; it is as if all the men present are of the same race, all are black men laughing to keep from crying. Alan thought he understood the absurdities of racism in a way that is possible only for a black person who has experienced it—"But only for an instant."

Upon hearing the tape immediately after the recording session, the black musicians insisted that the tape be destroyed or that their identities be hidden. "'Why, why?' I demanded. 'What could you be afraid of, way up here in the North?' 'You don't know those peoples down there,' they said" (473). (Lomax conflates two separate recording sessions here. The "Mister Prince Albert" story and Lomax's epiphany were recorded in Chicago when Big Bill Broonzy first introduced Alan to Memphis Slim and Sonny Boy Williamson. Lomax later brought all three to New York City and recorded them in a studio talking about the blues; it was at this second recording that they made their statements about keeping their identities hidden. The second recording is available on CD with notes by Lomax that make it clear that there were two separate sessions [A. Lomax 2003b].)

Lomax learns that being accepted as a black person cannot last. Ultimately, racial difference means that he cannot fully understand what it is to be black; all along he has claimed to understand southern whites, but according to these black musicians he does not "know those people down there" from a black perspective. Was this incident, then, an example of the positive possibilities of racechange? "Only when the boundaries separating black and white are perceived as demonstrably permeable does racial mutability lead to the undermining of race itself as a category" (Gubar 1997, 25). Although the concept does not depend on the process being two-way in every instance, this situation would have indicated greater undermining of racial categories if there were some evidence that the black men perceived it in the same way the white man did.

Lomax singing a prison work song seems to be received with ironic openness by Big Bill Broonzy, Memphis Slim, and Sonny Boy Williamson, leading them to the moment of cross-racial understanding, but the permeability appears to be one way. We do not have their subjective perspective on the experience, but they seem to maintain their distance from the educated white man with their chuckles and winks, and especially when they have to explain the dangers of the racist south to him. He may think that through mimicry and empathy he has become black, but they do not seem to accept him fully or "act white" themselves so that the permeability does not work both ways. Given their dark skin, passing for white would have been impossible for them on any kind of literal level, and there is no way to know if they ever imagined themselves as white. The undermining of race is mainly in the imagination of the white man. To Lomax's credit, he does not end the scene with the epiphany but with the recognition by all of them that racial difference supersedes the moment of commonality. "We knew we had made a real breakthrough and had opened up a dark period of history that had previously been hidden—they felt that as much as I did—yet a pall had fallen over our friendship." He kept his promise to hide their identities and did not reveal them until 1990 when all three men were dead (1993, 473).

Alan Lomax wrote many descriptions of black performers, but there are not many from their perspective about him, another function of the power differential in folklore fieldwork. However, because of the research of anthropologist and fiction writer John Stewart who collected and edited the life story of African American singer Bessie Jones, we do have at least one. Bessie Jones met Lomax in 1955 and gives him credit for her professional singing career: "Alan Lomax was the person who sent me out to the stage" (Jones 1983, 137). He encouraged her to go on singing tours and seems to have made decisions about her itinerary and who went with her (138–39). For instance, he did not want her group the Georgia Sea Island Singers to go with her on tour, and when she arranged for the other singers to join her, he was upset. "Then I told Lomax about it and he asked, 'What in the world did you do that for? Let those people go back home. Ain't nobody gonna be sending for a crowd of people that way.' He went on terrible" (139). He changed his mind when he heard a tape of them. Jones says, "And ever since then he's been wild over us. But left up to him, I would've been right there by myself, self-concerned, and I couldn't stand it, knowing that they could sing and what they could do," thereby representing blackness in terms of communality as opposed to white selfishness. She never showed the other singers the letter Lomax had written speaking "so deeply against them," "because I knew how it would have hurted them" (140). As he and his father had done with Leadbelly, he assumed the authority to make decisions for the folk performers that he had helped to make known, displaying arrogance and power in doing so.

After Alan Lomax's death on July 19, 2002, other perspectives on his attitudes toward African American performers began to appear. His friend and fellow folklorist Bruce Jackson wrote a loving tribute that contains an honest and understanding although critical description of Lomax's relationships with black people (Jackson 2002). He recalls a meeting in 1968 with Lomax, Ralph Rinzler, then of the Newport Foundation, and members of the Southern Christian Leadership Conference (SCLC) to help set up "Resurrection City" in Washington, D.C., as part of Martin Luther King's Poor People's Campaign. Rinzler asked the SCLC members how the foundation could help, and "Alan jumped up and gave everybody a lecture on the power of folk music, black folk music in particular." "Bevel and the others listened to Alan in polite, stony silence. . . . When the meeting was over, Bevel beckoned Ralph and me to the side of the room and said, 'You guys ought to do something about him.' 'I wish we could,' Ralph said. 'He means well, and he knows a lot.' 'I guess,' Bevel said" (Jackson 2002). Alan Lomax's eagerness to help black people combined with his white liberal certainty that he understood their needs led him to be arrogant about his right to speak for them, an assumption that caused black people to respond with contempt.

Jackson gives another example during the same period that shows another side of Lomax's displays of arrogance. There was a musical performance at Resurrection City, and after one group finished singing, Lomax asked Jackson in a loud voice about the high tenor in black male vocal music, "Do you think it has to do with repressed homosexuality?" "Several heads turned and stared. Another group sang. Alan tapped the shoulder of a woman in the back row and said, 'Those boys sure do sing good, don't they, honey?' I don't think he meant anything ill by it. It's just how he was. Several young men nearby had heard both his remarks and were looking at him hostilely" (Jackson 2002). Jackson left and when Lomax caught up with him and asked him why, Jackson told him that he "didn't want to be there when you got them *really* pissed off." Lomax seemed to understand, and explained his behavior by saying, "You don't know what it was like growing up in the Library of Congress." Jackson adds, "For some reason, I thought I knew exactly what he meant" (Jackson 2002), suggesting his understanding of the pressures on a young man who followed his famous father in devoting his life to crossing racial boundaries to try to comprehend black experience. This episode displays Alan's arrogant lack of self-awareness that seems grounded in his effort to be close to blacks and in his assumption that he has been accepted totally by black people, but a more uncertain vulnerable Alan Lomax is revealed behind that façade. Some part of him seemed to realize that he could never be black and that his bluster was all a role he played.

Popular music writer David Hajdu also wrote a posthumous assessment of Lomax's arrogance in his fieldwork relationship with blacks, but unlike Jackson, he has no sympathy for him. "Wheeling his sound-recording gear around Negro quarters of the segregated South, Lomax never realized how far he was from familiar ground. His writings show that his understanding of black culture was critically flawed, and that his attitudes toward African Americans were discomforting, no matter how virtuous he may have held his motives to be. His descriptions of his hosts and their environments are tainted with an air of superior bemusement . . . Lomax seemed to think that he was extending compliments when he was oozing noble-savage condescension . . ." (2003, 41). Evidence from Lomax's writings certainly support the general assessment here, but I think Hajdu has oversimplified a complex character by not viewing him within the context of his time and cultural background. Hajdu is simply wrong when he says that Lomax "was really a nineteenth-century figure—a domestic colonialist who mistook 'discovery' for creation and advocacy for ownership" (5). As I indicated earlier in this chapter, Alan was strikingly different than his father in terms of nineteenth- and twentieth-century politics of race although he and other twentieth-century folklorists had their own "colonialist" assumptions. Also, Bruce Jackson's more intimate portrayal of Alan suggests a complex psychological and emotional dimension to his character that Hajdu is not aware of.

The most controversial assessment of the ethics of Lomax's fieldwork methods came in a book edited by Robert Gordon and Robert Nemerov (Work 2005) based on their discovery of lost manuscripts by black scholars John W. Work, Lewis Wade Jones, and Samuel C. Adams, all of whom had been collaborators with Lomax on the Mississippi Delta field research. According to Gordon and Nemerov, despite the major contributions that the three black scholars made to the fieldwork, Lomax only mentions Work three times in *The Land Where the Blues Began,* including once in the acknowledgments "where his name is listed with Jones and Adams. Adams is not otherwise mentioned; Jones, who is cited several times, is the only one portrayed as an actual participant in the research" (24). Work was the original instigator of the Delta fieldwork, but you would not know it from the account in Lomax's memoir. Work convinced administrators at Fisk University where he taught that the Lomaxes should be brought into the project to make use of their extensive fieldwork experience and obtain financial support from the Library of Congress (8–10). Alan responded with interest, and when he met with the people from Fisk, "a shift in the control of the project from John Work to Alan Lomax" took place, and Lomax insisted that some of Work's field recordings be contributed to the Library of Congress. "Not only was Work's vision being *commandeered,* so were his recordings" (12, emphasis added). Lomax does not give credit to Work for instigating the project; instead he takes credit himself: "I approached Fisk University . . . with the idea of doing a joint field study with my department at the Library of Congress" (A. Lomax 1993, xvi). Gordon and Nemerov use the "commandeered" metaphor again when they describe the specific situation of a recorded interview Work and Lomax conducted together: "The only aural evidence of Work during that week" are the recordings of Muddy Waters. "Work conducts two of the four interviews with 'Stovall's famous guitar picker.' In the second, Lomax interrupts after several minutes, commandeering the questioning. In subsequent recordings, Lomax's is the only interviewer's voice heard." "John Work—a trained musician and a member of the ethnic group being studied—was kept from the heart of the project and, after the trip, retired to a room in the social sciences building at Fisk to transcribe the discs. From the enthusiasm in Work's voice and the relaxed responses of Muddy Waters in the few moments when Work has control of an interview, one can only wonder what may have been gathered had he been allowed to truly 'facilitate rapport with informants'"(Work 2005, 15). Despite the evidence of Work's skill as a fieldworker here and elsewhere, Lomax was critical of him in his field notes: "Rest of evening with John Work getting his records ready for deposit and trying to work out his problems—mostly of incompetence, laziness and lack of initiative on his part" (20). Also, in a letter to the president of Fisk in which he did not mention Work by name, Lomax questioned his competency to write the proposed book based on the fieldwork and called for more editorial supervision of him (21).

Despite Lomax's misgivings, Work, Jones, and Adams continued to write scholarly pieces about their fieldwork in the Delta, and Work eventually combined his research findings with Jones's in a manuscript that they expected to be published by the Library of Congress based on their negotiations before the fieldwork began. The manuscript was sent to the Library of Congress but was misplaced, then found, and lost again. The president of Fisk wrote letters about the manuscript to two different heads of the Archive of American Folk Song, but they did not seem to be interested in it especially after Alan Lomax left the archive, and the manuscript was never published (22–23). The world was not aware that the manuscript existed until Gordon and Nemerov found it "in the back of a file cabinet drawer in the Alan Lomax Archives at Hunter College in New York" with a cover that identified it as the property of Fisk University (29). "That the manuscripts were found in the Lomax archives six decades after they went missing may reveal much about how research is, and is not, shared, attributed, and published" (27). Gordon and Nemerov published the Work/Jones manuscript along with Samuel C. Adams' master's thesis as *Lost Delta Found* (2005).

In their introduction and notes to the book, Gordon and Nemerov make clear that Lomax used material from the manuscripts in *The Land Where the Blues Began* often without attribution (25), but they word their descriptions of the historical facts carefully to avoid a direct accusation about Lomax's motives in taking and holding on to the manuscripts. However, they imply that he took the manuscripts when he left the Archive of Folk Song and kept them to prevent their being published. A more forgiving explanation would be that the manuscripts were in Lomax's files at the Library of Congress and that he took them when he left thinking they would be published elsewhere.

A scholarly controversy followed the publication of *Lost Delta Found* that is still going on, and scholars disagree about some of the details in the book. For instance, an article in the *New York Times* (Weingarten 2005) about Gordon and Nemerov's findings caused a flurry of responses on Publore, the online discussion group of the American Folklore Society's Public Program Section. Matthew Barton (2005) points out that in correspondence on file at the Library of Congress, Lomax wrote in support of Work and shared credit with him for the field recordings of Muddy Waters. Barton also says that the Work manuscript Gordon found at Lomax's office was a copy and not the original, suggesting that the original was still available elsewhere and could have been published without Lomax's support.

Roger Abrahams wrote letters defending Lomax to the *New York Times* and the *Chicago Tribune* that Robert Baron forwarded to Publore with Abrahams's permission (Abrahams 2005). Abrahams says that Lomax was not trying to hide the manuscript; on a visit to Lomax's archive over fifteen years ago, he examined the Delta file at Lomax's invitation and read "the unfinished manuscript report and the letters from Work explaining why he hadn't finished it." Abrahams also read a letter from Work saying that he (Work) had misplaced his copy of the manuscript and that the Fisk University Library could not find their copy when Abrahams asked for it (ibid.). These statements help clarify some of the facts and undermine some of the negative implications about Alan Lomax's ethics in Gordon and Nemerov's research. However, when seen in the light of other evidence cited earlier in this chapter, their findings add to the complexity of the racial issues in Lomax's fieldwork. It is, at the very least, regrettable that Lomax had these valuable original contributions to the scholarly understanding of black southern culture from an African American perspective and did not take the initiative to have them published. He had a chance to be an early innovator in collaborative research across racial lines (see chapter 8); despite the fact that the field research started out as collaborative, Lomax soon took over and failed to acknowledge his collaborators fully.

Gordon and Nemerov do not do much analysis of this episode in racial terms, but Lomax's actions have to be considered within the context of race. Lomax's incomplete representation of the involvement of the three black scholars suggests the erasure of academic blackness from the ethnographic record, making it seem as if one white man did most of the fieldwork and scholarly analysis. His failure to give more credit to the essential fieldwork of his black collaborators in the research fits the ongoing historical pattern of white dominance over black. The broad cultural pattern is clear, but we need to look closer at the details of his behavior to explain his personal psychological and emotional motives. (I use the same psychoanalytic approach here that I have criticized in the white folklorists' interpretations of black informants; the difference is that Lomax and I are of the same scholarly and social groups, and I recognize that I make subconscious racial assumptions in my own research.)

That Lomax cut in and took over Work's interview with Muddy Waters and failed to give Work much credit in the memoir may indicate Lomax felt threatened, perhaps subconsciously, by Work. That would also explain his criticism of Work in his fieldnotes and in the letter to the president of Fisk, both of which are grounded in racial stereotypes about the laziness and incompetence of blacks. By seeing Work in stereotypical terms, Lomax asserts his white superiority, thus psychologically reducing the perceived threat of Work's academic expertise. John W. Work was academically trained as a musicologist and so was Lomax, but Jeff Titon thinks that Lomax was more of a "collector" and that Work was a better scholar: "Indeed, Lomax was incapable of Work's kind of scholarship, and Work knew it" (quoted in Work 2005, 21). I think Lomax may have felt this too, and his insecurity was one source of his neglecting to fully acknowledge the contributions of Work, Jones, and Adams to the Delta fieldwork. In racial terms, he slights the contributions of black scholars to construct whiteness as intellectually superior to blackness. Intellectual educated blacks did not fit Lomax's concept of black folk as illiterate. He felt more comfortable in fieldwork situations with uneducated black folk he could condescend to rather than with educated black men whom he feared might condescend toward him. Jones, Adams, and Work did not fit

Lomax's preconceived notions about black as folk and their contributions therefore had to be minimized in his book.

Lomax's conceptualization of the folk was narrower than that of the three black scholars. Lomax focused his field research on lower-class uneducated blacks in the Delta, but as Gordon and Nemerov point out, Adams, Jones, and Work recognized that "Coahoma County was a diverse community that included educated black Southerners able to articulate their ideas about their home. By devaluing their contribution, by emphasizing the culture of powerful but less articulate artists that he—Lomax—is required to 'explain' or 'interpret' for mainstream America . . . Lomax creates an appealing but static and nostalgic portrait of black Southern America" (25).

This is another example of Lomax's underlying assumption of white superiority. Lomax also concentrated on genres that he considered more authentically folk such as traditional spirituals while Work included current church practices and music that Lomax considered too modern (ibid.). Like Work, Samuel C. Adams also focuses on social change and urbanization; he says that his master's thesis "seeks to measure the effects of urbanism on the customary modes of behavior of rural Negroes in an area where there still exist many evidences of the sway of traditional life" (223). Gordon and Nemerov do not make a direct comparison with Lomax on this point, but there is a clear contrast between Adams's emphasis on social change and Lomax's emphasis on static tradition. For instance, like his father, Lomax saw radio and phonograph as contaminating influences on tradition while Adams saw them in a positive light: "Specifically the victrola, the radio, the juke box, the dance halls, the movies and the changes in technology make it possible for the plantation Negroes to have a greater access to broader worlds of experience than ever before" (223–24). As upwardly mobile educated blacks, Adams, Work, and Jones could perceive cultural change as positive for black people, but to Lomax change meant the passing of the old world and the death of the folk. As a white person he needed to hold on to the perception of black as folk since it reinforced his underlying sense of white as elite and superior to black, although Lomax seems to be unaware that he was doing this. One of the great ironies of his professional life was that on a political level he considered black people as equal to whites, but his underlying romantic concept of black folk as uneducated caused him to assume white superiority over them. Positive romantic notions contained hidden assumptions of pathology.

The way Alan Lomax imagined blackness as folk was also a significant and contradictory factor in his intense desire to be black. He maintained a sense of black inferiority, but at the same time he wanted to be black on an emotional level. To explain this more fully, we must return to the beginning of *The Land Where the Blues Began* and that scene early in his Mississippi fieldwork when he was walking through a black neighborhood. "I strolled along, wrapped in my Anglo-Saxon shyness and superiority. We had grabbed off everything, I thought, we owned it all—money, land, factories, shiny cars, nice houses—yet these people, confined to their shacks and their slums, really possessed America; they alone, of the pioneers who cleared the land, had learned how to enjoy themselves in the big, lonesome continent; they were the only full-blown Americans" (1993, 32).

Evidence exists here of Alan Lomax's underlying concept of racialized folkness: race and class combined to create "full-blown Americans" as if being dispossessed were a necessary quality for Americanness as well as for being a folk. The materialism of the white middle class seems unimportant when contrasted to the spiritual qualities associated with the folk and with blackness. There is also a significant point in understanding his racial desire here: he assumes that black people have the key to happiness and that Anglo-Saxons have lost it. His idea fits a larger cultural pattern in the dynamics of race, one outlined by bell hooks: "In the cultural marketplace the Other is coded as having the capacity to be more alive, as holding the secret that will allow those who venture and dare to break with the cultural anhedonia . . . and experience sensual and spiritual renewal." "Anhedonia" is a term coined by Sam Keen in his book *The Passionate Life* and defined by hooks as "insensitivity to pleasure, the incapacity of experiencing happiness" (1992, 26).

Alan Lomax definitely thought that black otherness held the secret of sensual and spiritual renewal, and this was related to his own sense of whiteness as being incapable of experiencing pleasure. Black life and African American culture were close at hand and held all of the sensual pleasures denied to whites by Puritanism. This was not a new idea for him in the early 1990s; he expressed something similar in the 1960 publication *The Folk Songs of North America*: "The full weight of Puritanism did not fall upon the Negroes, who came largely from cultures which placed a high value on erotic and aggressive behaviour and which provided vivid outlets for them in song, dance, and ceremonial" (1960, xix). Nor was it a new idea in the 1960s; scholars have traced this white concept of blackness in terms of sexuality back to at least the eighteenth century as part of the European colonial construction of the primitive (Torgovnick 1990). David R. Roediger sees the association of blacks with the primitive as a core feature in the development of working class whiteness in the nineteenth century: blacks were defined "as sexual but also without history and as natural, erotic, sensual and animal. Whiteness took shape against the corresponding counter-images, shunting anxieties and desires regarding relationships to nature and to sexuality onto Blacks" (1991, 150–51). Roediger is describing nineteenth-century working class Irish-Americans, but he could just as well be describing Alan Lomax in the 1950s.

Lomax's ideas about black sexuality were part of a larger intellectual merging of anthropological functionalism and Freudianism in terms of primitivism. "Ethnography, especially when influenced by Freud, collaborated with other aspects of our culture in perpetuating an image of the primitive that is still with us" (Torgovnick 1990, 3). Throughout *The Land Where the Blues Began* Lomax emphasizes sexuality as a defining core feature of African American and African culture reinforcing the construction of blacks as primitive. He then explains sexual behavior in functionalist terms; for instance, he sees promiscuity among Delta blacks as a result of social conditions—crowded communal living for men and women on the plantations, women encouraged to have children during slavery no matter who the father was, and pregnancy being seen as proof that a woman loved a man after emancipation (1993, 84). These functions are based on the principles of functionalism that emphasize immediate historical social context; however, Lomax also had a mythic conception of sexuality as ingrained in African cultures across space and time (1993, 84–86). He saw evidence of this in traditional cultural expressions such as the blues: "These blues couplets belong to the powerful undercurrent of African-American eroticism that has come to influence Western culture. Carried on the tide of black popular music, it broke past Western prudishness and has drastically liberalized sexual attitudes in the Unites States. In the Delta caste ghetto, where the blues were born, this African permissive pattern was simply taken for granted. Little boys and girls began their sexual lives early, and by ten, it is reported, were inured to intercourse with their playfellows" (85–86).

Lomax's contrast of African eroticism and European prudishness indicates how whiteness and blackness defined each other in his mind. He saw sexuality everywhere in black Mississippi including in children's rhymes. "Those young black girls sang 'satisfied' in perfect and saucy unison, with tremendous swing and an offbeat clap that sent chills up my spine . . . I can never forget those slim black girls, seeming almost to take wing as they skimmed the red dust on those golden summer afternoons, the verses exploding like firecrackers on the 4th." The nostalgic romantic language used to describe black girls at play takes on a sexual dimension because Lomax saw a sexual function for the rhyme they were chanting: "Sexually active at ten or eleven, with marriage maybe only a couple of years off, a Delta country girl needed to know how to sort through the males, and how to move between marriage partners." (89). He also discerned underlying sexuality in other cultural expressions such as the movements of black workers lifting and carrying heavy loads, a movement he called "rocking": "That this movement also mimes sexual intercourse endows rocking with pleasurable associations. In a word, it is at the very core of African cultural survival" (155).

On a more obvious level, Lomax also saw eroticism in African American dance. But it is not merely the connection he makes between dance and sexuality that has significance for his construction of blackness and whiteness; it is the language he uses to describe eroticism in dancing. Several descriptions of dances in the book emphasize the sexuality and Lomax perhaps inadvertently reveals more about his own desires than he realized. At one point, he and a crew were filming black men dancing in Mississippi, and he noticed how the dance was becoming increasingly more sexual: "At this point the black Mississippi sound man demanded that we stop shooting, and since I had enough for my film, I agreed. I understood his concern. The normal American audience might mistake this sexually hyperactive, virtually all-male dance for a homosexual orgy, which it most certainly was not. All-male erotic dancing has always been a part of African tradition" (342).

But Lomax does not seem concerned that this footage might reinforce stereotypes whites have about black sexuality in general. In fact, he seems to want to confront white puritan views, "Dance was music and music was dance, and both were powerfully and positively genital. These country people were having fun with their bodies—shaking it on down out there in the dark—fun that might shock Calvinist sensibilities, but which harmed no one, hurt no one, not even themselves. They were giggling, smiling, grinning, and laughing as they played their rhythmic sexual games, carrying on in ancestral ways" (343). In describing a trait he associated with blackness, he often directly projects an opposite trait for whiteness, and here it is black eroticism versus white sexual inhibition, "Calvinist sensibilities," a major and recurring example. A seemingly polemical tone comes through here, condemning puritanical views in order to espouse openness toward sexuality in a way that is reminiscent of Alfred Kinsey. Even when he does not explicitly mention white lack of sexuality, Lomax implies it in his descriptions of African American eroticism.

Although his language gets heated, most of his descriptions of erotic black dancing are from the point of view of the detached ethnographic observer who is not personally involved, and since this observer is white, we have an implied contrast of blackness and whiteness. He has a lot to say about a particular black dance popular in the 1930s and '40s called the "slow drag." "The couples, glued together in a belly-to-belly, loin-to-loin embrace, approximated sexual intercourse as closely as their vertical posture, their clothing, and the crowd around them would allow . . . The slow drag was, I believe, an innovation at that time, and it may well have been then the most erotic dance on earth" (364). Later he describes the scene at a juke joint he has just entered: "The blues—the slow drag—is probably the most licentious of all, for here the partners stay pressed as close together as possible, just as if they were in bed, belly-to belly, thigh-to-thigh, crotch-to-crotch, both arms round the other's neck and, holding this position, grind their hips together slowly so that their mounting sexual excitement may be coexperienced" (366).

This sexual display was going on all around him, but he remained, for the most part, an observer. He entered into it at only one point: "Their white whiskey ran down our gullets like fire and brought on a sweat. There was local barbecue for sale, spicy and delicious. People were having fun" (ibid.). He and his cohorts take part in the drinking and the eating, but he does not indicate if they danced. The eating and drinking, though, seem like a metaphor for the erotic dancing—whiskey whose "fire" "brought on a sweat," and barbecue "spicy and delicious." The sexual desire seems to be displaced, but the detailed language he uses to repeatedly describe the eroticism of the dancing makes the element of white desire clear.

Erotic dancing, like other traits of African American culture, is given a mythic dimension through Lomax's language. His description of another dance illustrates this. First he establishes the erotic nature of the dance movement called "balling the jack" by citing a woman dancer: "rotating her hips and squatting lower and lower till her dress tail stirred the dust" (330). Then he describes a dance by fife player Ed Young:

> The sweet African sounds washed across the sandy yard and Ed, too, began to ball the jack, turning while he sank slowly toward the earth, until he was close enough to reach out and caress the ground with a wide sweeping gesture. Then, while he slowly spun erect again, he drew the fingers of his right hand across his brow, leaving there a powdery trace, as if, by this token, he declared himself to be a child of Mother Earth, and as he rose like a bird from the dust, out of his cocked flute poured raptures of goat cries, bird songs, and lovers. We looked on with brimming eyes as this black sprite of a man magically recalled his ancestry in this bit of African choreography. (331)

It is all here: the sexuality, the romance, the mythic link to Africa, the magic connection to the earth, the unbridled African American performance, and the European American emotional response "with brimming eyes," all indicating that this cultural expression transcends race at the same time that it reinforces racial difference. This description encapsulates Lomax's white desire for blackness.

From his father describing Alan's fieldwork contacts with black prisoners when he was seventeen to Alan's own reminiscing in his seventies about his fieldwork among blacks in the south, a constant theme of fascination with African American culture runs through his life. That fascination reveals deeper levels of the cultural processes whereby race concepts are created and maintained in America. Alan Lomax was like many other American white men in the nineteenth and twentieth centuries whose attraction to blackness was grounded in a desire to be black; that desire was itself created out of imagining blackness and whiteness to be at opposite ends of a spectrum of pleasure and denial. In *The Land Where the Blues Began*, the actions of white and black characters represent deeper cultural and racial traits, some of them related to existing cultural stereotypes. The book could have been unintentionally racist, but I think it is more racial than racist because of Lomax's strong sense of identification with black life. Toni Morrison says that her vulnerability as a black writer "would lie in romanticizing blackness rather than demonizing it, vilifying whiteness rather than reifying it" (1992, xi). I think that Alan Lomax had such a powerful identification with blackness that he tried to write as if he were black; in *The Land Where the Blues Began* he romanticizes blackness and vilifies whiteness. The stereotypes are still there, but they are romantic stereotypes framed by a sense of the social reality of the oppressive racist conditions in which blacks lived.

Lomax's representations of black and white relationships in the south in his memoir undermine a basic concept of whiteness as goodness and light (hooks 1992, 169). This may have become so ingrained in white self-concept that some whites also thought that blacks saw whiteness as benign. (hooks quotes Richard Dyer's essay "White" [1988] on this point, but the entire quote is not in Dyer's essay.) Alan Lomax is clearly an exception to this white perspective: he recognizes both that whiteness does not represent goodness and that black people do not see whiteness as benign. Hazel Carby makes the point that pain, oppression, and lynchings are usually left out of white representations of blackness making African American art a safe "aesthetic commodity for white consumption" (1998, 98). Alan Lomax has resisted this form of commodification of black art: his major representations of African

American song as art, *The Land Where the Blues Began,* is unrelenting in its cataloging of atrocities perpetrated by whites against blacks. In fact, he saw black suffering as integral to the development of blues as an art form. Despite his reifying of blackness as mythic and timeless in its expressions of pleasure and eroticism, he also examined the interactions of whiteness and blackness, at times through self-reflection, in ways that anticipate developments in critical race theory at the beginning of the twenty-first century.

Even more directly significant was Alan Lomax's influence on the blues revival of the 1950s, '60s, and '70s. His romantic ideas about African Americans were taken up by a new generation of young white blues fans and musicians who then represented African Americans as Exotic Other in their writings and performances.

5

Bongo Joe, Lightnin' Hopkins, and the Blues Revival

> What I really like about the jungle
> is I ain't there.
> —Bongo Joe

One of the first field-recorded record albums I bought in college in the 1960s, "Roots of the Blues" (n.d.), was from Alan Lomax's fieldwork in Mississippi. Instead of an obscure "folkie" label. a major commercial label released the record because of the growing popularity of rural folk blues at the time, a phenomena that later came to be called the blues revival. I remember being struck by how "African" some of the performances sounded, especially those by Ed and Lonnie Young that were also later featured in the film *The Land Where the Blues Began* (1988c). I had bought into Alan Lomax's mythic representation of African Americans. But he was not the only white writer who was projecting images of black people as folk. The recording industry was producing numerous folk blues albums with extensive liner notes, and publishers were releasing books on the blues as well; for example, Samuel Charters, *The Country Blues* (1959); Frederic Ramsey, *Been Here and Gone* (1960); and Paul Oliver, *Blues Fell This Morning* (1960); and numerous albums by Mississippi John Hurt, Furry Lewis, Son House, Robert Johnson, Lightnin' Hopkins, and so forth.

Historically African American folk performers had to rely on white producers to represent them to an audience beyond their own communities. In Texas in the 1940s, '50s, and '60s Lightnin' Hopkins needed white record producers to get his music heard beyond Houston's Third Ward. Later, he was represented in books by blues writer Samuel Charters, in the folk music revival of the '50s and '60s by several writers of album liner notes, and in documentary films by Les Blank. Another Texas performer, George Coleman, better known as Bongo Joe, was recorded and written about during the same period. The way white writers portrayed Lightnin' Hopkins and George Coleman depended on the specific political, economic, and social context of the time as well as the history that informed that context. The assumptions and motivations of individual cultural producers determined to a great extent how black entertainers were perceived by the outside world.

Bongo Joe was a street performer who played steel drums on Seawall Boulevard in Galveston and at the Alamo Plaza in San Antonio. I interviewed him twice, once in Galveston in 1967 and again twenty-eight years later in 1995 in San Antonio. On the second occasion, I sent him a copy of an article I had written about him in 1970 and asked him what he thought of it. He was not openly critical of what I said about him although he may have had some thoughts that he did not express. As a public performer he seemed more interested in the attention the article might have drawn than in the nuances of racial representation. When I interviewed him the first time in 1967, he definitely wanted to reach a wider audience; within a year Arhoolie Records owner Chris Strachwitz released a record album of his music (see Skoog 1968). As with Lightnin' Hopkins, Bongo Joe's image as a black performer was being shaped to some extent by white mediators, both scholars and popular producers, for a mainly white audience. By examining the way whites such as Samuel Charters, Mack McCormick, Les Blank, myself, and others represented Lightnin' Hopkins and Bongo Joe during their careers, we can begin to see how the folk revival absorbed attitudes about race from earlier writers such as Newbell Niles Puckett and John and Alan Lomax and adapted them to the political and social changes taking place in the 1950s and '60s.

I first heard Lightnin' Hopkins's music on record when I was in college in Beaumont, Texas, in the early 1960s, a time when I was collecting blues records and beginning to write about African American music. I read a paper on "soul music" at the 1964 meeting of the Texas Folklore Society in Houston, and afterwards John Lomax, Jr., asked me if I liked Lightnin' Hopkins's music. "Of course. I'm a big fan of his." "How would you like to meet him?" A young white blues fan's fantasy come true. He gave me Hopkins's telephone number and told me if I invited him to our hotel and promised him a bottle of gin, he would come and play for us. I called and had a brief conversation with Hopkins, but he was scheduled to play at a club in Arcola south of Houston that night. I talked to him on two other occasions, once at the Match Box, a club in Austin where he was performing, and at the Ash Grove, a popular '60s folk revival club in Los Angeles. He was always courteous and friendly, seemingly open to what were to him probably naive and frequently heard questions from a fan.

As a college student in Beaumont, I first heard Bongo Joe in person. Along with many other college students at the time, I went to Galveston for the beach and the beer drinking. I heard Bongo Joe play his drums and do his routines on Seawall Boulevard; later when I was in graduate school at the University of Texas looking for a folklore fieldwork project, I thought about Bongo Joe and went back to Galveston to record him. I spent an afternoon and part of an evening interviewing him and watching his performance in front of an audience of mainly white tourists. The essay I wrote about him, "A Negro Street Performer: Tradition and Innovation," appeared in 1970 (Mullen 1970).

My brief encounters with Bongo Joe and Lightnin' Hopkins gave me only superficial information about them, but I assumed the authority to write about them as did Samuel Charters, Mack McCormick, and others with Hopkins. White writers and scholars had a great deal of interest in African American folk performers during this period. The late 1950s witnessed the beginning of the blues revival, and writings from the revival have influenced perceptions of African American culture since. White writers perceived black performers based not only on fieldwork interviews and observations but also on certain shared assumptions about African American life, and black performers responded to this white interest in particular culturally shared ways.

According to Jeff Todd Titon, who was a white participant in the blues revival, "Those of us who participated in the revival thought we had discovered an object called blues, which we then set out to think about, document, analyze, and, in some cases, perform. Instead, by our interpretive acts, we constructed the very thing we thought we had found" (1993, 222–23). This is not to deny the existence of blues music in the African American community, but to recognize that the music and the culture from which it came were transformed through the prism of race into a cultural product for white consumption. Since I was writing about African American music at the same time, I also was constructing a version of this product. Politically, all of us were rebelling against our conservative middle-class backgrounds by identifying with what we perceived as a marginal culture with different values that challenged our parents' and teachers' values (223). Lightnin' Hopkins and Bongo Joe became symbols of this rebellion, but to make them fit our political and aesthetic purposes, we reshaped their images into our image of their culture. These representations were often based on wide knowledge and deep understanding of African American culture on the part of white researchers, but they could not help being influenced by underlying cultural assumptions.

As I discussed in earlier chapters, one of the patterns of race representation is related to a larger romantic concept of folklore which goes back to the eighteenth century—the creation by antiquarians and folklorists of a pure folk, a pastoral ideal thought to be disappearing because of social change, industrialization, urbanization, and developing technology. This early folk pastoralism was applied to African American culture in the nineteenth century, but the immediate precursor to the 1950s and '60s blues revival use of it was probably John Lomax's southern pastoral view of the black singers he recorded for the Library of Congress in the 1930s and '40s (Hirsch 1992; Porterfield 1996; also see chapter 3). Lomax and blues revival writers saw African American culture as a pastoral ideal and black performers as representatives of a simpler rural time and place. The very title of my piece on Bongo Joe indirectly reflects this: "A Negro Street Performer: Tradition *and* Innovation" (emphasis added). By suggesting that tradition and innovation are separate entities, I implied that black tradition is a pure inheritance from the past. In the article, I stated, "Thus in Bongo Joe's role as a street entertainer, in his sound, and in his instrumentation he is a traditional folk performer, but the influences of jazz and mass media have made him a popular performer. He is between a pure folk and a popular tradition" (Mullen 1970, 95). I assumed that the pure oral folk tradition was separate from popular mass media, implying that popular culture could contaminate folk culture.

Born in a rural part of Texas, Lightnin' Hopkins spent the first thirty three years of his life playing music in agrarian and small town settings throughout East Texas (Wheat 1996, 256–60). He settled in Houston's urban Third Ward right after World War II and was first recorded about the same time. His 1940s and '50s recordings were aimed at the black record-buying public, but from the late '50s on he was increasingly marketed for the white revival audience (260–61). David Benson, Lightnin' Hopkins' road manager for ten years, said that in his later years, "99 per cent of the time Lightnin' played for white audiences who were romanticizing blues music and saw him as bigger than life" (269).

The white-revival blues fans were clearly the audience for Mack McCormick's liner notes for several Lightnin' Hopkins's albums of the late '50s and early '60s (1959, 1960a, n.d.) and in articles he wrote for *The Jazz Review* (1962) and *Sing Out* (1960b). Despite the urban and commercial components of Hopkins's career, McCormick preferred to emphasize his rural and oral culture roots as the basis for his authenticity. McCormick followed John Lomax's model in constructing a pastoral ideal of the black folk singer. On a 1959 album, he called Hopkins a "genuine folk artist"; his criteria for what made Hopkins genuine included country roots and a pure oral tradition. In the *Jazz Review* article, McCormick quotes Hopkins reminiscing about picking cotton, singing in church, and playing blues in rural East Texas before he moved to Houston (1962, 313–15). In liner notes (1959), he described Hopkins's country roots poetically, giving them an almost mystical air: East Texas "is a magic spring from which the great blues minstrels have flowed in an unbroken line." Not only the singer but also his audience had this rural communal base: "Like many of those who make up his audiences, beneath the sharp urban manners he is pure 'country.' He belongs to the East Texas cotton lands in an almost tribal sense." In the *Jazz Review* article, McCormick describes Hopkins in a similar way: "A man with a tribal sense of belonging to his culture, he is outside the modern dilemma" (1962, 313). The repeated phrase "tribal sense" is especially revealing of McCormick's romanticizing of the African American past, suggesting not only rural but primitive sources. Hopkins's "urban manners" are merely a facade over his pure country roots. Most of the evidence of McCormick's romanticizing of Lightnin' Hopkins comes from the 1959 album and the *Jazz Review* article; subsequent liner notes indicate less of a tendency in this direction.

Les Blank's film *The Blues Accordin' to Lightnin' Hopkins* (1967) maintained the view of Hopkins as a rural blues singer. The film opens with a shot of farmland and cows; it then shifts to Hopkins, blues singer Mance Lipscomb, and harmonica player Billy Bizor playing on a dirt road, with shots of chickens and a rooster interspersed. The film was shot in Houston and Centerville, Hopkins's birthplace, but the main emphasis is on rural and small-town settings even though Hopkins no longer lived there. There is a suggestion that this is a Centerville homecoming for Hopkins, but the viewer does not get much sense of his then current urban environment. Although the Third Ward at this time was a "surprisingly country-like environment of pastured lots and [stores and houses] lying just across the freeway from the city's downtown skyscrapers" (Wheat 1996, 266), the Houston scenes in the film seem to be framed to exclude freeways and skyscrapers.

The purity of African American folk tradition was assumed by other writers of liner notes and reviews of Lightnin' Hopkins's albums and concerts. Chris Albertson (1964) called him "one of the few blues artists on the scene today who has never resorted to commercialism," which again suggests he is uncontaminated by media influences. Russ Wilson (1966) called Hopkins one of the "real folk artists" without defining the criteria for real folk music but suggesting purity in its essence. Albertson said Hopkins's blues "have all the qualities that are so sorely lacking in the pseudo-folk music which clutters today's market," and this album "is worth fifty anemic-sounding 'folk' singers on your own private shelf." Like Russ Wilson, Albertson never explained what constitutes "pseudo-folk music" or why the singers are "anemic-sounding," but the implication is that these are imitations of the real thing—the pure unadulterated black blues.

To these critics, the purity of African American folksong was threatened by commercialism, popular music, technology, and urban influences. The genuine folk artist had to be isolated from these influences and innocent of the workings of the contemporary world. McCormick refers to Hopkins living in "isolated Negro wards of a southern city" in his *Jazz Review* article (1962, 313) and in the liner notes says that Hopkins "is a strangely innocent man, isolated and oblivious to much of contemporary life, and ignorant in some astounding ways. (Until the time of this recording he had never heard of long playing records even tho [sic] an LP reissue of his early recordings was on sale within a block of his home)" (1959). Another liner note writer, Lawrence Cohn (1964), says the same thing about Hopkins, "charming and coy—possessed of an unbelievable naivete in respect to many worldly considerations and matters." For Hopkins to be folk for these writers, he has to be isolated from mainstream society, and his ignorance of long-playing records (if in fact he was ignorant of them) makes him part of a purer oral tradition. McCormick recognized that the oral tradition had been influenced by recordings when he said, "There has been since the 1920s a tremendous interchange between regional traditions and records," and he specifically mentioned that Lightnin' Hopkins learned the song "Jailhouse Blues" from a Bessie Smith recording (McCormick n.d.). However, his need for a pure tradition, free of media influence, caused him to write, "[Lightnin' Hopkins's] roots are not the motley impressions of phonograph records but the distinct heritage of his birthplace" (McCormick 1959).

McCormick set up a dichotomy that was widely accepted by folklorists and blues scholars: the modern world of recordings and other technological developments on one side and the traditional oral world of the isolated rural folk community on the other that he construed as "outside the modern dilemma" (1962, 313). This is, I think, a false dichotomy; the traditional and the modern, oral and media transmission, are not isolated entities; they have always interacted with one another because tradition is a concept of the past that is constructed in the present (Handler and Linnekin 1984). Folk processes have always included the incorporation of technological developments; for instance, printed broadside ballads became part of the traditional process of ballad transmission after the invention of the printing press, and blues singers were influenced by recordings from 1923 on. Lightnin' Hopkins learned directly from Blind Lemon Jefferson, Texas Alexander, and others, but he also heard blues recordings on phonograph and radio. The recognition of media influence did not keep McCormick and most folklorists in the 1960s (myself included) from constructing a pure oral tradition that was exemplified by African American performers.

This belief meant that technological realities of the recording industry had to be ignored or condemned. In the *Jazz Review* article, McCormick says, "Recording directors have consistently forced tasteless material, amplified guitars, and heavy-handed drummers on [earlier Hopkins recording] sessions" (1962, 316), and in liner notes, "Lightnin was first recorded in 1946 by a firm devoted to the jukebox trade. Since then, increasingly pursued by amplifiers, echo chambers, and thudding drums, he has appeared on a dozen labels. His near pathetic attempts to conform to the gimmick-oriented demands of these firms . . . have resulted in nearly 200 selections of a nondescript Lightnin in competition with the rock n' roll industry" (1959). Music archivist and blues scholar John Wheat makes a different aesthetic judgment of these early recordings; he sees them as a more accurate reflection of the black community: "Though less polished in performance and technical quality than some of the later recordings, they project a raw, rough-edged vitality that lies closer to the marrow of Hopkins' musical origins" (1996, 261). The electric guitar had been a part of the blues tradition since the 1940s, and Lightnin' Hopkins was playing an electric guitar when McCormick first encountered him, but blues revival producers recorded blues singers with acoustic guitars because it fit their and the audience's notion of folk music. This also happened to John Lee Hooker at about the same time (Titon 1993, 231).

Bongo Joe was playing a drum made from a used steel barrel when Chris Strachwitz and I recorded him, but he was not playing it by choice. He told me that he was denied a job at a Houston club because he did not have his own drum set, and that he fashioned his own out of available materials. He was not trying to sound primitive; rather it was a choice dictated by his economic circumstances. Bongo Joe's use of homemade steel drums appealed to a white audience and to white folklorists because it reinforced their concepts of African American folk music, seeming vaguely Caribbean in nature even though Bongo Joe played in a different style and denied any influence from Trinidad steel drums. Lawrence C. Skoog's notes to the Bongo Joe album (1968) indicate the primitivist concept of African American drumming: "George Coleman is a Drum beater, a man who uses the drum to send important information over long distances, he is the logical extension of this primitive art into modern culture."

Mack McCormick's need to preserve Lightnin' Hopkins's performances as pure folk music extended to the recording techniques he used. "For these recordings, engineering finesse was happily sacrificed in order that no inhibiting technical process dampen his rough edged moods" (1959). It was as if pure folk music demanded simple recording techniques. McCormick's imagined pure folk music caused him to denigrate any popular influences or technologically advanced recording techniques. Recordings by B. B. King in the late 1960s and John Lee Hooker in the early '90s show that traditional blues artists do adapt to technological change just as they did with the move from acoustic to amplified guitar in the '40s.

White critics selected aspects of African American social reality that conformed to their preconceived notions, offering a narrow, oversimplified view of the culture as a result. "Rejecting conformity to middle-class values, blues revivalists embraced the music of people who seemed unbound by conventions of work, family, sexual propriety, worship, and so forth . . . The romantic strain projected a kind of primitivism on the blues singer and located him in a culture of natural license" (Titon 1993, 225). In other words, even though their impulse was liberal and well intentioned, these writers reinforced racial stereotypes of blacks. For instance, in *The Country Blues* Samuel Charters's description of Lightnin' Hopkins includes the detail that Hopkins was drinking straight gin (1975 [1959], 16). Jeff Todd Titon sees this selection of detail as a significant construction: "I do not doubt that he drank the gin; what concerns me is why this detail is selected and others omitted" (1993, 230). By emphasizing this detail, Charters was reinforcing the view of blues singers as part of a "culture of natural license," fulfilling white revivalists' need for a symbolic alternative to a repressed white society. I always mentioned Hopkins's gin drinking when I told the anecdote about talking to him on the phone in Houston; I too needed a symbol of escape from repression because of my imagined white middle-class restrictive background.

Mack McCormick falls into the same cultural pattern in depicting Lightnin' Hopkins: his songs reveal "his easy familiarity with the enforced poverty, the quick violence, policy slip gambling, mojo charms, and empty gin bottles" (1959). As with Charters's description, these details are part of the reality of Hopkins's community and undoubtedly reflect predominant themes in blues songs, but blues do not represent the entire spectrum of black experience. Descriptions that concentrate on the gamblers and drinkers leave out the church-going people, those who have steady jobs and teach their children the work ethic, and countless other blacks who belie the stereotype of violence, gambling, and drinking. When McCormick quotes Hopkins, he selects excerpts from interviews where Hopkins discusses his many common-law marriages, trouble with the law, and prison time, all of which fit with common themes in blues songs. This represents a narrow focus on African American society that oversimplifies the complexity of the overall culture.

In my article on Bongo Joe, I painted a picture of him as a victim of racial discrimination: "The trapped black man usually can see no way out of his predicament, but that does not keep him from raging against it through expressive forms such as songs, tales, and comic routines" (Mullen 1970, 98). This was and is an accurate statement, but by seeing Bongo Joe and other African American performers only as victims, I denied them individual dignity and self-determination. History is full of examples of black men and women who overcame racial discrimination and achieved personal and cultural success, and this includes Bongo Joe and Lightnin' Hopkins. My emphasis on the black man "raging against" racial discrimination was influenced by the Black Power movement of the late 1960s, in ways similar to Roger Abrahams's racial politics during the same period (see chapter 6). In the late '50s and early '60s, writers such as McCormick and Charters portrayed a more passive black performer. McCormick sees Hopkins as withdrawing from racial conflict: "Bound to the city and detesting the Yessuh behavior demanded of a southern Negro, he chooses to seclude himself within his own segregated society with its self-sufficient mores" (1959). Shifts in white representations of blacks took place as the political climate changed, but there was a consistency in the stereotyped image of African Americans as Exotic Other.

I reinforced other stereotypes by focusing on Bongo Joe's sexual persona in performance and on his itinerant life. "As with the Negro male in general in American society, he has been highly mobile" (Mullen 1970, 91–92). This statement may contain some truth for men from lower socioeconomic classes, but it neglects the experiences of millions of upwardly mobile and middle-class black men. I concentrated on a sexual theme in his performance: "Both of these routines are expressive of the sexual attitudes of urban Afro-American culture. In them the words through the use of clever conceits and suggestive metaphor take on sexual power; language becomes a male control device in any contest of the sexes . . . [Bongo Joe] is proving his manliness to the audience at the same time as he entertains them" (100). Again, there is some truth to this, but the problem comes from generalizing Bongo Joe's performance to all "urban Afro-American culture," and focusing on his sexuality to the exclusion of other facets of his performing persona. In this tendency to generalize about all black men from a small sample I was like other white social scientists at the time (Duneier 1992). White male folk performers also deal with sexual themes and project sexual images, but in general folklore scholarship does not emphasize this as much as it does with black men.

Some white interpreters of African American folk music were not knowledgeable about the tradition, and they made incomplete interpretations of the performances they observed as a result. Gerald Davis is critical of filmmaker Les Blank's 1967 presentation of Lightnin' Hopkins because it lacks sufficient context. Davis doubts that "the viewer has any enhanced sense of the historically long tradition Hopkins represents (an important, necessary context), or of the griot/commentator/observer/aesthetician/innovator/composer/gender-bearer/dynamic 'man-of-words' nature of the bluesman" (Davis 1992, 115). Jazz critic Ralph Gleason also seems unaware of this tradition in a review he wrote of a Lightnin' Hopkins concert: "Hopkins has now worked out a little vignette of storyline to introduce each tune, which is really a drag and quite pretentious" (Gleason 1966). What was "pretentious" to Gleason was part of Hopkins's traditional role as a blues singer—to be a griotlike storyteller within his performance. Mack McCormick was more knowledgeable about the tradition than Gleason; he recognized the storytelling element in Hopkins's art in a description of his street corner performances: he "involves his listeners with impromptu narratives and asides tossed out with a knowing grimmace [sic]" (McCormick 1959).

However, McCormick was like the Lomaxes and most other white blues critics in applying Euro-American aesthetics to an African American art form or in seeing the art as "mythic" and beyond aesthetics. "Subject to the pitfalls of an unreflective art, he may drift into banal repetition in one moment, and in the next strike out with some deep intimacy, stunning with humor or melancholy insight" (ibid.). What McCormick sees as "banal" may not be perceived by a black audience in the same way. To maintain his image of Hopkins as a genuine African American folk artist, McCormick had to view his art as unreflective, as coming from a "magic spring" instead of from conscious artistry. He made no distinction between Hopkins's various identities: "Lightnin' the man is the same as Lightnin' the artist" (1962, 313). Samuel Charters made a similar judgment when he failed to see Robert Johnson's intensity as "calculated art" because he confused the singer with the person (Titon 1993, 229). Charters also applied Euro-American intellectual concepts to Lightnin' Hopkins, seeing him, in Titon's words, as a "romantic, even existential, artist-hero" (ibid.).

All of the white writers during this period saw African American folk music as culturally unique but at the same time as transcending racial and cultural differences; white critics were romantic idealists who represented music as a universal language. This was not a new ideal; 1930s populist folksong collectors such as Alan Lomax and folk festival producers such as Sarah Gertrude Knott saw folk music as a bridge between different races and cultures (Cantwell 1992, 284; Hirsch 1992, 202–3). McCormick's description of a Lightnin' Hopkins' concert before a white audience illustrates the ideal: "Artist and audience, who moments before had been ignorant of each other, had found common ground thru [sic] the impact of Lightnin's personality, the self-evident spontaneity of every moment, and the deeply personal expression of a vital people's music" (1960a). I did the same thing in my description of Bongo Joe's street corner performance: the crowd is "a mixture of both young and old, with many family groups. Most are white tourists who are in Galveston for the day; there are only a few Negroes. Most of the people laugh, tap their feet, and generally seem to enjoy the performance. A few teenagers even dance to the rhythm of the drums" (Mullen 1970, 92). I see this as an accurate description of what happened, and I have no doubt that McCormick's description is factual too; however, in emphasizing the white audience's reaction, we were illustrating our own white liberal idealism about the possibility of racial harmony. According to Lightnin' Hopkins's black road manager David Benson, black performers did not always share this idealism: "Although young white guys may be enamored of the blues and in love with the image of Lightnin' Hopkins, he couldn't quite believe that . . . He came from that era of lynchings . . . from a world where there were no known good white people . . . [This was] not a paranoia, but a certified feeling that he never was able to transcend" (Wheat 1996, 269).

Following in the tradition of Alan Lomax, white writers set themselves up as mediators between black and white, as tour guides who crossed over into another culture, learned the culture, and came back with a message about racial understanding. Undoubtedly many of these writers, including Mack McCormick and me, were knowledgeable about African American culture and understood racial politics better than most whites at the time. White and black researchers performed a great cultural service by bringing black performers to the attention of a wider audience and by creating a better understanding of cultural difference. The unrecognized problem in all this was that the mediators by framing and shaping the artists and performances in the way they did were reinforcing unintentionally some of the audiences' stereotypes about African Americans. The liberal attempt at integration was undermined by the way African American culture was presented and perceived in stereotyped terms. The image of the bluesman as isolated, primitive, and free of societal restraint often was generalized to the whole black population. This was a problem during the blues revival of the 1960s and, despite a greater awareness of the complexities of identity politics today, is still a problem whether at folk festivals, on television situation comedies, or in movies.

To this point, I have emphasized how white mediators shaped black images, but this was not a one-way activity; African American performers negotiated their own identities and manipulated the white producers as part of this cultural process. In most cases, the white writers and filmmakers seem to have been unaware of this; I know I was not conscious of any manipulation. Gerald Davis has pointed out how Lightnin' Hopkins drew upon African American traditional knowledge about dealing with white people to pull verbal and visual tricks on Les Blank and his film crew. During a scene in Blank's *The Blues Accordin' to Lightnin' Hopkins* Hopkins, while eating a watermelon, offers a fork to a white man. Davis says, "In the film there is no indication that the Anglo male either understands or appreciates the humorous jibe to which he has been subjected" (1992, 114). Hopkins was playing with the stereotype of the watermelon-eating Negro, ironically turning it around by suggesting that the white man eat with a culturally appropriate utensil for white people. "The young Anglo male was an outsider. As such, he was probably shielded from critical bits of valuable information" (115). An African American viewer of the film likely would pick up on the joke, a white viewer likely would not. This scene was not in the 1967 version of the film I saw. Davis cites the date as 1969; this may reflect different cuts of the film. Blank's film on Mance Lipscomb, *A Well Spent Life,* also has a biracial watermelon-eating scene. Hopkins may have been manipulating in a similar vein when he told Mack McCormick that he did not know about long-playing recordings, thereby satirizing McCormick's expectations of the isolated country black man.

Bongo Joe was a master of this technique, and I made some incomplete interpretations of his performance as a result. He performed a routine in which the jungle is the central image.

> What I like about the jungle [drums]
> —all them wild animals,
> forests,
> trees,
> marsh,
> Everglades,

woods [drums]
—well, jungles
—that covers all that,
don't it?
Wild animals and beasts and things.
Get in the middle of the jungle,
and you don't have to worry about protection.
Texas rangers won't mess with you out there [drums].
You don't have to worry about our present-day situation [drums].
Out there in the jungle you ain't got nothing but peace [drums].
You don't have to hang no sign on your door
talkin about "Please don't Disturb" [pause].
Might have to hang one on a tree [drums].
What I like about the jungle is,
all them barks,
and roots,
and herbs [pause],
and berries.
I could drink or eat as much as I want to.
Didn't have to worry about no federal control and
prescription and all that stuff.
They served their purpose for two,
ah, twenty thousand years.
Two hundred years did a good job of keeping one of them a secret,
til the Americans come over,
bombarded,
confiscated,
brought it over here,
slapped a label on it,
and called it LSD [loud drums].
What I really like about the jungle [pause]
is [pause]
I ain't there [laugh, drums]. (Mullen 1970, 97)

In 1970, I interpreted the jungle as a metaphor for Africa and saw political meaning in it. "In Joe's routine the jungle is pictured as a paradise in contrast to the corrupt civilized world of America. This almost seems to echo the current desire of many blacks to find a cultural identity in Africa although Joe may not consciously be aware of it" (98). I think now that he was not only aware of this possible meaning but of others as well. Seeing the jungle as "his ideal of a more primitive state" led me to interpret the ending in one particular way: "Paradoxically Joe's final words tell us that with all the advantages of the jungle, he prefers not to be there. He seems to recognize that although Africa is a good dream, ultimately the black man must make his place in America" (ibid.). If, on the other hand, Bongo Joe was playing with white expectations and stereotypes as Lightnin' Hopkins had done, there was another meaning entirely that I missed. Instead of the jungle being an African American ideal, it was a means of signifying (Abrahams 1985, 6–7; Gates 1988, 44–88) on the white stereotype of the African American as primitive. When he says, "What I really like about the jungle is I ain't there," it could be a literal statement, a rejection of the white stereotype of him as primitive. The irony is in the two perspectives of the jungle as metaphor. Bongo Joe was manipulating his audience, the folklorist who was recording him, and by implication all the white blues scholars and music writers who used him, Lightnin' Hopkins, Robert Johnson, and other black performers to construct a primitive image of African American culture.

I missed yet another meaning in the text, one that seemed obvious once Mary Manning, a student in one of my graduate seminars, pointed it out to me. I might have seen it if I had considered the social and political context of 1967 more carefully. The references to foreign jungles, bombardment, drug use, and Americans should have been enough for me to realize that the poem is also about U.S. involvement in Viet Nam. I opposed the war in Viet Nam, and I used my student deferment to avoid the draft throughout the 1960s. Why did I not see the connection? Perhaps my white liberal guilt was a factor. A black man was expressing his attitude toward the war, and I felt guilty because the draft board in my hometown had more than enough lower-class young black men to meet their quotas and never bothered middle-class white college students like me. No wonder Bongo Joe said what he liked best about the jungle was that he wasn't there. That was true for me as well, but I was not subject to conscription to the same extent as he was.

I let my romanticizing of black performers overcome my knowledge of political reality. I was part of a long-standing and deeply ingrained tradition that romanticizes other racial cultures as exotic so that I was unable to see how different our positions were. Power and privilege along racial and cultural lines are taken for granted, and liberal abstract ideals can be diminished or destroyed in a moment when confronted with the concrete reality of racial prejudice (Cantwell 1992, 293). We white folklorists of the 1960s were convinced that our well-intentioned liberal politics kept us from misrepresenting African Americans, but a closer look at the scholarship of a major folklorist of the period, Roger Abrahams, will show how wrong we were.

6

Roger Abrahams and
Racial Politics in the '60s

Highlighting traditions of resistance also served
the larger task of alerting the general reader
to the existence of these vital alternative
voices and practices.
—Roger Abrahams

The political changes taking place in the 1960s that so influenced Lightnin' Hopkins, Bongo Joe, me, and other black performers and white blues scholars were also bringing about changes in folklore scholarship that we did not always recognize at the time but that are easier to see in retrospect. Roger Abrahams was a key figure in the theoretical and political changes that took place in folkloristics in the '60s, and his research among African Americans was central to these changes. He was important in the reconceptualization of folklore to include urban as well as rural areas; he was a major theoretical thinker in the paradigm shift from textual to performance approaches, and he was part of the movement from a conservative to a liberal and leftist political orientation in folklore studies that had started in the 1930s but reached its fullest expression in the '60s and after. I think that '60s politics were a significant part of the context in which the other changes took place.

At the beginning of the 1960s, folklore research on African American culture concentrated almost exclusively on rural settings. As I pointed out in the last chapter, even the writings on such urban blues performers as Lightnin' Hopkins and John Lee Hooker focused on their rural background. Newbell Niles Puckett, John Lomax, Alan Lomax, and other white folklorists conducted their fieldwork far away from cities because of an assumption that folk equaled agrarian. There were exceptions to this rural emphasis, but the scholars and writers who collected folklore in urban areas were usually black—Arthur Huff Fauset's research in Philadelphia in the 1930s and '40s (1971 [1944]), Ralph Ellison's fieldwork in Harlem for the Federal Writers' Project (Banks 1981, 243–45, 250–52, 254–60), and Langston Hughes's and Arna Bontemps's inclusion of "Harlem Jive" and "Street Cries" in their collection *Book of Negro Folklore* (1958). White folklorists, though, continued to restrict their conception of folklore to rural areas. In fact, as late as 1970, Richard Dorson still titled an article "Is There a Folk in the City?" His answer was "yes," but even asking the question indicates that this was still an issue in the definition of the folk (Dorson 1970). Roger Abrahams was one of the folklorists whose research made it possible for Dorson to answer "yes." His fieldwork among blacks in South Philadelphia in the late 1950s and subsequent publication of *Deep Down in the Jungle . . . Negro Narrative Folklore from the Streets of Philadelphia* (1964) altered the course of African American folklore scholarship.

That book also contained intimations of the theoretical shift toward performance in folklore studies. Abrahams, along with Dell Hymes, Richard Bauman, Dan Ben-Amos, and others, formulated the performance approach based on the ethnography of speaking from sociolinguistics. Since much of this theoretical shift took place during the late 1960s and *Deep Down in the Jungle* was written earlier in the decade (published in 1964), it can be considered a transitional document from older approaches to performance theory. As the decade passed, Abrahams saw the need to revise the book to correct some of the problems he perceived in it and to make it fit his changing theoretical perspective; a new edition was published in 1970. I shall examine both editions along with other books he wrote during this period to more fully explain changing scholarly representations of African Americans as folk in the shift to urban research and performance theory. In identifying the underlying assumptions of Abrahams's academic constructs of blackness, I am not trying to identify instances of racism; rather, I am attempting to more thoroughly understand the way prevailing attitudes about race influenced even the best-intentioned writings about African American culture. Also, in saying that certain political ideas were based in romantic concepts about African Americans, I am not arguing against those ideas— some served necessary political purposes in terms of "strategic essentialism" (Spivak and Rooney 1993); rather, I am trying to analyze specific ways that cultural assumptions influenced political interpretations. This will not be an examination of Abrahams's entire career but a look at key works from the 1960s and early '70s that exemplify the shift of theoretical paradigms in folklore studies at that time. An interview I conducted with Roger Abrahams in 2002 provided many insights into the scholarly processes of the '60s and '70s (Abrahams 2002). The interview took place at my home initially with just the two of us. Aaron Oforlea, a graduate student who had been in one of my seminars, joined us later; he brought an interesting black perspective to some of the questions.

In the first edition of *Deep Down in the Jungle*, Abrahams follows an "eclectic" model (1964, 4); he draws on older theories such as comparative, functional, and psychoanalytic, but also demonstrates innovative thinking about rhetorical and linguistic approaches that suggest an emerging performance theory. I shall deal with the functional and psychoanalytic approaches first. Abrahams acknowledges the functional approach with a caveat: "To analyze the strategic effect of any piece of folk-literature is to consider its function. However, by insisting on such considerations I am not espousing any strict functional approach" (8). Within the functionalist model, he emphasizes psychoanalysis: "To discuss a story in psychological terms is to recognize that the tale is a physical embodiment of an internal experience of the individual, and through psychological considerations we can firmly establish the relationship of the story and its inherent values to the lives of those telling or listening to it" (14). This is in keeping with what William Bascom pointed out in 1954—that folklore functions psychologically as an escape from repression and socially to reinforce cultural values (1965 [1954], 290–92).

As we saw in Alan Lomax's case (chapter 4), theory informs racial representation: his functional, Freudian, and Marxist ideas influenced his perceptions and representations of African Americans. Roger Abrahams's link to Alan Lomax is that both suggested an underlying pathology as a result of their use of the Freudian approach. As Abrahams acknowledged, Gershon Legman's Freudian treatment of sexual folklore was a major influence: "Legman's immense contribution to this work will be further testified to in the copious quotations from his letters and works which I have included" (1964, 1; also see Legman 1963 [1949]). When I interviewed Abrahams in 2002, I asked him where he got the idea to use the psychoanalytic approach with the African American material he collected in Philadelphia. He replied, "Well, the psychoanalytic came from the only literature then that was available on black families in America, that was run by, you know, was interviews were run by psychoanalysts and so at that point, of course, the black family was regarded as the crucible of social illness, you know, dysfunctionalism, so on. So I kind of bought into that especially because, because so much of the folklore that I collected was oriented at mother bashing, you know, so that seemed like it was significant" (2002). He applied this approach to the traditional

African American male adolescent verbal contest "playing the dozens" in which the insults are often directed at the opponent's mother (1964, 56–58). "I came down heavy on the way in which the young men used the mother baiting as a way of achieving some kind of personal liberation. I think some of that is there, but I think mostly it's poppycock. I think it's simply a fun and games situation, playing the dozens. I don't think it has anything to do with mothers" (2002). He came to reject the psychoanalytic approach as he recognized problems inherent in it, but in the original edition he used it to paint a pathological portrait of black men.

One of the problems with the psychological functions approach is that the scholar assumes a position of superiority over his or her informants, discerning subconscious meanings in their behavior and cultural expressions of which they are unaware, and often these meanings are identified as pathological (B. O'Connor 1995, 42–44; Mullen 2000c, 128–29). While recognizing this inherent flaw in the psychoanalytic approach, I also think that it can provide insights into various behaviors; the problems are universalizing from the paradigm in ways that ignore different cultural contexts and applying the psychoanalytic model to identify behaviors always as pathological. In the first edition of *Deep Down in the Jungle,* Abrahams interprets the behavioral patterns of his informants as revealed in their narrative poems (toasts) and jokes as deeply pathological. The resulting representation of urban black men is that they are psychologically handicapped.

The chapter on "The Heroes" in *Deep Down in the Jungle* provides a revealing example of psychological interpretation as cultural representation because Abrahams closely links the performers and the heroes of their narratives: "The heroes and the narrators are even more closely related than in most fictive expressions of other groups because of the importance of the narrators' word control in the psychic release afforded by the pieces" (1964, 65). He believes that when the heroes commit antisocial acts, it reveals something about the psychological problems of the storytellers. I agree that connections exist between storyteller and characters in the story and that there are psychological meanings; the problem lies in viewing these connections as necessarily pathological. Abrahams concentrates on two hero types: the trickster is "amoral" and "childlike" and the badman is a "perpetual adolescent" (68–69), and in both cases this reflects back on the storyteller. Abrahams places the storytellers in their social context to explain their identification with such heroes.

> The trickster provides a full escape for those Negroes who have been offered
> no opportunity to feel a control over their own lives, no method for develop-

ing their egos through a specific action. As such, the trickster may reflect *the real childlike state of a severely stunted ego,* or a veiled revolt against authority in the only terms available. (69, emphasis added)

[With the badman] we have the open defiance which we are able to see exhibited *in real life among the Negroes* in the activities of their gangs and the establishment of their gang leaders, and, with some of them, later in their lives as criminals. The values of this group in revolt are implied in the conduct of their badman heroes. (70, emphasis added)

Significantly, Abrahams uses the word "real" in both these quotes to make the connection between the fantasy world of the stories and the everyday lives of the storytellers. For Abrahams, fantastic and immoral acts of the heroes directly reflect the attitudes, desires, and behaviors of the storytellers.

According to Abrahams, the trickster figure was more popular in the south and the badman in the north. His explanation for this suggests some positive social and psychological development, but both heroes are still explained in terms of sexual pathology. "[Earlier southern black men's] trickster protagonists existed in a permissive, childlike, neuter world, divorced from sexual conflict completely. To regress was the only way in which these men could express aggressions at all, and thus their fictive expressions had these aggressively infantile heroes" (73). Here Abrahams moves from the characters in the fictive world to the storytellers in the real world and back again to the fictive realm, reinforcing his argument in a circular way. Because he is in a dominated position, the southern black man must regress to a presexual stage becoming "the impotent man" (ibid.). Northern urban black men rejected this image and replaced it with the more aggressively masculine badman image, which also had sexual problems according to psychoanalytic theory. Abrahams's major example of the badman, "Stackolee," is antagonistic toward both men and women, and he does not hesitate to kill anyone who crosses him. Abrahams sees his acts as "an extension of his disturbed ego" and his sadism as "an outlet for repressed male sexuality" (80, 81). Again, the real men are reflected in the fictional hero: "The lack of a transforming experience in the lives of the Camingerly [Abrahams's name for the black neighborhood] men, then, is mirrored in the circular emotional state of their hero" (82).

As I pointed out earlier, implicit in the functional and psychoanalytic approaches are the assumption of a superior position. John Roberts says that in general white folklorists' interpretations of black folk heroes in the 1960s and '70s were informed by superior ethnocentric biases: "In essence, folklorists who have studied the black badman tradition have either implicitly or explicitly made Anglo-American cultural norms and heroic values the standards by which the black badman tradition is to be evaluated. In the process, they have concluded that the black badman's characteristic actions threaten rather than support American values" (1989, 184). Roberts goes on to interpret black heroes within the context of African American history and values thereby undermining the pathological view. Psychoanalysis was especially ethnocentric and prone to see other cultural behaviors as pathological because its followers assumed the model was universal and therefore they did not perceive the cultural bias within their approach.

One way to get at the effect of the psychoanalytic approach on racial representation is to view the use of Freudianism by folklorists such as Alan Lomax and Roger Abrahams as a theoretical model that suggests a social drama with the scholar as white psychoanalyst and the folk informant as black patient. The analogy is not exact, and psychological analyses of folkloric material did not always follow this model, but in some cases viewing the ethnographic relationship as doctor and patient reveals significant underlying assumptions. First, the scholar/psychoanalyst assumes the existence of pathology; from the beginning he or she is trying to understand a cultural and individual problem: why are black men behaving in this antisocial way? The problem then becomes finding out what causes this behavior, and the doctor/folklorist looks at the patient's jokes and other cultural expressions for evidence just as Freud looked at jokes and myths. The psychoanalytic folklorist's assumption of the authority to determine the problem and analyze a solution places him or her in a superior position to the patient who the doctor assumes does not understand what is going on. This hierarchical relationship parallels the long-standing dichotomy between ethnographer and folk: the white psychiatrist represents control, the black patient represents chaos; the white psychiatrist is mature, the black patient is infantile. Abrahams's characterizations of black social life as chaotic and black men as childlike or adolescent follow from the psychoanalytic model with which he started. Just as we saw with Alan Lomax's representations of African Americans, the cultural construction of race is dynamically reflexive: blackness as infantile chaos constructs whiteness as mature control.

Recently, when I taught Abrahams's chapter on heroes in a graduate seminar, the black students were incensed that his psychoanalytic interpretation of African American heroes represented black male storytellers as childlike and adolescent. They saw this as part of the history of cultural representation of adult black men as children. I reminded them of the historical context of the late 1950s and early '60s when this was written, especially the appeal of the psychoanalytic approach at the time, and that Abrahams himself had rejected this approach in the 1970 edition of the book. Abrahams says that in revising the book he removed "most of the psychoanalytic baggage": "The imprint of Freud, Jung and Campbell, and Erikson as it led to certain ethnocentric judgments will not be so evident here," and he admits that Jung and Campbell especially led him to some false conclusions (1970a, 30).

In my interview with him, Abrahams also gave some personal reasons for rejecting the psychoanalytic approach.

> At some point in that era, somebody must have said to me, "Why are you reading blacks through German-Jewish people? Is this an ethnocentric act on your part?" And I'm sure that that really hit hard. I don't remember, but I decided yeah, you've got to look at yourself and what's going on, and you've got to listen to your informants much more closely. So that's when I began giving up on the psychoanalytic, especially the pathological side.

Abrahams was also sensitive to criticism from blacks about *Deep Down in the Jungle.*

> And, also, I also remember Bernice Johnson Reagon coming to, with the Freedom Singers, coming to the Folk Song Society, to the Folk Song Club [at the University of Texas]. They gave a concert, must have been '64, '65, because the book was out . . . And she came up to me afterwards and she said, "I hate that book. How could you write that book?" And you know I really had to take that seriously. It took me a little while to figure out why a black woman would take such exception to it. I realized how gendered it was at that point, you know, I was just writing into the dark. (2002)

Even in the first edition of *Deep Down in the Jungle,* Abrahams had moved beyond the functional and psychoanalytical approaches and into the realm of performance by bringing Kenneth Burke's rhetorical theories (1950) into the mix: "And the function of words is more than to entertain or communicate. Words exist to persuade, court, control. Viewing society agonistically or dialectically, words in formal arrangement then exist primarily for rhetorical purposes" (1964, 8). He does not limit himself to function in Bascom's anthropological sense of cultural solidarity on the macro level but has shifted the focus to the function of language in specific situations on the micro level, thereby bridging the gap between the cultural concerns of anthropology and the aesthetic concerns of literary studies. The emphasis on rhetoric and aesthetics led him to examine "syntactical patterns" and "how the method of constructing word groups in narrating differs from conversational speech patterns" (13–14). This seems to be an early articulation of the theoretical principle that performance is "an aesthetically marked and heightened mode of communication, framed in a special way" (Bauman 1992, 41). Finally, the most fundamental breakthrough Abrahams made was in his shift from the concept of folklore as static text to folklore as an ongoing part of cultural processes (1964, 8–9).

Abrahams's training up to the time he wrote *Deep Down in the Jungle* had been mainly literary, and he later came to see Burke as a connection between the literary and anthropological approaches. When I interviewed him, I commented, "I thought by using Burke and a rhetorical approach you were in some ways anticipating some principles of performance approach, and then by the time you did the revision that had become more full-blown." He replied,

> That's exactly right. What happened, I guess, and this is hard for me to recall in terms of the actual timing of it. I had been—because I was an English major in undergraduate school—I had continued to read in the lit-crit area too, you know, mostly monographic studies of individual writers, but when I was at Columbia . . . somewhere in there, I encountered *A Rhetoric of Motives* (1950) of Kenneth Burke, and it must have been around the same time I was working on riddles and proverbs because it just leaped at me that these were like ballads and folk tales—ways of naming social situations in which creative energies could be channeled into what today I would call "they say" stuff, that is, put into the impersonal voice and given the mark of authenticity and age. . . . Burke gets into the language proverbs work in their social settings, and I just thought, "Well this is, this is, you know, here is the connecting point that I need." (2002)

He said that in the early '60s he had not read much anthropology except for Melville Herskovits, but he met anthropologists at the University of Texas who led him to read British social anthropologists such as E. R. Leach and Mary Douglas, and he saw the connection with Burke and with literary New Criticism since they treated culture as text. Through this meeting of literary criticism and anthropology beyond the functionalists, the groundwork was laid for his rhetorical approach to folklore.

Between publication of the first edition of *Deep Down in the Jungle* in 1964 and the second edition in 1970, Roger Abrahams moved away from the psychoanalytic model and toward the performance model that his early interest in rhetoric and sociolinguistics had indicated. A section on "Style and Performance" and several long examinations of rhetorical strategies in telling toasts and jokes appear in the first edition, but performance becomes even more important in the second edition with added material foregrounding the approach. For instance, the following statement is found only in the 1970 edition: "The toasts are devices to call attention to performance abilities, and most of the stylistic criteria will reflect the personal perspective: the performer must be able through his improvisational abilities, his artful control over the active vocabulary, and his repertoire of commonplaces and themes to hold the audience" (1970a, 112). Some of the defining elements of performance theory are articulated here: the display of communicative competence, the ability to enhance experience to create a special intensity, and the evaluation of the performance by an audience (Bauman 1984 [1977], 11). By 1970, psychological meanings were not as important as rhetorical ones for Abrahams; the focus had shifted from the black man as someone with a flawed ego to the black man as performer, as artist. This suggests a turn from a pathological representation of race to a romantic representation that was in keeping with the emergence of black performers as culture heroes in the 1960s (Keil 1966).

To critique racial representation in performance studies, I am going to use the later Abrahams to examine the earlier Abrahams. This is in keeping with the reflexive dimension of his research from the 1960s when he first critiqued his earlier fieldwork. His postmodern ideas from the 1990s have relevance for understanding the shift from modern to postmodern scholarship that was taking place in the '60s and '70s. By the '60s, folklorists were beginning to abandon the old romantic agrarian concept of the folk, but, as Abrahams pointed out in 1993, "an equally romantic story has taken its place as folklorists have collected directly from tradition-bearing performers. By recording and transcribing the 'actual words' of an informant, we aver that we make a vital connection with some spiritually pure resource" (1993, 13). When Abrahams recorded black men in an urban setting in the late 1950s, he implicitly rejected the romantic agrarian model of the folk, but maintained another romantic model of the folk as performers whose spirit could be captured in the recordings of their artistic expressions. The roots of this model go back to the beginning of the invention of folklore in the eighteenth century when some ballad scholars insisted on verbatim texts without literary rewriting (12–13), but the invention of electric recording in the twentieth century intensified the concept of original performance as the means of tapping the essence of the folk. Once the recording machine became portable, John and Alan Lomax and others could strike out for the cotton fields to record African American singers motivated by two overlapping images of the folk—one as agrarian and communal and the other as individual and artistic.

And the rest of us followed, some into the same fields the Lomaxes had plowed and others into city streets, the first group maintaining the ideal of the agrarian folk, the second rejecting it but holding on to the field-recorded performance as evidence of authentic folkness. To folklorists, city folk had other things in common with rural folk: both had maintained a sense of tradition that modern mainstream society had abandoned. Folklorists, then, were taking part in a quest to recover what had been lost. In racial or cultural or class terms, educated white people could learn something from uneducated black people in the ghetto, and the recorded performance was a means of finding out what that was. One of the problems with this approach was its basis in the old folk/elite dichotomy because civilization caused us to lose our traditional knowledge in the first place. The folk may have some answers, but those answers are a direct result of being uncivilized and closer to primordial sources—whether they live in the country or the city. The romantic artistic performer model still contained a hidden pathology.

In his writings in the 1990s, Abrahams recognizes the persistence of the agrarian vision (folk as preindustrial and premodern) in folklore studies and that the concept logically can be extended to emerging concepts of the urban folk: "The folk are constructed as 'indigenous Others,' peoples who live within the orbit of metropolitan centers but who have maintained a sense of cultural distinctiveness that is apparent to both the group itself and to those with whom they come into contact on a regular basis" (27). The black people in Abrahams's 1950s fieldwork lived in a modern setting and in all likelihood some worked in industry, but they were perceived in some ways as preindustrial and premodern because of their recent migration from the rural south and because of their race. Race and cultural distinctiveness also made them susceptible to construction as "indigenous Others." These racial ideas from the broader white society were also the assumptions of folklorists doing research among urban African Americans, and the assumptions persisted after performance theory became the dominant paradigm in folklore studies.

Statements Abrahams added to the second edition of *Deep Down in the Jungle* illustrate the persistence of the old dichotomy: "One of the major cultural differences between the white middle class and ghettoized Afro-Americans is that the latter have preserved an oral-aural world view while the former have invested their creative energies and imaginations in books, in the typographic-chirographic world" (1970a, 39). (This concept is from Walter J. Ong's *The Presence of the Word* [1967]. By 1993, Abrahams had disavowed this "big bang theory of cultural development" [1993, 13].) Abrahams admits that all of his black informants could read, but "reading simply did not enter their lives very often" (1970a, 39). This concept represents, I think, a means of maintaining in performance theory the dichotomy of modern self versus traditional Other from older paradigms. Abrahams constructs the dichotomy so that it appears to be a means for typographic whites to gain insight into African American worldview. "Many ethnocentric judgments about blacks stem from the white man's inability to understand or appreciate the creative aspects of living in an oral atmosphere. He neither understands nor remembers the ways in which an effective talker-performer may strongly influence our attitudes. He does not value words effectively used in speaking events enough to confer high social status on the effective speaker. . . . a good talker as judged by ghetto Negroes is often regarded by whites as hostile and arrogant" (ibid.).

It is significant that the white man does not *remember* the influence of effective talking; this suggests that a kind of cultural evolution is at work—the white man in his modern typographic world has evolved beyond the traditional oral world of the black man. The white folklorist is then in a position as mediator to bring understanding of this lost traditional oral existence to modern whites, and the performance approach offers a theory and methodology for examining that oral world. The cultural evolution of John Lomax and Newbell Niles Puckett had been reframed to fit the performance approach.

Like such functionalists as Alan Lomax, performance theorists also brought political beliefs to their work with minority groups, and these beliefs must also be considered in analyzing the way they constructed racial representations. Speaking about himself and the other founding fathers of performance theory, Abrahams in a 1990s critique identifies some of their underlying political assumptions. He emphasizes folk group self-identification as a basis for theory building:

> That this sense of groupness was produced through a confrontation with other cultures dramatized the usefulness of analyzing folklore in its political, social and cultural contexts. Mexican-Americans . . . and African Americans . . . were performing in counterpoint to mainstream American practices. We underscored the countervailing voices and acts of resistance within these traditions because they were discernible in actual practice. Highlighting traditions of resistance also served the larger task of alerting the general reader to the existence of these vital alternative voices and practices (1992, 35–36).

I happen to agree with this political perspective, and my own work with Bongo Joe exhibits a similar ideology (see chapter 5), but I would also suggest that a certain amount of political romanticizing is going on here in the tradition of leftist perceptions of the disenfranchised. There is a link to the functionalist/Marxist approach of Alan Lomax ("vital alternative voices" sounds close to Lomax's "giving voice to the voiceless"), but there is something new in the way Abrahams has incorporated performance as the voice of political resistance. Group political identity can be discerned in the expression of an individual's artistic performance; the performance becomes a microcosm of the larger sociopolitical macrocosm; the specific performance stands in a metonymic relationship with general social conditions. By concentrating on the performance situation and the process of communication, the scholar could be a means for these "alternative voices" to be heard thereby advancing the cause of the cultural revolution that was taking place in the 1960s.

The political stance of some performance theorists is clear in a statement Abrahams added to the 1970 edition of *Deep Down in the Jungle*. After saying that ghetto adolescents have "no new areas in which they may utilize" their verbal skills, he adds: "This situation has changed somewhat since I collected my data with the growth of black militancy among the ghetto men. Their rhetorical skills have become extremely useful in the developing confrontation with the power structure of the white world. Thus, some of the frustration of the good talkers that I observed in the late fifties has found a creative outlet, though it is not always recognized as such by whites" (1970a, 42). Since Abrahams conducted his 1950s fieldwork before the development of 1960s black militancy, his examples of black expressive culture in the second edition of *Deep Down in the Jungle* are not directly political, but he frames them as political by placing them within the larger context of white racism. "The man of words is immensely important as a representative of the dispossessed men of Camingerly. By exhibiting his wit, by creating new and vital folkloric expression, he is able to effect a temporary release from anxiety for both himself and his audience. By creating playgrounds for playing out aggressions, he achieves a kind of masculine identity for himself and his group in a basically hostile environment" (60). Psychoanalysis merges with performance theory to give psychological functions political meanings. Traditional verbal expressions not only provide a release from anxiety but at the same time form political identity for dispossessed performers and their audiences.

At the center of this model is the performer: social context and audience response are important, but no performance occurs without the performer. Who is this performer? In particular for our purposes, who is this African American male performer? He is an artist, but he is also the voice of the people; aesthetics and ideology are both important in analyzing his performance. Abrahams compares the street corner and pool hall performers he recorded with the better-known popular black performers of the day—the artists that

Charles Keil identifies as black culture heroes such as James Brown, B. B. King, and Bobby "Blue" Bland (1966). They are more than entertainers; they are representatives of the concerns of their people. The star entertainers were all widely known in the black community and even to some outside; but the street corner performers were known only in their neighborhoods. The folklorist could bring knowledge of them to the outside world thereby educating the white community about this nearby but unknown world. Again, this model already existed in the field research, publications, and commercial recordings by the Lomaxes of such performers as Leadbelly, but Abrahams and other folklorists such as Bruce Jackson were not interested in popularizing the performer as much as communicating his message beyond the ghetto (Jackson 1974).

In 1970, the year the second edition of *Deep Down in the Jungle* appeared, Abrahams also published *Positively Black,* a book that was primarily a political "applied folklore" endeavor. In it he takes the political implications of the first edition of *Deep Down in the Jungle* and applies them to some of the same folkloric material to address race problems that were in the forefront of American consciousness at the time: "This book has been written in an effort to educate whites about certain aspects of Negro culture that seem essential to an understanding of lower-class black life" (1970b, 10). Again, the white folklorist who has insider knowledge is seen as the mediator between black and white; because he understands the significance of African American performance, he can contribute to the political revolution that was taking place in the 1960s and '70s. According to Abrahams, that contribution starts with the recognition that one of the main problems of race relations was a lack of communication between blacks and whites. "These failures of communication all too often lead to the widening of a social gap which threatens the foundations of our existence as a nation. But these are great times precisely because the foundations *are* being threatened, because our basic cultural assumptions are being questioned and tested." This threat to American foundations did not seem to frighten Abrahams as it did most "straight" Americans; rather, he saw it as a time for revolutionary change: "The *square world* rejects this [cultural] diversity; it insists on viewing life in an outmoded and essentially ethnocentric perspective" (20, emphasis added).

The solution is to embrace the very black culture that frightens white Americans: "But fortunately for our collective cultural sanity we have a home-grown and constant reminder of diversity and possible choice. Living in our midst, and in numbers far too great to ignore, are blacks who remind us with every

word, movement, gesture, that we are a culturally heterogeneous country"
(ibid.). Knowing that Abrahams was a singer and guitarist who was part of
the folk revival of the 1950s and '60s helps explain his ideology. He shared
certain attitudes about race with those revivalists, especially those who sought
political answers in African American music. As I discussed in chapter 5,
Jeff Titon, another revivalist who became a folklorist, identified this pattern:
"Rejecting conformity to middle-class values, blues revivalists embraced the
music of people who seemed unbound by conventions of work, family, sexual
propriety, worship, and so forth. The blues revival was a white, middle-class
love affair with the music and lifestyle of marginal blacks. The romantic strain
projected a kind of primitivism on the blues singer and located him in a culture of natural license" (1993, 225). This love of secular black music became
generalized to a love of what was perceived as black lifestyle. Especially if one
had leftist political leanings, he or she would tend to look for an alternative
to the middle-class "square" world in the "exotic" culture of blacks.

During our 2002 interview I asked Roger about the connection between
the "square" metaphor and the folksong revival: "You frame it [*Positively
Black*] in a way that I thought was interesting where you say something like,
you refer to the white middle-class world as 'the square world' or 'the straight
world,' or something like that." He agreed, "Right, both," and I continued,
"And you're offering black traditional style as an alternative, and it struck
me, and I wanted to know what you thought about this, as something very
close to revival kind of thinking, that a lot of the white singers were interested in doing blues as an alternative to the straight white world. Did you
see it that way?" "That was in the folk song movement, definitely. I mean
there was certain white performers that were attracted to folk song strictly
because they wanted to do black stuff, and they went to school to Reverend
Gary Davis or to Lightnin' Hopkins or to various blues people that were in
New York." He seemed to recognize the pervasiveness of the influence but to
downplay the direct relevance to his work, and I tried to get him to be more
specific. "Well, when I read that, your statement about the straight world,
I was, the image that came to my mind is, Roger is like the Lenny Bruce of
the folklore world [laughing]—you know, straight, you know kind of critical
of the straight world and the square world. It was like you were advocating
hipsterism by—." And he gave a more detailed explanation, "I can't say that
I wasn't conscious of that, and I wasn't playing to that crowd that wanted to
go black. On the other hand, I had a bread and butter sermon by that time
which was called something like that, the circle in the square in which I got
into hipness and the circularity of the body movement." Someone could be

aware of this attitude toward race and write about it without necessarily accepting the underlying dichotomy.

However, Abrahams did offer the performance approach as a way at getting at the truth of black life: "This book [*Positively Black*] is primarily made up of analyses of expressive—rather than the usual institutional—culture, but this approach seems essential to an understanding of American Negro lifeways because of the central importance of performers and performances in the everyday life of blacks" (1970b, 19). Abrahams labeled the central African American performer the "man-of-words," and he based this cultural type on thorough ethnographic documentation within African American society, both in the United States and later in the West Indies. But as ethnographically accurate as it is, it is still a white invention in the sense that it is an academic construction that originated in the mind of a white scholar, and as such it reveals underlying white assumptions. For instance, as in *Deep Down in the Jungle*, the heroes in *Positively Black* are drawn from urban and often criminal black street life; the "badman," the "cat," and the "gorilla" are identified not just as fictional characters but as "social types" who directly reflect the values and behaviors of the performers (1970b, 84–96). Ultimately, these types are presented as pathological; Abrahams carries over some of the psychoanalytic baggage from his earlier studies. As with all academic constructions, a problem occurs in the man-of-words as a cultural type: significant aspects of black social life are left out. Generalizing from part of the population distorted the picture of black society. Sociologist Mitchell Duneier speaks to this problem: "No generalization about human nature substitutes for a reminder that the black community, and black men in particular, constitute a diverse group. Progress in our conceptions will occur, not by replacing one particular stereotype with another, but rather by eliminating the notion that any generalization will suffice for a category so diverse, embedded in so many situations" (Duneier 1992, 184). The working poor in the black ghetto who may have less flamboyant heroes (fathers, coaches, athletes, ministers, and so forth) were not part of Abrahams's research base. One reason may be that these heroes were more closely aligned with the square white world and thus did not fulfill the exotic traits expected by white negrophiles of the 1960s.

Abrahams was a part of the liberal white scholarship on African Americans in the 1960s and '70s that Duneier criticizes for their misrepresentations of ghetto culture (137–55). He bases his critique on Shelby Steele's concept that innocence is power: "By innocence I mean a feeling of essential goodness in relation to others and, therefore, superiority to others. Our innocence always inflates us and deflates those we seek power over. Once inflated we are entitled; we are in fact licensed to go after the power our innocence tells us we deserve. In this sense, *innocence is power*" (Steele 1990). In racial terms this is similar to Toni Morrison's point about white "magnanimity" in cultural representations of blacks (1992, 17). Duneier says that, "The sociologist's success at conveying his or her 'essential goodness in relation to others' most commonly by simply advertising that his or her books present a less stereotyped view of blacks, or by embracing a liberal political program, has afforded a license to make generalizations about the black population that are not supported by firm evidence" (1992, 139). Along with such scholars as Ulf Hannerz (1969), Elliot Liebow (1967), and Charles Keil (1966), Roger Abrahams in *Positively Black* generalized about young urban black men as resisting white middle-class values about work and responsibility in ways that created stereotypes even though the scholars' motivations were "innocent."

As in *Deep Down in the Jungle,* Abrahams places the black man-of-words within the context of an oral/illiterate culture in *Positively Black,* again suggesting a dichotomy with white print/literate culture (1970b, 17–18). Clearly differences exist between the African American cultural emphasis on oral performance and the European American emphasis on literacy; the flaw is in seeing the oral/print categories as too rigidly dichotomous—black lower-class culture on one side of the divide and white middle-class culture on the other, ignoring the complex cultural processes whereby orality and literacy interact. The oral/literate dichotomy has been under attack in the scholarship for years, but it has persisted. Grey Gundaker sees the man-of-words figure as significant in the persistence of the dichotomy:

> The obvious importance of men-of-words and good talking among Africans and African Americans has provided a warrant for the divide between oral and literate and, more recently, a kind of "yes, but" attitude that questions the descriptive adequacy of polar divides in literacy theory but falls into them in practice all the same. Frequently scholars substitute one divide for another; for example, replacing a cognitive divide—preliterate versus postliterate—with a communicative one: orality versus literacy. Since the idea of evolutionary progress is built into those aspects of literate ideology most concerned with identity, this tendency is difficult to avoid; orality and literacy remain poles between which much purported cultural relativism oscillates. (1998, 138–39)

In *Deep Down in the Jungle,* Abrahams suggests an evolutionary dichotomy between oral black and literate white (1970a, 39), and this dichotomy persists as a "communicative divide" in *Positively Black* (1970b, 18–19). Gundaker offers a way out of this dilemma with his concepts of "conventional literacy" and "vernacular practice" as cultural processes that continuously interact. Vernacular practices are more than oral expressions and include music, material culture, belief and custom—any activities that are "indigenous" and "often noninstitutional" (1998, 4); in other words, the range of traditional cultural expressions that folklorists term "folklore" or "folklife." Conventional literacy includes "a maze of institutionally sanctioned practices and events" related to "Roman script literacy." These are seen as in a constant state of "expressive interaction," as part of a process of "recurring differentiation and cross-fertilization" (3).

When the African American man-of-words is conceptualized within this cultural matrix, he becomes more than a representative of oral/aural culture; his performances can be seen as complex intricate events that incorporate knowledge of and responses to both written and spoken language (ibid.). "By tracing [the] interaction [between outsider conventional literacy and insider vernacular practices] we can see how African Americans have used literacy and its artifacts to construct cohesions, distinctions, and differences that elude description through familiar 'divides' like orality versus literacy, literate versus illiterate, or writing versus marking" (4). From the beginning of his performance studies, Abrahams recognized the influence that literate European culture had on African American oral culture, and he analyzed performances of the man-of-words in the West Indies with that influence in mind. Gundaker makes extensive use of Abrahams' research to reinforce his argument about oral/literate interaction (136–38). However, an underlying assumption of an oral/print dichotomy still remained in Abrahams's conceptual model.

The Man-of-Words in the West Indies: Performance and the Emergence of Creole Culture (1983) is Abrahams's most fully realized application of performance theory to African expressive culture in the New World. He began his fieldwork in the West Indies in the 1960s as a way to test and expand his findings about black performers in South Philadelphia (xv). To do this he turned away from urban environments and followed a well established folklorist's pattern of the past: "The dimension of the problem I was most concerned with investigating—the distribution of performance styles and traits—could best be carried out in remote agrarian communities" (xviii). "I was self-consciously looking for the most archaic material in the most removed and backwater areas of Afro-America" (xix). In the interview he said something similar: "So I decided then that I would understand the material better if I lived in a different kind of, more villagey, Afro American community." From the perspective of the present, this suggests that for Abrahams the Philadelphia black neighborhood was not "oral/aural" enough, that, at least initially, he went to the West Indies to find the purest sources of African American verbal creativity; in other words, this was a search for authenticity that had some similarities to John Lomax's attempt to find Negroes untainted by civilization. However, because Abrahams was more reflexive ("self-consciously looking") in his ethnographic quest, he was able to recognize the strong influences of literacy on Afro-Caribbean expressive culture. Still, he frames literacy as existing within an "*essentially* oral culture" (emphasis added) thus maintaining the dichotomy between the two. "Vincentian peasants retain an essentially oral culture in spite of the high degree of literacy in the community, one in which word power is seen to reside more in controlled speaking than in the mastery of writing and reading. Books do, indeed, enter into Vincentian life, but mainly as a source for developing recitations and instituting glosses" (80). Gundaker used evidence from Abrahams's fieldwork to indicate that writing and reading were not peripheral to an essential oral culture, but were, in fact, part of a central cultural dynamic with orality (1998, 136–38).

Abrahams also continued his interpretation of certain aspects of African American culture as a politically subversive alternative to established white culture in *The Man-of-Words in the West Indies,* this time framed in terms of play versus respectability. He posited that both play and respectability are found within the black community, but play is culturally associated with black society and respectability with white. The dichotomy starts with work versus play: work is related to home and women, play to public places and men. According to Abrahams, "play . . . comes to be *the* activity by which Afro-American individuality is asserted and maintained." "Because it is public and individual, play is regarded as inappropriate in areas dominated by respectability values, especially the home" (51). The contrast between play and respectability within black society is related to a larger black/white dichotomy: "Playing in Anglophonic Afro-America means not only switching styles and codes characteristic of all types of play, but also switching downward to roles and behaviors regarded from household (and Euro-American) perspectives as 'bad' or improper. . . . Playing then means playing *bad,* playing black, playing lower class" (1983, 53).

This seems to revert back to the psychoanalytic dichotomy between order and control that Abrahams had posited in the first edition of *Deep Down in the Jungle;* the psychological model has been transformed into a social one, but blackness imagined as chaos still implies whiteness as control. The difference is that instead of being viewed as pathological, black chaos is now seen as a positive alternative to white control. The politics of the 1960s have intervened to turn negative pathology into positive romance. The "square" world of middle-class white America needs to be undermined by the "bad" and "improper" world of lower-class blacks. This romantic view may have caused Abrahams to overemphasize the political results of play; as Richard D. E. Burton points out, "Perhaps . . . Abrahams romanticizes the subversive purport of the culture of play and reputation, failing to grasp the ease with which, even in the supreme instance of carnival, the ludic is absorbed and neutralized by the established order" (1997, 173).

My critique of Abrahams's representations of race in his scholarship in the 1960s and '70s was made easier by his self-critiques throughout that period and later. Before reflexivity became standard practice in ethnography and folkloristics, Abrahams practiced reflexive ethnography. He came to recognize the ethnocentric bias of the psychoanalytic approach in the 1963 edition of *Deep Down in the Jungle* and made the necessary changes in the later edition. He was even more reflexive in *Positively Black,* and by 1976 he could state directly, "But recently we have begun to recognize the inadequacies of our past methods and models" (1976, 2). He framed his book *Talking Black* (1976) with a statement on ethnocentrism and the pathological model:

> Any method of cultural or social analysis which defines the other group in terms of what it doesn't do or doesn't have is playing the same game as the stereotyper, for it is not just describing the other group in terms of differences, it is prejudging them as well and relegating the differences to the category of inadequacies.
>
> The essence of this prejudgment is that the group possesses *no* order, since it departs from our own system of order, our culture. Hence, stereotyped groups are classed as precultural creatures like children, barbarians, or animals. (1976, 2)

By establishing more self-awareness about the position of the ethnographer in regard to the people he or she was studying, Abrahams prepared the next generation of white folklorists to do a better job of research and interpretation. However, reflexivity alone is not enough to solve some of the deeper problems of cultural representation; in fact, postmodern approaches may have gone too far in the other direction, concentrating so much on the way scholars have created academic constructions of reality that we have lost sight of the reality.

In the 1960s and '70s Abrahams and other scholars represented urban black men in romantic and pathological ways; we sometimes idealized criminal behavior as political resistance, and at other times we saw antisocial behavior as a pathological norm in inner-city black neighborhoods. These were clearly flawed as representations of African American culture, but we have to recognize that pathological behaviors occur in all cultures and that black ghettos in the 1960s contained criminal and antisocial behaviors that were deeply ingrained and that have become even worse since then. Just because white folklorists interpreted these patterns in ways that reflected back on their own racial assumptions does not mean that the patterns did not exist. We now recognize that our research findings did not represent everyone in a community, but it did represent some.

Our postmodern emphasis on the misrepresentations of white observers should not ignore the social realities of those black communities and the way they influence cultural performances. For instance, folklorists and other social scientists need to consider the connections between the 1960s badman heroes in "toasts" such as "Stackolee" and current rap and hip-hop lyrics that romanticize the "gangsta." White folklorists still bring preconceived notions about blackness to their field research, but being aware of that reflexively is not enough. We need to listen to people in the community, share our interpretations with them, and consult with black scholars about our findings. We should be working collaboratively with black ethnographers and the people we study to get it right this time. I began to do this somewhat tentatively in recent field research on black children's rhymes and in a more rigorous way with a black minister about his life story. The last two chapters will examine these collaborative fieldwork situations in more detail.

7

Children's Rhymes
from 1971 to 2001

I went downtown
To see James Brown.
He gave me a nickel,
I bought me a pickle.
The pickle was sour,
I bought me a flower.
The flower was dead.
You know what I said?
I said, "Ooo-she-wah-wah
I got Black Power."
—African American children's rhyme

Racial politics were so pervasive in the 1960s that they eventually influenced African American children's rhymes and in turn influenced the way folklorists interpreted the rhymes. At that time white folklorists such as Roger Abrahams, Bruce Jackson, Margaret Brady, and me conducted our research in ways that implicitly sought the approval of black scholars and critics, and as a result we interpreted African American folklore within the frame of black power politics. Black children's rhymes contained enough militant content to offer evidence for our ideological interpretations, but there was a problem in our approach: we ended up representing children as actively advocating militant ideas and ignoring other meanings in the rhymes. In this chapter I want to critique white folklorists' scholarship on African American children's folklore (including my own) in the late 1960s and early '70s and update it with research from the 1990s and 2000s.

Roger Abrahams included traditional children's verbal play in *Positively Black* (1970b), and that influenced my decision to conduct field research in 1971 at a predominantly black school in Columbus, Ohio. Almost thirty years later, in 2000, I again did fieldwork with the same race and age group in Columbus with the idea of comparing the social and political issues reflected in the rhymes of the two different periods. The 1971 study included seven girls and three boys ages eleven to twelve at Gladstone Elementary School, and in 2000–2001 six girls ages ten to twelve. To expand the research base, I supplemented the 1971 fieldwork with rhymes collected from African American students at Ohio State University who remembered them from childhood and with variant rhymes from published sources (Jones and Hawes 1972; Brady 1974, 1975; Eckhardt, 1975). I also have found variants of the 2000–2001 rhymes in publications from the 1980s and '90s (Merrill-Mirsky 1988; Riddell 1990; Gaunt 1995, 1997, 1998, 2006) indicating that they have been widespread among black children in the United States for the last ten to fifteen years.

I published the results of the 1971 research in an article titled "Black Consciousness in Afro-American Children's Rhymes: Some Ohio Examples from the Early 1970s" (Mullen 1979–81). The Columbus Public Schools District denied my requests to conduct follow-up research at Gladstone Elementary in 2000, so I arranged to record and interview children outside the school setting. The six girls I interviewed came from five different schools, and their rhymes are probably the same ones currently being recited at Gladstone because the rhymes are widespread among black children in Columbus and throughout the United States. Beginning in 2000, I recorded sisters Clarrissia and Scherazade Fleming (ages ten and eleven and in grades five and six in the Columbus Public Schools), with the help of their mother Mickey Williams who had been in a graduate seminar I taught on race and representation. When I brought up the subject of African American children's rhymes in the seminar, she mentioned that her daughters frequently recited them. She brought the girls to my office one day so that I could record them. The atmosphere of an academic office was far from the usual context in which they played the games, and their performances were somewhat constrained as a result. I met with them again in July 2001 so that they could help me in transcribing the words to the rhymes. Mickey Williams has continued to act as a research assistant on this project by setting up recording sessions and commenting on my interpretations of the material.

In 2001 I continued the research with Carina Drakes, Shara Simmons, Deanna Dorsey (all age ten and in grade five), and Dana Dorsey (Deanna's sister, age twelve and in grade seven). Carla Wilks, program coordinator at the Ohio State University African American and African Studies (AAAS) Community Extension Center, arranged for me to record these girls at the center, and she has continued to help with the research by reading and commenting on drafts of this chapter. One of the girls attended a Catholic school and the rest Columbus Public Schools; one was in the same school as Scherazade Fleming. The AAAS Community Extension Center was a more relaxed and spontaneous space for recording than my office. The larger group of girls and the community setting helped them get over their initial shyness sooner; they had more room to move around than in the narrow confines of my office. Wilks also helped them to feel at home by providing snacks. I met with the girls again in July 2002 to check my transcriptions and to ask some follow-up questions.

The children from 1971 and 2001 were different in many of their attitudes, and their rhymes reflected these differences, but groups from both eras were alike in their vitality and enjoyment of play. Even the shyest children were transported from the mundane to another level of pleasure through hand clapping, dancing, and chanting the rhymes. The presence of boys in the '70s group caused some gender friction with the girls dominating in a realm of behavior that was seen by both girls and boys as a girls' domain. At one point when the girl in the center of a ring game was twirling to choose the next "it" and chose her best friend, one of the boys complained loudly, "Aw you always choose her." Overall, though, the children got along well as they played. The all-girl groups in 2001 and after played together without conflict and from my perspective were engaged in female bonding, expressing through performance their common interests and attitudes. This is a significant factor in considering the role of gender in their play in both eras, an element that the 1960s and '70s scholarship neglected because of the emphasis on racial politics. The presence of a white male adult inhibited all groups at first; but eventually they became relaxed and more spontaneous, especially the larger group in the '70s. The smaller groups of girls in 2001 never became as free in their behavior but did loosen up considerably as they got used to my presence.

The political nature of African American children's rhymes and scholarly ideological perspectives toward them shift over time with changing political contexts suggesting the importance of the following questions: What were the racial assumptions of white folklorists studying black folklore in the early 1970s? How did those assumptions influence the representation of African American culture? And how do those assumptions and representations change over time? (For more on the subjective assumptions of white folklorists about race see Mullen 1999.)

My fieldwork on children's folklore in 1971 took place within a larger institutional context: I was conducting field research for the Smithsonian Institution's American Folklife Festival, which featured the state of Ohio that year. I concentrated on African American folklore in Columbus, Cleveland, and Cincinnati, and children's games and rhymes seemed a fruitful area to explore. Gladstone Elementary was close to where I lived on the near northeast side of Columbus, so one day I went to the school and talked to the principal, Leon Mitchell (who happened to be black), about doing field research there. He put me in touch with Jean Hannah, a white fifth-grade teacher, who in turn gave me access to students in her class. I spent several weeks at the school recording the children on the playground, in the gym on rainy days, and in individual interviews in the hall outside their classrooms.

Ralph Rinzler, director of the festival at the time, agreed to invite ten children to perform their games and rhymes on the National Mall in Washington, D.C., as part of the festival. With the help of Mitchell and Hannah, I chose the following ten black students to make the trip: Robbie Harris, Charlene Morgan, Pam Carter, Dorothy Moye, Lisa Feaster, Lynn Johns, Lorraine Fields, Yvonne Davis, Lam Hairston, and Steve White. Hannah accompanied them, and they all seemed to have a great time. The audiences responded positively to their performances, and they were able to meet other children, both black and white, and share games and rhymes with them. At the time I thought it was a very successful exercise in applied folklore within a public sector context, a way to educate white people about African American culture, and to promote racial understanding and harmony. In spite of professional folklorists' present awareness of social and political problems inherent in such public folk festivals (Feintuch 1988; Baron and Spitzer 1992; Cantwell 1993), I still think they are worthwhile.

I collected a total of twenty-three rhymes from the children at Gladstone, but concentrated my article about them on only three, plus four others from college students and published sources that contained ideological references. These examples of hand clapping, jump-rope, and ring-game rhymes from the early '70s directly expressed militant political attitudes that were widespread in the 1960s. A good example is the following rhyme collected from an eleven-year-old girl about the 1968 U.S. presidential election:

> Humphrey, Humphrey, he's our man.
> Nixon belongs in a garbage can.
> Paint it blue, paint it white.
> Blow it up with dynamite.

The girl who recited this indicated her understanding of the political meaning when she looked around to make sure the teacher would not hear her; other children expressed their awareness of the politics through more direct statements. A black college student reported another rhyme with violent content that she had heard from eight- to fourteen-year-olds in New York in 1971; other students said it was used as a cheer in Columbus high schools in the early '70s.

Ah, beep beep, walkin' down the street.
Ungawa, Black Power.
Destroy white boy.
I'm a cool, cool nigger
From a cool, cool town;
Takes another cool nigger
To knock me down.
Soul sister number nine,
Sock it to me one more time.

Scholars in the late '60s and '70s such as Roger Abrahams (1970b, 53–54, 72–73), John Horton (1972, 31), Paulette Cross (1973), Bruce Jackson (1974, 31, 34), and me (Mullen 1979–81, 3) found verbal expressions such as rhymes and jokes to be evidence of a tendency toward violent behavior among black adolescents and young adults, especially males. I now think the rhymes expressed attitude much more than actual behavior. Black Power allowed African American people to express ethnic and racial pride in the form of superiority over whites and to express it metaphorically through violent references in traditional verbal forms. A child or adolescent who chanted "destroy white boy" was not necessarily going to act this out through violent behavior. This is not a simple functional explanation, though; hostile verbal expressions were more than an outlet for repressed emotions. The games, dances, rhymes, and other traditional expressions of oppressed people can be seen as rituals that have complex meanings and purposes in terms of the group's relationship with the oppressor. What dance scholar Jacqui Malone (citing Albert Murray) says about the functions of African American vernacular dance can be applied to the entire spectrum of African American folklore: "African American public dance [is] a ritual of purification, affirmation, and celebration. It helps drive the blues away and provides rich opportunities to symbolically challenge societal hierarchies by offering powers and freedoms that are impossible in ordinary life" (1996, 1). These expressions do not just help to maintain the stability of the larger culture by allowing for release of repressed anger (Bascom 1965 [1954]); they are also part of a cultural process that protests and brings about change.

The Black Power movement of the 1960s was part of broader intellectual and theoretical changes that opened up the possibility for such radical readings of folk culture. Black Power influenced many white scholars at the time, including me; we wanted to be part of the movement, and militant rhetoric became a part of our scholarship. Black and white scholars alike made black adolescents and even children into avatars of "Black Rage" (Grier and Cobbs 1968) on the basis of jokes and rhymes. There was undoubtedly much anger and hostility toward whites at the time—that was clear in direct statements and behavior—but it now seems extreme to have projected it onto children. Black children could identify with the leaders and the political ideals of the Black Power movement through their rhymes (as they did in a rhyme that ended with "I got Black Power") without joining in street protests (although they may have taken part as they grew older); they could express their own sense of anger and injustice without committing violent acts.

Other rhymes I collected in 1971 had an underlying structural pattern that suggested ideological meanings about racism. A comparison of white and black variants of one rhyme makes the political meaning of the black rhyme clearer.

White: I went downtown
To see Mr. Brown.
He gave me a nickel
To buy a pickle.
The pickle was sour,
I bought a flower.
The flower was yellow,
I gave it to my fellow.
My fellow was sick.
I gave him a kick.
And that was the end of my dirty trick.

Black: I went downtown
To see James Brown.
He gave me a nickel,
I bought me a pickle.
The pickle was sour,
I bought me a flower.
The flower was dead.
You know what I said?
I said, "Ooo-she-wah-wah
I got Black Power." (also see Abrahams
    1969, 93–94; Riddell 1990, 137–45)

The most obvious content differences are the references to black soul singer and culture hero James Brown and Black Power in the African American version, but there is a less obvious and significant underlying structural pattern that I identified as attempt-negative outcome. The attempts to buy a pickle and a flower in the black version have negative outcomes since the pickle is sour and the flower is dead. The attempts in the white version have both negative and positive outcomes: the pickle is sour, but the flower is yellow. In the black version, the negative outcomes have a resolution, Black Power, which seems to suggest a political answer to recurring problems. Did the black children who recited these rhymes understand the political meaning completely? I don't know. They may have understood on some level but were not capable of articulating the meaning, or I failed as an interviewer to ask them to explain their meaning.

The same solution was offered in another rhyme from black school children in Columbus in 1971, except that here the solution was couched in symbolic terms.

Winstons taste good
Like a cigarette should.
Winstons taste good
Like a oo eye
I wanna piece of pie.
The pie too sweet,
I wanna piece of meat.
The meat too tough,
I wanna ride the bus.
The bus too full,
I wanna ride a bull.
The bull too black,
I wanna ride his back.
I said, "oo ah ah
Oo ah ah, oo ah ah
Oo, oo, oo."

Here we have the same attempt-negative outcome pattern: the pie is too sweet, the meat is too tough, but when the bull is described as too black, instead of rejecting it, the speaker wants to ride his back thus symbolically accepting and using the bull as a symbol of Black Power. Also significant, I think, is the reference to the bus being full; children would have been aware of the importance of buses during the Civil Rights era and of Rosa Parks's refusal to give up her bus seat to a white person in Montgomery, Alabama, one of the pivotal acts in the history of the civil rights movement. Carla Wilks remembers hearing a variant when she was a child: "Bull too black / I want my money back," suggesting the importance of economic power in the struggle for civil rights.

The Attempt-Negative Outcome pattern was not new in the 60s and 70s; it can be found in African American rhymes that go back to the nineteenth century. The "I wanna piece of pie" rhyme goes back at least to the 1910s and '20s Mississippi childhood of Richard Wright who uses it in his short story "Big Boy Leaves Home."

> Bye n bye
> Ah wanna piece of pie
> Pies too sweet
> Ah wanna piece of meat
> Meats too red
> Ah wanna piece of bread
> Breads too brown
> Ah wanna go t town
> Towns too far
> Ah wanna ketch a car
> Cars too fas
> Ah fall n break mah ass
> Ah'll understand it better bye n bye (Wright 1938)

This older version of the rhyme contains the same attempt-negative outcome pattern, but the ending seems to signal resignation rather than protest.

Bessie Jones reports a rhyme that goes back even further in time; her grandfather told her one that was recited in slavery times.

> Juba this and Juba that
> And Juba killed a yellow cat
> And get over double trouble, Juba.
> You sift-a the meal, you give me the husk,
> You cook-a the bread, you give me the crust.
> You fry the meat, you give me the skin,
> And that's where my mama's trouble begin.
> And then you Juba,
> You just Juba.
> Juba up, Juba down,

Juba all around the town.
Juba for ma, Juba for pa,
Juba for your brother-in-law. (Jones and Hawes 1972, 37–38)

What is described here was the common practice in slavery of giving the poorest cuts of meat and the poorest quality food to slaves. As Bessie Jones explained, "You see, so that's what it mean—the mother would always be talking to them about she wished she could give them some of that good hot cornbread or hot pies or hot whatnot. But she couldn't. She had to wait and give that old stuff that was left over" (Jones and Hawes 1972, 37–38; also see Douglas 1962 [1892]; Jackson 1967, 3; Talley 1968 [1922], 9).

Another traditional rhyme that has the attempt-negative outcome structure is "Hambone." Roger Abrahams collected the following in Philadelphia in the early 1960s:

Hambone, Hambone have you heard?
Poppa's gonna buy you a mockingbird.
If that mockingbird don't sing,
Poppa's gonna buy you a diamond ring.
If that diamond ring don't shine,
Poppa's gonna buy you a bottle of wine.
If that bottle of wine gets broke,
Poppa's gonna buy you a billy goat.
If that billy goat runs away,
Poppa's gonna buy you a stack of hay.
If that stack of hay gets wet,
Poppa's gonna beat your butt I bet. (Abrahams 1970a, 139–40, see also
     1969, 125; Parrish 1965 [1942], 114–15; Jones and Hawes 1972, 220)

Carla Wilks remembers a variant from the '70s:

If that diamond ring don't shine,
Poppa's gonna take you to the five and dime.
If that five and dime don't sell,
Poppa's gonna take you to the wishing well.

This seems to be a reference to the civil rights sit-ins at five-and dime-stores that would not allow blacks at the lunch counters. There is recognition of the problem of racism, but instead of protest, there seems to be a self-aware escape into fantasy. In all the versions of "Hambone" and "Juba," and in the early version of "I wanna piece of pie" there is no resolution suggesting that perhaps the inclusion of a resolution in rhymes of the '70s meant that black people perceived the Black Power movement as offering a new solution to problems caused by racism.

The attempt-negative outcome structure of the rhymes is clearly related to the social structure of lower socioeconomic black Americans. My interpretation here is related to meanings Abrahams and other 1960s folklorists saw in African American performance. As I pointed out in chapter 6, performance theory posits that group political identity is expressed in particular artistic performance; in this case the chanting of rhymes has a metonymic relationship with the social conditions of oppression and poverty.

> Blacks repeatedly experience negative outcomes because of prejudice and racism. For example, the attempt by blacks to acquire adequate shelter often has been negated by the slum conditions of many buildings in the ghetto. Even new federal housing projects turn out to be poorly constructed. Also, in attempting to feed her family nourishing food, the black mother often is defeated by high prices and poor quality goods at ghetto markets. Finally, blacks seeking employment often have met with the negative outcome of failing to get a job for which they are qualified or getting lower pay than whites holding the same job. (Mullen 1979–81)

This quote is from my original article on black children's rhymes. I would like to be able to report that things have changed since the 1970s, but unfortunately many of these problems remain the same. Gladstone Elementary School (where I did the original field research) is even more predominantly black now than it was then and is one of the poorest schools in the Columbus Public School District. My scholarly representation of ghetto culture in the '70s had some flaws, but the description of poverty and racism was accurate then and is still accurate today.

"I Went Downtown to See James Brown" is not as widely known today, and the girls I interviewed in 2000–2001 did not know the black bull part of it. I collected a version of "I Went Downtown" from ten-year-old Carina Drakes but with notable differences from the '70s version.

> I went downtown
> To see James Brown.
> He gave me a nickel
> To buy me a pickle.
> The pickle was sour.
> So I bought me a flower.
> The flower was dead.

So this is what I said
I said bang, bang, choo-choo train
Wind me up and I'll do my thing.
No peanut butter, no Reese's cup,
Mess with me, and I'll kick your butt
All the way to Pizza Hut.

One children's rhyme cannot stand for the social and political changes that have taken place from the early 1970s to the early twenty-first century, but it is tempting to see this rhyme as a metaphor for the depoliticizing that has occurred since the '60s. From "Black Power" to "Pizza Hut" seems to suggest that consumer culture has replaced political culture. The communal call of "Black Power" has been replaced by an emphasis on the individual in "I'll do my thing" and "I'll kick your butt." The attempt-negative outcome pattern is still there, but the resolution is personal rather than communal. On the other hand, this interpretation depends on selecting only a narrow range of examples from the two eras. There were plenty of individual-oriented rhymes in the '60s and '70s; the 2001 rhyme expresses an anticonsumer attitude: "No peanut butter, no Reese's cup." The child is not going to Pizza Hut to buy a pizza, only kicking someone's butt on the way. Still, I think it is significant that none of the children that I interviewed in 2000 and 2001 knew the "Black Power" part of the rhyme.

Less-direct references to racial politics are in two of the 2000–2001 rhymes, "Shame, Shame, Shame" and "Tweedle, Leedle, Lee" ("Rockin' Robin"). There were two versions of "Shame, Shame, Shame," one about Mexico and the other about Hollywood. Both groups of girls recited the one about Mexico, but only the group of four girls did the one about Hollywood.

Shame, Shame, Shame.
I don't want to go to Mexico
No more, more, more.
There's a big fat policeman
At my door, door, door.
He grabbed me by the collar,
Made me pay a dollar.
I don't want to go to Mexico
No more, more, more.
(also see Merrill-Mirsky 1988, 45)

Shame, Shame, Shame.
I don't want to go Hollywood
No more, more, more.

There's Michael Jackson
At my door, door, door.
He grabbed me by my hips,
Made me kiss his lips.
I don't want to go to Hollywood
No more, more, more.

"Mexico" seems to be about fear of the police. Is this racial? No evidence in the rhyme or in the girls' comments suggests that it is, but the rhyme makes clear that the policeman is corrupt and demanding payoffs. It may be about drug smuggling, and the bribe is to cross the border. Any interpretation like this has to be symbolic; the children themselves do not seem to be aware consciously of these meanings. They are aware of the anti-Michael Jackson meaning of the other version. I asked them, "What do you think of Michael Jackson? Is he somebody that kids like nowadays?" They all said no, and one of them said, "I like his songs" but added, "I don't like him." They did not elaborate, but social context suggests that "He grabbed me by my hips / Made me kiss his lips" is a reference to the sexual abuse allegations made against him, and the rhyme is a reflection of their concerns about sexual abuse of children. "I don't want to go to Hollywood" might be seen as a rejection of popular culture, but other rhymes embrace it.

Both groups of girls performed "Tweedle, Leedle, Lee," but the group of four girls broke off before finishing it. This is the complete version by Scherazade and Clarrissia.

Tweedle, leedle, lee
Skeeball
Tweedle, leedle, lee
That's all.
Tweedle, leedle, lee
Popsicle
Popsicle.
Your breath stinks.
Going rockin' in a tree top
Rockin' all night long.
A-huffin' and a-puffin'
And a-singin' that song.
All the little birds on Jay Bird Street
Love to hear the robin go tweet, tweet, tweet.
Rockin' Robin,

Tweet, tweet, tweedle, lee,
Rockin' Robin,
Tweet, tweet, tweedle, lee.
Mother's in the kitchen
Stirrin' that rice.
Daddy's on the toilet
Shootin' that dice.
Brother's in jail
Raisin' that hell.
Sister's in the corner
Goin' fruit cocktail.
Rockin' Robin,
Tweet, tweet, tweedle, lee,
Rockin' Robin,
Tweet, tweet, tweedle, lee.
Batman and Robin
Flyin' in the air.
Batman lost his underwear.
Batman said, "I don't care
"Cause Mama's gonna buy me
"A six-pack pair [beer?].
Rockin' Robin,
Tweet, tweet, tweedle, lee,
Rockin' Robin,
Tweet, tweet, tweedle, lee. (also see Merrill-Mirsky
        1988, 172–73, Riddell 1990, 188–200)

The other group of girls started to trail off when they got to "Daddy's in the toilet." I could make out the lines through "Raisin' that hell" but nothing after that. Perhaps they thought this was too risqué to recite in front of an adult. In fact, this rhyme is typical of certain children's folklore that expresses taboo subjects—toilets, shooting dice, jail, raising hell, and "goin' fruit cocktail," if this is a sexual metaphor. Cecilia Riddell says that a group of girls she recorded in the Los Angeles area changed "raising hell" to "ringing a bell" when the teacher objected (Riddell 1990, 414). Back in the '70s, I might have interpreted this rhyme as a reflection of ghetto crime and a racially based dysfunctional family with the mother hard at work while the father is gambling, the son is in jail, and perhaps the daughter is engaged in prostitution. Now I see it more as a cross-cultural expression of taboo subjects. Many rhymes collected from middle-class white children also contain such taboo references (Knapp and Knapp 1976, 179–90).

One of the major flaws of representation in the original study was that I ignored gender as a factor, and my recent field and library research convince me that gender and sexual politics are essential to understanding the rhymes. Most of the participants in the 1970s study were girls; it was clear at the time that girls were the main tradition bearers of the rhymes and games as they are today (Merrill-Mirsky 1988, 71; Gaunt 1995, 291–92). Many scholars at the time neglected gender in their theoretical models; for instance, Richard Bauman did not consider gender in his influential formulation of differential identity (Bauman 1972). I had a similar blind spot when it came to the folklore of women and girls; much of my field research had been with male storytellers and within the masculine occupation of commercial fishing (Mullen 1978). Feminist folklore publications in the 1970s and '80s pointed out the gender bias in folkloristics (Farrer 1975; Jordan and Kalcik 1985), but gender issues continued to be neglected into the '80s. Many of the rhymes I collected in 1971 had to do with the culturally based interests of girls such as boyfriends, fashions, and dancing, and many key characters were female such as Donna, Miss Lucy, the "Sentorita" [sic] at the old Kentucky fair, and mother figures. I relegated these rhymes to an appendix of the original article so that I could focus on the militant black power rhymes in the body of the article.

Shifting the focus of analysis to feminist concerns requires other theoretical shifts. The scholarship of ethnomusicologist Kyra Gaunt has been useful to me in making that shift. She articulates a broad approach that focuses on African American girls' games as a major component of the construction of black women's identity.

> The construction of a gendered ethnicity and/or an ethnicized gender is defined generation after generation by African American girls as young as age five. This generational tradition seems to go back as far as the mid-1940s, based on the age of those I interviewed. This oral tradition has existed primarily with little or no direct adult intervention. Black girls created unique social arenas of play where they freely extrapolated the musical sound, texture, and movement that defined their cultural experience in racial terms . . . These games function as a tool of expression that signifies black femaleness in urban, and also rural, contexts (1998, 275).

Gaunt and other vernacular dance and ethnomusicology scholars (Koskoff 1989; Malone 1996) did important research on girls' folk games with an emphasis on kinesics and music. They mention the rhymes in passing, but did not concentrate their analyses on the way the words and dance movements come together as a process of identity formation. I shall use their approach but will apply it more directly to the verbal element of play.

One of the jump-rope rhymes the group of four girls recited illustrates very directly how play activities are part of the process of racial and gender identity formation. It involves some call and response between the girls turning the rope and the one who is jumping.

> Jump in, jump out.
> Turn yourself about.
> Jump in, jump out,
> Introduce yourself.
> My name's Carina. (Yeah)
> I want to be a singer. (Un huh)
> And a model. (Yeah)
> For the rest of my life. (For the rest of her life.)
> Jump in, jump out.
> Turn yourself about.
> Jump in, jump out,
> Introduce yourself.
> My name's Dana. (Yeah)
> I want to be an actress. (Un huh)
> And a (hesitation) big.
> For the rest of my life. (Laughter)

Clearly they are projecting not only who they are as children by giving their names but also who they want to become as women by stating their career goals. All the professions named have to do with performance, and that may have something to do with popular culture influences or because they are doing a play performance, but each kind of performer career role named is culturally gendered. Perhaps the rhyme suggests that career aspirations for African American girls are higher now than they were in the 1960s, but the roles are still limited to show business, which has traditionally been a career choice for some black people. This desire to be in glamour professions such as entertainment or sports is not limited to black children though; white children have the same aspirations.

I may have neglected gender concerns in the 1970s, but Scherazade, Clarrissia, Carina, Shara, Deanna, and Dana would not let me ignore their concerns as girls in 2000 and 2001. They may be more assertive about gender issues than the girls I dealt with in 1971, but I think my attitude has changed as well. I am more interested in the significance of gender in folklore studies, and I am more theoretically aligned with the perspective of individual agency than with cultural determination. Their individual concerns and personalities are a bigger part of my analytic focus than in 1971 when I was thinking of the children mainly as part of a cultural group. Despite these significant differences, many links between the rhymes they are reciting today and those chanted in 1971 can be seen above in "I Went Downtown to See James Brown." As with folklore in general, both continuities and discontinuities occur in the transmission of children's rhymes.

One of the Fleming sisters' rhymes is directly related to one I collected in 1971, but as their mother pointed out, it has a perspective not found in the earlier rhyme. First the one from 1971:

> My mother, your mother live across the street.
> When they get in a fight, this is what they say:
> They say, "Ennie meenie just a peenie
> Ooo wha shah mileenie,
> Achie pachie Liberace, I love you.
> Take a peach, take a plum,
> Take a stick of bubble gum,
> Don't like it, don't take it.
> Do the Alabama twist.
> Mr. Clean, Mr. Clean, I hate you."

What are the two mothers fighting about? Symbolically, at least, it could be over a white man since both Liberace and Mr. Clean are white. Mr. Clean was a bald white man wearing a white T-shirt in television commercials at the time, and Liberace was a popular television star. The rhyme expresses love of Liberace and hatred of Mr. Clean suggesting, perhaps, the ambivalence the women have toward white men. All of this is complicated by the fact that Liberace was widely perceived as gay.

Neither Mr. Clean nor Liberace is mentioned in the 2000 versions, but the rhyme as recited by Scherazade and Clarrissia is still about gender relationships.

> Your Mama, my Mama live down the street,
> Eighteen nineteen Blueberry Street.
> Every night they have a fight
> And this is what they say, hey hey:
> Boys are rotten and made out of cotton.

Girls are sexy, made out of Pepsi
Boys go to Jupiter to get more stupider.
Girls go to college to get more knowledge.
Girls take a shower to get more power.
Boys take a bath to get more mad. (also see Brady
     1975, 51, Merrill-Mirsky 1988, 105)

Mickey Williams: Sounds like a feminist made that one up.
Scherazade: The last part, the last part, like, it changed because
     it used to be, "Boys take a bath, to get more dirtier."

According to Carol Merrill-Mirsky, a similar version she collected in the late
1980s contains "a definite prejudice in favor of girls":

Girls are handy, made out of candy,
Boys are rotten, made out of cotton,
Girls go to Mars, to get more candy bars,
Boys go to Jupiter to get more stupider. (1988, 105)

Margaret Brady collected a version of this rhyme in the early '70s, but the
attitude toward boys is different:

My mama, your mama live across the street
Eighteen-nineteen Carmel [Marble] Street
Every night they had a fight and
And this is what they say:
Boys are rotten just like cotten [sic].
Boys are dandy just like candy.
Akawasaboos, Akawasaboos
Akawasasodawater, I love you! (Brady 1975, 51;
     also see Abrahams 1969, 135)

In both the '70s and later versions of the rhyme, the core gender relationship part of the rhyme is framed by mother figures, suggesting girls' concern
for what their mother might think about the opposite sex. Brady points out
the importance of black mothers as role models for girls and that this is
reinforced in their play (Brady 1975, 13–14). Clarrissia's 2000 version does
seem, as Williams says, more feminist than the two 1970s versions in one
sense—girls are represented as superior to boys in terms of sexuality and
intelligence—although not in some of the other meanings of feminism. The
'70s rhyme I collected does not have direct statements about gender superior-

ity, and the '70s rhyme from Brady seems ambivalent—boys are both sweet and rotten. Is the change in the rhyme indicative of the feminist revolution that took place between the '60s and today? The militant rhymes of the '70s suggested black superiority to whites; now there is a female superiority to males. Merrill-Mirsky collected this rhyme from African American, European American, Latino, and Asian students at all five schools where she conducted research in Los Angeles (1988, 210) indicating that the feminist attitude is widespread.

One thing is certain, children's rhymes across cultures have been concerned with gender and sexuality for a long time, sometimes expressed innocently as in "I like the little boy and he likes me" and sometimes more explicitly as in

> Down in the valley where the green grass grows,
> There sat Sally without any clothes.
> Along came Billy swinging a chain,
> Down went his zipper and out it came. (Abrahams 1969, 43)

Earlier collections of children's rhymes offer wide-ranging evidence that sexuality is a theme of children's folklore across cultures although collections from the Victorian era such as William Wells Newell's would refer to "love games" or "courtship" rather than sexuality (Opie and Opie 1959, 93–97; Newell 1963 [1903], 39–62; Knapp and Knapp 1976, 82–91). As with blues songs, the temptation was there for white scholars to read African American children's rhymes as evidence of black sexuality. Brady quotes an unpublished manuscript by Abrahams to stress the cultural difference between African Americans and Anglo-Americans in regard to sexuality: "Abrahams states that the most constant theme of conflict in Black life is the 'independence and consequent opposition of the sexes.'" She applies this to children learning adult behavior: "Early in the lives of many young girls, a distinction is learned as to how one should relate to a boy. Boys, then, become *sexual* persons at an early age. The asexual character which is described to exist between middle-class preadolescent boys and girls disappears more rapidly in the Black community" (1975, 14).

I think that just as we overemphasized black militancy in the scholarship of the 1960s and '70s, we also overemphasized black sexuality. White preadolescent children were also expressing concerns about the opposite sex in their rhymes and learning about adult behavior in a play context. More overlap exists between the two cultures than folklorists, sociologists, and anthropologists were willing to admit; commonality of children's culture across racial lines continues today. Many of the rhymes I collected from black girls also have been widely found among white girls, sometimes with differences in wording that is culturally based, other times with almost exactly the same words: "I Went Downtown," "Down, Down, Baby," "Miss Mary Mack, Mack, Mack," "Miss Lucy Had a Baby," and "Rockin' Robin" have all been collected across cultural and racial lines, again with differences in some of the rhymes when it comes to race references.

A rhyme recited by all six black girls in the 2000s was, according to white college students in my classes, also widespread among white girls in the 1990s. Both white and black versions deal with sexuality, but the black version brings sexuality and race together in an explicit way. This seems to be a concern that has been around for a while since Brady collected a similar rhyme in the 1970s:

> 1970: Down, down, baby
> Down, down the roller coaster
> Sweet, sweet baby, please don't you let me go
> Shimmy shimmy cocopuffs
> Shimmy shimmy pow
> Shimmy shimmy cocopuffs
> Shimmy shimmy pow
>
> I like the coffee; I like the tea
> I like the little boy and he likes me
> Step back, Jack; your hand too black
> You look like a nigger on a railroad track.
> To the front, to the back, to the side by side
> To the front, to the back, to the side by side
> Ladies and gentlemens, childrens too,
> This little lady's gonna boogaloo
> Gonna shimmy shimmy til the sun goes down . . .
>   (Brady 1975, 51)
>
> 2000 (Clarrissia's and Scherazade's version):
> This train goes down, down, baby,
> Down by the roller coaster.
> Sweet, sweet, baby,
> I'll never let you go.
> If you want to kiss me,
> Just say you love me.
> Shimmy shimmy coco pop,
> Shimmy shimmy rah,

Shimmy shimmy coco pop,
Shimmy shimmy rah.
I like coffee,
I like tea,
I like a white boy [black boy],
And he likes me.
So step back black boy [white boy],
You ain't shy.
I bet you five dollars
I can beat your behind.
Last night, and the night before,
I met my boyfriend at the candy store.
He bought me ice cream,
He bought me cake,
He brought me home with a bellyache.
I said Mama, Mama, I'm so sick.
Call the doctor, quick, quick, quick.
Doctor, Doctor, shall I die?
I closed my eyes and I count to five.
I said a-one, a-two, a-three, a-four, a-five.
I'm alive on channel five.
I said a-six, a-seven, a-eight, a-nine, a-ten.
I'm dead on channel ten. (also see Merrill-Mirsky 1988,
     109, 211; Riddell 1990, 251–63)

(The version recited by the other four girls was almost
     the same except for the ending:
I'm alive on channel five.
Scooby Doo on channel two,
All the rest on CBS.)

Both the 1970s rhyme and the two versions from 2000–2001 express attitudes toward interracial relations. The '70s rhyme does not state that the "little boy" she likes is white, but it suggests a preference for white over black in the next two lines: "Step back, Jack, your hand too black / You look like a nigger on the railroad track." The rhyme recited by Clarrissia and Scherazade in 2000 indicates individual choice about race and sexuality within a traditional rhyme: the younger girl, Clarrissia, said "I like a black boy" while Scherazade said "white boy" at the same time. Their mother commented at the end, "That was kind of a racist one wasn't it?" and the girls explained what they meant.

Scherazade: Like really and truthfully, I would prefer
    white boys, and she would prefer black boys.
Mickey Williams: When did this happen?
Pat Mullen: You mean in terms of boyfriends?
Scherazade: Yeah.
Pat: Not just in the rhymes?
Scherazade: When I get older.
Pat: Okay. Your personal preference, you'd like to have
    a white boyfriend?
Scherazade: Yeah.
Mickey: You would?
Pat: And you'd like to have a black boyfriend?
Clarrissia: Yeah.
Mickey: You would? Why, because I prefer a white man? [She laughs]
Scherazade: No, because I think they're more nice and sweeter, and,
    and, you know.

Williams went on to defend black men by pointing out that the girls'
twenty-one-year-old brother was a "gentleman" and a "wonderful" person.
In this instance, the discussion we had afterwards indicates that the content
of the rhyme reflects actual attitudes and behavior of these two girls. In this
rhyme as recited by Dana, Deanna, Shara, and Carina, they all said, "I like a
black boy" and "Step back white boy." I asked them if they ever said, "I like a
white boy" or had heard anyone else say this, and they all replied negatively.
The possibility still exists for each girl to change the words to fit her individual
preferences.

Here again, attitudes seem to have shifted since the 1970s: then there were
references to boyfriends in the rhymes but not many to race and sex together,
and they were not as specific in sexual terms. Interracial relationships and
marriages are much more common in the 1990s and the 2000s than they
were in the '60s and '70s (Fears and Deane 2001, A1–2), and society's openness is culturally condoned in both the rhymes and in the girls' comments.
Even though this rhyme was also collected in Los Angeles and other parts of
the country, I cannot conclusively state that a shift from militant politics to
sexual politics has taken place because there are too many variables. Brady
collected similar sexual rhymes in the 1970s (1975, 51), and sexual themes
were apparent in children's rhymes even earlier.

The black girls I interviewed in 1971 may have known sexual rhymes that
they were unwilling to recite in front of a white man. Clarrissia and Scherazade may have been more open with me because their mother has a master's

degree in education and seems to be a liberated woman herself. Her presence made it much easier for the girls and me to speak freely although it is also clear that she is learning some of the girls' preferences for the first time. As their mother she is present in both the context of their performance and in the text itself. I think it is interesting that as a result of the girl's involvement with a boy in the rhyme she gets sick and has to call on her mother and the doctor for help. This could be a metaphoric reference to the possibility of pregnancy. The other four girls were willing to recite the rhyme but only answered briefly when I asked them about race and sexuality in it.

Other sexual attitudes are at play in this rhyme: the references to dancing and the dance movements that accompany the rhyme enhance the sexual meaning already established by the lines

> Sweet, sweet, baby,
> I'll never let you go.
> If you want to kiss me,
> Just say you love me.

The dance referred to was related to a song, "Shimmy Shimmy," that was popular in two different versions in the 1950s and '60s by Little Anthony and the Imperials (1959) and the Orlons (1964). This is a point where the words of the rhyme come together with the movements of play, and kinesics must be considered in the analysis. Kyra Gaunt says that, "Many of the game songs black girls played contain conscious and unconscious articulations about the female body as a source of musical and sexual power" (1998, 282). As the girls recite the rhyme and dance to the rhythm established by their chanting, they are doing more than expressing racial and gender identity; it is part of a cultural process of constructing that identity. When the girl says in the 1970s rhyme "This little lady's gonna boogaloo" or in the 2001 rhyme "Wind me up and I'll do my thing" it is a declaration of who she is, and her body movements reinforce that claim at the same time. Williams was aware of a sexually explicit rhyme that her younger daughter knew and even requested that she perform it to be recorded.

> Mickey Williams: What's your little nasty one that you do?
> Scherazade: I don't know it.
> Clarrissia: Okay. This one's me by myself.
> Mickey: Go on over there, girl. And then I want to know
>   where you got it from. Go ahead.
> Clarrissia: Britanny.

My boy friend made me do it.
He really, really, really sent it to me.
He really, really, really do it to my motion.
He really, really, really criss crossed me down.
He really, really, really took me to his house.
He really, really, really gave me on his couch.
He really, really, really
Hoosh, aash,
Hoosh, aash, hoosh
(She breaks out laughing)

Clarrissia: Britanny taught me that one.
Pat: They got to learn that sometime.
Clarrissia: I don't do that.
Mickey: What does it mean? Do you know what it means?
Scherazade: Sheena told her that.
Clarrissia: Nasty, that's all I know.
Scherazade: Sheena told her that; you know how she is.
Mickey: Okay.

Clarrissia is younger but seems to be more interested in sexuality. Williams explains this in terms of the different personalities of her two girls: she calls Scherazade her "tomboy" because of her interest in sports and Clarrissia her "hoochie mama." Scherazade seems to be easier to deal with while Clarrissia gives her more trouble: "She thinks she's Tina Turner or Whitney Houston or something . . . she's very defiant and belligerent." Perhaps Clarrissia is trying to defy her mother when she recites such sexually explicit rhymes. My sense is that the rhymes do not mean that she has begun to engage in any of the sexual activities that are described.

This is in keeping with Kyra Gaunt's findings on black girls' games. "In girls' game playing, beyond any institutional control, sexual behavior and references to sex are neutralized and do not reflect actual behavior. 'Doing your thing' here does not mean doing the thing, having sex" (1997, 157). Ethnomusicologist Ellen Koskoff sees women's traditional musical expressions about sexuality as often being coded and not matching outward behavior (1989, 11). The dynamic between the two girls and their mother offers evidence that the sexuality in these rhymes is metaphoric, but there is also an implicit suggestion of sexual behavior at some point in the future. The metaphoric rather than actual nature of the references seems to be reinforced by the presence of sexual repression in their performance and the ensuing conversation. Repression can be discerned in both mother's and daughters' use of the word "nasty," in Clarrissia's breaking out in laughter at the end of the erotic sounds in the rhyme, in Scherazade's suggesting that the girl who taught Clarrissia the rhyme is a bad girl—"you know how she is"—and in the fact that the girls have withheld information about their sexual knowledge from their mother. The other four girls were even more hesitant to discuss sexual references openly, and I did not feel comfortable pursuing that line of questioning with them—repression on both sides.

This evidence of sexual repression counters a long-standing stereotype of black girls and women as primarily sexual beings in cultural representations of African Americans in folklore scholarship. For instance, as I pointed out in chapter 4, Alan Lomax saw sexual references and movements in black girls' rhymes and games in Mississippi as a way for girls to learn about sex and as directly linked to behavior. After describing a particular game and quoting the accompanying rhyme, he states, "Sexually active at ten or eleven, with marriage maybe only a couple of years off, a Delta country girl needed to know how to sort through the males and how to move between marriage partners" (1993, 89). I think in the case of Clarrissia, Scherazade, Dana, Deanna, Carina, and Shara, learning is going on in that children's games and rhymes in general are part of learning about adult behavior, but it is a mistake to equate sexual references with actual behavior and thereby reinforce racial stereotypes.

As I indicated earlier, both continuities and discontinuities exist in African American children's games and rhymes. Evidence occurs of certain changes in attitude toward race, gender, and sexuality between 1971 and 2001, but not as much as I thought there would be. The continuity between children's play in the early '70s and their play in the early twenty-first century struck me as even more significant. Black girls are still learning how to be black women through their games and rhymes. Scholars, including myself, in the '60s and '70s were talking about games and rhymes as part of a socializing process; scholars today see these same activities as part of the social construction of racial and gender identities. Back then the emphasis was on militancy or sexuality, with a tendency to overemphasize cultural difference. Now the emphasis is on cultural and sexual politics, with a tendency to overemphasize difference. Whatever theoretical terms we use, we are still talking about folklore as a traditional activity in which young people are becoming themselves, individually and culturally. Black children were doing the "Shimmy" and the "Boogaloo" in the 1960s and '70s, and they are doing it today. They were chanting "Down, down, baby / Down, down the roller coaster" in the '60s, and they are chanting it today.

This suggests that children's game rhymes can be considered as rituals in Barbara Myerhoff's sense, as repeated patterned behaviors that are symbolic enactments dramatizing abstract conceptions (1984, 305). George Lipsitz says something about rock and roll as ritual that I think applies to children's games; "Songs with references to familiar folk tales and sagas or to everyday speech or street-corner games tended to include listeners in a community of improvisation and elaboration. The songs came from life and easily blended back into it. As the members of the audience remembered and repeated, they ritualistically confirmed the commonality of everyday experience" (1990, 114).

As black children are playing they are ritualistically confirming their commonality with both the African American community and with other communities. They are making the connection between their individual identities and cultural identities as black people and as Americans. They were doing it in the nineteenth and early twentieth century with "Juba"; they were doing it in the 1950s and '60s with "Hambone"; they were doing it in the '70s with "I Went Downtown to See James Brown"; and they are doing it today with "Down, Down Baby," "Rockin' Robin," "I Don't Want to Go to Mexico," and more, drawing on the past, creating in the present, and preparing themselves for future roles. Girls, who are the primary tradition bearers of the rhymes and games, are constructing their racial and gender identities through ritual, reinforcing cultural and racial differences and at the same time connecting across racial lines to other girls their own age.

One of the unnoticed recurring themes in the scholarship on black children's rhymes over the last twenty years is how much rhymes and games have crossed cultural and racial lines. Merrill-Mirsky collected five different rhymes from African American, European American, Latino, and Asian students at all five schools where she conducted research in Los Angeles (1988, 210). Riddell's field research in the Los Angeles area in the late 1980s also indicated a broad cultural sharing of children's rhymes. She concentrated on one class of fifth graders in which thirty-two out of thirty-three of the students were African American, but she concluded that, "My prior experience collecting singing games had confirmed that children of diverse ethnic backgrounds share many, if not all, of the same playground games in Los Angeles." As proof she cited a collection from a predominantly white school in the area that produced "tunes, texts, and movements" that were "virtually identical to those collected from" the black school she studied (1990, 11). The collecting I have done among white and black college women in my folklore classes at Ohio State also supports this point; many of them remember similar rhymes from their childhoods although differences occur when it comes to direct references to race.

This cross-racial and cross-cultural sharing is further evidence that Gubar's process of racechange (1997) and Murray's concept of Omni-Americans (1970) are taking place, that cultural hybridization has developed an American culture that is mainly African American, blurring the differences between cultures, leading to the breakdown of racial distinctions, and perhaps ultimately to the abolition of whiteness (Ware and Back 2002). This does not, however, necessarily mean that cultural distinctions will disappear: black girls seem to have maintained strong identities as African Americans in the cultural sense even as their rhymes and games have been assimilated by Hispanic, Asian, and Caucasian girls. It remains to be seen if the loss of racial consciousness also means the loss of cultural distinctiveness, but along with many other scholars I think that cultural identity can be maintained even as we destroy the concept of race as a natural category.

My understanding of African American children's rhymes was facilitated enormously by Mickey Williams and Carla Wilks who collaborated with me in the field research. Having members of the African American community helping me to find children to interview and record and then commenting on my interpretations of the material was an invaluable part of the research. This kind of collaboration across racial boundaries offers a new paradigm for the future of African American folklore scholarship, a topic I will explore in more depth and detail in the next chapter.

8

Collaborative Research Across Racial Lines

The Lord sent it even if
the Devil did bring it.
—Jesse Truvillion

The preceding seven chapters have critiqued past folkloristic practice in terms of cultural representations of African Americans. In this last
chapter, I concentrate on directions African American folklore scholarship
can take in the future, specifically the potential of collaborative research
between white scholars and people in the black community to correct some
of the past mistakes of representation. As I suggested in the introduction,
self-representation by African Americans is necessary to correct the past
mistakes made by white folklorists, and recruiting black students into the
scholarly discipline of folklore studies is essential in achieving that goal. Students should train with folklorists from multiple racial and cultural groups
to learn about cultural difference *and* commonality. Academic training is
itself ideally collaborative so that collaboration, whether between white and
black folklorists or with members of the community being studied, has to
be part of the model for research in African American culture in the future.
This kind of cross-racial and cross-cultural collaborative research already
proved valuable in Native American Studies (Foley 2001), and there have been
earlier attempts by ethnographers to include black subjects in the creation
of the ethnographic text (Valentine 1978) although such collaborations have
not been practiced widely since.

I have had experience in collaborative research across racial lines in the
past with mixed results. Examining one of my recent efforts at biracial collaboration will be productive since the ethnographic process was documented
in some detail from the perspectives of both collaborators in a special issue

of the *Journal of Folklore Research* (Mullen 2000a, 2000b; Truvillion 2000a, 2000b). As I identify mistakes my collaborator and I made in that research, I consider how they relate to larger theoretical issues in reciprocal ethnography (Lawless 1992). As in the rest of the book, I include only those personal details relating directly to scholarly concerns. This is especially important in this situation because to do otherwise would violate the privacy of my collaborator. As we are no longer in contact with each other, I have no way of verifying his perspective on the research process after the time we ceased communicating. All of the information about him in this chapter has been published previously in essays that he wrote.

Meeting Jesse Truvillion (the son of Henry Truvillion) in 1995 not only provided an opportunity to do research on John Lomax's relationship with a major African American folk singer (see chapter 3) but also opened up the possibilities of collaborative research across racial and cultural lines for Jesse and me. As a folklorist, I was excited about the opportunity to work with a black minister to explore the historical relationship of a black minister and white folklorist of an earlier generation. As I started to interview Jesse, details of his own life emerged, and we realized that the collaboration could extend into an ethnoautobiography: I would tape record narratives about his life, and we would write a book about it. I thought collaborative research could be at least a partial solution to problems of racial representation in folklore studies; the white folklorists' interpretations could be guided and critiqued by someone within the black community. We could practice Johannes Fabian's theory of intersubjectivity: since absolute objectivity is impossible, scholars must strive to negotiate different subjective views to arrive at intersubjective understanding (1971, 1994). This process would, I thought, be easier because my relationship with Jesse was very cordial, and we were becoming friends as well as collaborators. Unfortunately, after we began sharing our research with other folklorists, complications arose that ended both the research and our friendship. In this concluding chapter, I examine what went wrong. How did such a potentially rewarding professional and personal relationship end in acrimony and misunderstanding, and what are the implications of this failure for African American folklore scholarship? Since Jesse and I were collaborating on a past study of African American culture, issues of historical cultural representation intersected with the current issues of collaborative research; I deal with both, focusing on cultural representation first while recognizing that they cannot be completely separated. Before delving into those issues, though, I will establish the background of the collaboration.

A mutual friend, Bob Russell, introduced Jesse and me. Bob and Jesse are both Presbyterian ministers who have known each other for many years. Bob knew that Jesse and I have a common interest in African American history and culture as well as a common regional background: Jesse grew up in the Big Thicket of East Texas about seventy miles from my hometown of Beaumont. Bob invited us to lunch on March 1, 1995, and this was when I first learned that John Lomax recorded Jesse's father, Henry Truvillion, for the Library of Congress in the 1930s and '40s. Jesse had vivid memories of Lomax's visits to the family home in East Texas. As we talked, we became aware of more than geographical similarities in our backgrounds: we are both from working class families, we both attended college in Texas, we both attained doctoral degrees, and we both left Texas to pursue our careers. I point out these similarities not to deny racial and cultural differences, but to establish the numerous bases for a collaborative relationship.

We arranged to meet later at my office to record Jesse's account of his life and his memories of his father and John Lomax. We met six times in 1995, either at my Ohio State University office or my home (a five-minute drive from Jesse's home in Columbus). While class difference was not a factor in our relationship as much as it was for John Lomax and Henry Truvillion, other differences in cultural and racial backgrounds continued to be significant for Jesse and me. We both grew up in the segregated South of separate schools, blacks in the back of the bus, and "colored" waiting rooms—but with obviously opposite perspectives. During our interviews, Jesse recounted harrowing personal experiences with racism in Texas, Mississippi, Alabama, and New Jersey. Our education, migration, and upward mobility removed us both from the segregated world where we grew up and created a context in which our conversations could be, as far as I could tell at the time, relaxed and open.

Our interviews were interrupted when Jesse moved to Jacksonville, Florida, to begin a new ministry, but we continued our collaboration by telephone and fax. We wrote separate papers that were accepted for the 1995 meeting of the American Folklore Society. We read the papers at the meeting in Lafayette, Louisiana, which were well received by those in attendance. Mary Ellen Brown, editor of the *Journal of Folklore Research* (JFR), asked us to submit them for possible publication; she eventually decided to devote an entire issue of the journal to our essays with an essay by Roger Abrahams that situates Lomax in the context of American folksong scholarship (2000), and commentary by Olivia Cadaval, Elaine Lawless, and Nolan Porterfield (John Lomax's biographer). During this process, the first misunderstanding occurred between Jesse and me, and he stopped responding to my faxes and phone calls. The following account of the incident is from my point of view;

the only information I have about Jesse's perspective is from an essay he wrote as a response to commentaries by me and the other folklorists published in the special issue of the journal (Truvillion 2000b).

The scholars who commented on our essays raised issues that helped me to view interracial collaborative research in a more complex way; unfortunately, their comments also introduced issues that led to misunderstandings between Jesse and me. We were all engaged in a responsible and principled scholarly exchange of ideas, but problems occurred for a number of reasons. Although we folklorists recognized content and stylistic differences, some of us addressed at least parts of Jesse's essay as if they were the same kind of scholarship we were writing. Jesse is an academically trained religious and historical scholar, but the language of ethnography and folkloristics was foreign to him in many ways. The situation was further complicated by his personal experiences as an African American and by the history of racism in America, including racism within academic research.

One of the many ironies of the situation is that the breakdown of the dialogue between Jesse and me led to a continuing scholarly dialogue because the research process was documented in print. Amy Shuman taught several folklore graduate seminars at Ohio State University using the special issue of JFR as a textbook to explore matters central to folklore fieldwork. Comments by Jesse, me, and the other scholars opened up new ways of examining the process of collaborative research. For instance, Olivia Cadaval in her commentary on Jesse's and my essays makes the point that collaborative research requires a foundation in reflexive ethnography: "By choosing a reflexive mode, we are committing to explore ways to represent these complex negotiation processes, including what is unmediated and left out, as well as the different ideological perspectives of agents involved" (2000, 191). In this chapter, I present more details about our "ideological perspectives" and about what was "unmediated and left out" of our original account. In this way, I hope to advance the scholarly understanding of the concepts of reciprocal and collaborative research.

In his commentary on our essays, Nolan Porterfield points out one area where collaborative research and cultural representation overlap. He states that ethnographic accounts, like biographies and life histories, are attempts to impose a "narrative truth" on an "objective truth" (Porterfield 2000, 180; Talbot 1999, 6). John Stewart offers "ethnographic fiction" as another means of describing the lived experiences of the subjects of field research that standard ethnographic accounts fail to adequately provide (1989, 1–24). Indeed, as Porterfield observes, we can never determine the "True Story" of Henry

Truvillion and John Lomax, and it is difficult to determine the "Whole Story" (2000, 182); neither will we determine the "true story" of Jesse Truvillion and Patrick Mullen. We can only attempt to interpret past events by trying to reconstruct the social context of that time, recognizing that our own positions in the present will influence that interpretation. Because this was a collaborative effort, our separate versions of the same past events had no glaring conflicts—but important underlying differences made reciprocal ethnography difficult.

Both of our original essays portray cultural representations of race relations in the south in the 1930s and '40s through an exploration of the relationship between Henry Truvillion and John Lomax, but because of our different perspectives the compositions differ significantly. Jesse's essay details his childhood in the Big Thicket; his narrative addresses the activities and values of his family members and is informed by his wide-ranging knowledge of African American history and culture. I concentrate more on the fieldwork relationship, with a special focus on the way the Anglo-American John Lomax represented Henry Truvillion as an African American (see chapter 3). In Jesse's account, Lomax is a relatively minor character who is not part of the family's everyday life; he is remembered as an occasional visitor who developed a friendship with Jesse's father. Jesse's essay provides a rich account of Henry Truvillion and his cultural milieu; this information contrasts with Lomax's limited view of Truvillion as a railroad foreman who led his track-laying crew in singing work songs. Jesse's perspective may be unique in scholarship about major folklore informants, which historically has always privileged the ethnographer's perceptions.

Other differences in our representations of African American life in the Big Thicket in the 1930s and '40s arose from our perspectives as insider and outsider. Jesse described his own family and community in terms of his intimate experience of them; I described them based on information gathered from listening to Jesse and from reading the work of John Lomax and other scholars as well as examining Lomax's field notes and recordings at the Library of Congress. Jesse brought another kind of sensitivity to his representation of his own culture, one learned through the experiences of being black in America. He self-consciously avoided stereotypes of African Americans, describing his family life with details that undermine what many whites may think about black rural life in that period. For instance, while he acknowledged the poverty that existed in the area, he also revealed that this was not the monolithic culture of the stereotype. For my part, I hoped that I had been sensitive to my own culturally learned assumptions about race and folklore—but none of us can step completely outside our own worldview. Undoubtedly, underlying assumptions crept into my descriptions just as they were embedded in John Lomax's.

If Jesse's and my cultural sensitivities differed, so did our writing styles: I am a scholar/teacher and he is a scholar/preacher; our writing reflects our different purposes. In his article, Jesse uses stories to make moral points much as he does when he preaches a sermon; his narrative style is effective in both written and oral media. I shall never forget the audience's response to Jesse's presentation at the 1995 American Folklore Society meeting in Lafayette; people wiped tears from their eyes as they stood to give him a long ovation. He made his points about the respect and love he feels for his parents in ways that are beyond my rhetorical abilities.

Our perspectives differed most obviously in the sense that Jesse seemed more favorably disposed toward John Lomax than I was. Perhaps this "interpretive difference" (Lawless 1992) regarding Lomax stems from the fact that my article focuses on fieldwork methods, while Jesse's addresses the concrete results of Lomax's work and the context that made it possible. We wrote our papers mainly via telephone conversations and faxes from 1995 until the essays were finished in 1999. We sent each other drafts, asking the other to comment and suggest changes. After listening to field recordings at the Library of Congress, I suggested some relatively minor changes in the way Jesse represented a conversation between his father and John Lomax, and he made those changes. After reading Jesse's paper with its favorable portrayal of Lomax, I softened some of my harsher criticisms about Lomax's racist behavior. I sent drafts to Jesse with requests to criticize or disagree as he saw fit. Since his responses were not critical, I took this to mean that he agreed with what I said about his father and Lomax and with my general representation of African American culture in East Texas during the 1930s and '40s.

Upon further reflection in the years since, however, I realized that there were underlying problems. When I asked Jesse to point out anything in my paper he disagreed with, his silence could have meant that he agreed with what I had said, that he valued our friendship in such a way that he did not want to question my reading, or that he deferred to me in my area of expertise. I deferred to his particular vision of the past out of fear that I might offend him, perhaps being overly sensitive about race. Hence racial difference complicated what were already potential problems in any collaboration. Underlying issues, including still unresolved disagreements about a document in the Library of Congress, surfaced after 1995, and in particular during the period of preparing the special JFR issue, causing conflict between us. Some of these issues had to do with race and others did not, although I will deal with the always subtle underlying connections later in this chapter.

Collaborative research in folklore is directly related to reciprocal ethnography in that the scholar consults with the "informant" about the ethnographic process with the intention of sharing all results with him or her, and this sharing will be reflected in the final product (Lawless 1992). As Elaine Lawless makes clear in her original formulation of the concept, reciprocal ethnography is a complex process, and ethnographers are just now beginning to experience and examine the difficulties of attempting such research. In her comments on our essays, she points out that reciprocal ethnography does not necessarily include friendship (2000, 201)—although as I have found out, friendship can be a complicating factor. As friends, Jesse and I were sensitive to each other's feelings to such an extent that it interfered with our research purposes. We tried so hard to agree with each other that we ended up creating what Allesandro Portelli calls a "pretense of reciprocal identification," undermining the ideal of maintaining two distinctive voices between researcher and subject (1997, 2).

Ethonographers must, as a matter of principle, be consciously aware of difference at all times to avoid pretended agreement. All voices must be granted an equal opportunity to be heard to achieve the "broadening and democratizing" of the scholarship that Cadaval, drawing on the work of Américo Paredes and others, calls for (Cadaval 2000, 186–93). We must remain open to different kinds of discourse and the differing orders of knowledge they engage and produce. At the same time, the family memoir, the sermon, and the academic paper should be subject to different kinds of evaluation. Different genres reveal the different roles and goals behind them; the roles of minister and professor have to be considered in evaluating individual writing content and style. As a minister, Jesse emphasizes racial harmony and forgiveness (what Cadaval calls" truth and reconciliation") in his representation of the relationship between his father and John Lomax, while I emphasize Lomax's faults as a researcher.

Cadaval points out that "native" and "ethnographic" perspectives have to be negotiated in terms of power and position: "Each can claim authority within his or her own discourse, arrive at a conclusion different from the other's, but still, within the larger collaborative framework, contribute to broader perspectives on ethnography and cultural production" (187). My own "show trial" of John Lomax, as Cadaval calls it, is within the scholarly frame of critiquing disciplinary history, and Jesse's "truth and reconciliation" is within the tradition of family memoir and sermon, but "dialogue emerges between the interstices of these two very different styles" (192). The interplay between different voices advances our understanding. This is a critical issue for someone doing reciprocal ethnography with anyone other than his or her own gender, social class, ethnic group, profession, and so forth. The value of such collaboration lies as much in the spaces between the two individuals as it does in the joining of their creative energies. Both need to respect the other's difference without losing sight of personal, moral, and political positions.

That is the ideal of collaborative research between people of different ethnic, class, and racial backgrounds, but as I found out, the actual experience can make it difficult to achieve. I did not consider carefully enough issues of power and position in my relationship with Jesse. Although much more reflexive than Lomax, I still assumed certain power without considering the consequences. I know that the history of racism in America and Jesse's own experiences of "paternalism, condescension," and "hidden [white] agenda[s]" are behind his negative reactions, and I agree with him that there should be no place for these in collaborative research (Truvillion 2000b, 220).

Some of our conflicts were partially attributable to our different professions. Because Jesse is a minister and a scholar of religion and African American history and I am a trained folklorist, we did not discuss ethnographic theories such as reflexivity, cultural representation, and the constructedness of life history except on the most informal and surface level. I do not believe Jesse was prepared to have his writing about his father evaluated in terms of scholarly frames that viewed personal-experience narratives as "fictionalized" (Titon 1980). I agree with Jeff Todd Titon's idea that life stories are selective and artistic, constructed out of memory to engage a listener in the present; I used the concept in my book on life stories of the elderly (Mullen 1992), but I was not willing to tell Jesse at the beginning stages of our collaboration that in theoretical terms his life story was "fictionalized." My thinking at the time was that we have enough problems in overcoming difference in fieldwork encounters without complicating the process by bringing in scholarly jargon having the potential to undermine the relationship. John Stewart, in his evaluation of this book in manuscript form, aptly terms this "intellectual paternalism."

In writing about Jesse's representation of his father and Lomax, I brought in the concept of fictionalizing but only in indirect ways. In the original paper in JFR, I made the point, without using the potentially insulting word "fictionalize," that Jesse and I were constructing versions of the past. I wrote, "There is the possibility that Jesse's memory is faulty in this because it does not fit his present image of his father" (Mullen 2000b, 162) and suggested that Jesse's "portrait [of his father] is . . . a cultural representation based on memory and emotional attachment. . . ." (156). I also recognized how my own fictionalizing had an impact on the facts: "undoubtedly, underlying assumptions have crept into my descriptions . . ." (121). I hold firm to the idea that life stories and ethnographic accounts are not objective, but are instead subjective constructions of the past—for me or for anyone. As Porterfield reminds us, "Stories are always a violation of objective truth" in the sense that narrating is a subjective process to give meaning to the original experience (2000, 182). However, because I did not introduce this idea into the private dialogue between Jesse and me, we were not prepared to deal with it when it became part of a public scholarly dialogue. Jesse and I used our collaboration to create a narrative about the past that was agreeable to both of us although it did not fully represent my theoretical principles. I compromised those principles to a certain extent to maintain a personal harmony between Jesse and me that turned out to be illusory. I still believe in the principles of collaboration and reciprocal ethnography, but differences between the theories of the scholar and the philosophical and religious beliefs of the collaborator will continue to provide stumbling blocks to the process.

Once Lawless introduced the term "fiction" in her commentary for the special issue of JFR (2000, 200), I responded in kind (Mullen 2000b, 210). This was a legitimate part of our scholarly discourse as folklorists but a problem for the only nonfolklorist among the authors. Despite my efforts to explain via fax that in using the term "fictionalize" I was not saying that he had fabricated his life story, we were unable to resolve this issue. An ethnographic problem that could have occurred between a folklorist and an informant of the same race became foregrounded as a racial issue. In statements Jesse made in his final published response, he brought to the surface the underlying issue of race that we had both suppressed: "What I have written is not fiction, but redemptive fact. There is no reason for me to fictionalize any event or experience that demonstrates our existence as persons in a context that often denied us personhood" (2000b, 216). Even though this indicates a misunderstanding of the theoretical concept, Jesse makes a valid moral point: such scholarly concepts have been used in the past to maintain academic superiority over the subjects of study, and scholars need to consider what we do as hegemonic discourse at every turn. The misunderstanding was, in other words, on both sides. To say that someone's life stories are fictionalized without first discussing what that means has the effect of denying their personhood, and if that person is of a different race then the problem may become racial. I now believe there is a need to bring in these academic and disciplinary concepts early on as part of the process of establishing friendship and trust in the collaborative relationship. Jesse and I shared our research findings with other scholars before we were ready: we had not dealt with the issues of fictionalizing and representation first to prepare ourselves for broader scholarly inquiry.

Part of the folkloristic understanding of the process of fictionalizing is the tendency to romanticize, and I agree with Lawless that Jesse's account is "a romantic, positive remembering" (Lawless 2000, 201). Jesse might have been trying to provide me with the story he thought I wanted to hear just as I was trying to defer to his version of the events. In this case, racial difference and our training as children to be civil in race relations may have led to accommodation on both sides. In romanticizing his childhood memories, Jesse is no different than most of us; I know that I have the tendency toward "a romantic, positive remembering" when I talk about my childhood in southeast Texas. However, despite these commonalities in our intellectual and emotional thought processes, my position as ethnographer and Jesse's as subject re-created the power differential that exists in all such relationships. Like all scholars who study other people, I assume a superior position over them, in this case by claiming enough postmodern distance from my own past to identify my stories about it as romantic while implying that Jesse lacks that distance. The problem could have been mitigated if Jesse and I had thoroughly discussed scholarly concepts related to the social construction of reality at the beginning of the collaborative research process. There was some paternalism in my not being willing to discuss theoretical issues with him, but to avoid paternalism now, at those points where I do not agree with Jesse's interpretations of the situation, I must be respectfully critical of him.

Jesse's original essay did not romanticize race relations as much as Elaine Lawless and I indicated: he balances his romantic emphasis on racial harmony with several references to racism. For example, he frames a story about getting lost on a white man's property as a child with this statement: "Racism haunted the thicket, much like the bigoted mindsets" of people in an all-white town in Florida whose residents set fire to an African American town, resulting in the "killing of many adults, children, babies, and a dog. All of this was fresh memory for my dad . . ." (Truvillion 2000a, 134). Jesse told me he faced racism throughout his adult life, sometimes as part of being active in the struggle for equal rights. In other kinds of narratives not included in his essay, he emphasizes racial oppression over harmony. Stories of racism are in the life history we began to compile, but their scarcity in his published essay should not be taken as evidence that he overlooked the sufferings of black people in

America. In his response to the folklorists' comments on his work, he makes very clear that he is acutely aware of racism in African American life: "How much truth will it take for the sun of understanding to rise out of these songs, sayings, rituals, and memories from a time in the Thicket when a White face carried with it 'approval' and 'righteous passage' and a Black face carried the shadows of slavery, segregation, and second class-ness?" (216). In fact, I think he used the opportunity of the written response to balance what some of us had seen as a romanticized view of race relations in his earlier essay.

Problems of power and position other than the fictional representation issue contributed to the breakdown of our collaboration, and he mentions these in his final response to all the scholarly commentaries in the special issue of JFR. His essay is full of powerful and revealing metaphors. If Toni Morrison's call to look closely at the language of whites in terms of racial implications is a necessary scholarly procedure, then we also must apply the same scrutiny to black writing. Jesse opens with a story about a hungry poor woman who is praying for bread. Two boys overhear her and decide to play a joke. They buy a loaf of bread and throw it over her fence. She starts to thank God for answering her prayers, and one boy yells out, "God didn't bring you any bread, we did." She responds, "The Lord sent it, even if the Devil did bring it" (215). Jesse's metaphor constructs whiteness as evil but recognizes some benefits from white magnanimity. I think the metaphor is apt for me and for folklorists in general because of the mixed results of our endeavors over the years—folklorists provide benefits to the people we study, but at the same time we do harm through condescension and misrepresentation. Unlike the boys in the story, we usually are well intentioned in our work with minority people. In fact, many of us view ourselves as advocates for the powerless, the disenfranchised, and the poor (recognizing that not all minority people fit this description), but we made mistakes and continue to make mistakes that result in exploitation of the people we are trying to help (Kodish 1993).

Some of Jesse's harshest criticisms of me spring from a footnote in my response to the folklorists' commentaries. Jesse says, "This footnote feels like a slave collar locked around my neck" (2000b, 221), a metaphor that goes to the heart of racial power and position in folklore research. In the footnote I intended to verify that Henry Truvillion could read and write, but by citing a document in the Library of Congress, I unintentionally contradicted Jesse's statement that the Library of Congress had never informed his father or the family about the recordings being in the Archive of Folk Song (Mullen 2000b, 213). My explanation for this affront was that it was unintentional and a result of my not paying enough attention at the time, but this explanation is yet another example of white "innocence" as a source of power over the Other (Duneier 1992, 138–39, also see chapter 6). Like John Lomax, Alan Lomax, Roger Abrahams, and other white folklorists, I let my good intentions mask a deeper exercise of power; Jesse's slave metaphor was more appropriate than I could recognize at the time.

Our attempt at collaborative research was such a debacle that Jesse could say, "Rather than feeling part of a collaborative pursuit of reciprocal ethnography, I feel more like a prisoner of war being questioned for the wrong reasons. Folklorists should realize that they sometimes ask the wrong questions and are there at the wrong times: they might not get detailed or 'straight' answers from 'informants' because they won't understand the answer" (2000b, 220). His language here suggests a construction of blackness and whiteness that is related to Morrison's concept of black enslavement as a source of white "meditation on problems of human freedom" (1992, 37) but from Jesse's perspective as a black man. Whites such as the Lomaxes used black imprisonment to enhance their own sense of freedom, making whiteness the central consciousness, but Jesse uses the "prisoner of war" and "slave collar" metaphors to suggest his own imprisonment by white folklorists. The interview process becomes an interrogation rather than a conversation between equals. This statement is like many others that he makes in his published response in that it contains a truth about folklore research expressed as a result of personal feelings of betrayal. I agree with him that folklorists do ask the wrong questions at the wrong time and that we do not always understand the answers. Reflexive ethnography has made us more aware of this concern, but obviously problems still need to be worked out.

The "communicative blunders" (Briggs 1986, 26, 109) between us were significant in the ethnographic process, but equally important in our collaboration were racial dynamics on a personal level. Jesse and I made individual decisions grounded in underlying assumptions about race. We played certain roles in a racial social drama, roles that we were not aware of at the time but that seem more apparent in hindsight. However, we cannot blame our failure on culturally learned racial assumptions alone: we must take moral responsibility for the scholarly and ideological consequences of our actions. As I have argued throughout this book, cultural process as symbolic action is not a deterministic model; rather, it recognizes that humans create culture in the present based on interpretations of received knowledge and attitudes from the past. We may have constructed reality from received cultural assumptions, but the consequences of our actions were real. Jesse and I had choices at every turn and often made the wrong ones. One of the ironies here is that Jesse and I behaved in ways related to our common social class and regional backgrounds, especially in our imagining ourselves as folk, and we ended up mirroring each other's racial identities, reflexively constructing blackness and whiteness on a symbolic level.

We both came from working class backgrounds in southeast Texas, and we both were upwardly mobile in terms of education. These circumstances caused us to form identities at least partially based on our imagined folkness. As we separated ourselves from our parents and family through advanced education and leaving the area where we grew up, we felt a need to cling to our working-class roots, to construct our selves in the present by identifying with what we conceived as a traditional past. We both imagined our parents and grandparents as authentic folk who had passed on to us traits we associated with folkness (especially hard-working physical labor related to economic upward mobility)—values that we saw as part of our success in the present. The stories I tell about family history offer concrete evidence of this, and Jesse told similar stories in the interviews I recorded with him and in published essays about his family (Truvillion 1996, 2000). I often tell how my grandmother on my mother's side scrubbed floors in a downtown office building to earn money to raise her children after she divorced my grandfather, and how her father left the tenant farm he grew up on in Alabama to migrate to Texas to work on a tenant farm there. My grandparents on my father's side were born and reared in the Ozark Mountains of Arkansas, and my grandfather was a ballad singer—family history that I talk about as proof of my "hillbilly" roots. I published an article about the ballads he sang, proudly displaying my own folk authenticity that in my imagination made me a more authentic folklorist (Mullen 1972).

Jesse was equally proud of his father as a folk singer who received the acclaim of John Lomax as one of the best folk performers he ever recorded, and Jesse is also proud of the work ethic of his parents, often referring to his father's job as the foreman of a track-laying crew. We both take these historical facts and romanticize them. For instance, Jesse writes about watching, "the Pine Knot-Special (with the great black train engine) go from the sawmill out into the forest to bring back the logs on the rails that Daddy's crew had laid. He wore his red bandanna every day, but it always seemed new. He looked like 'a man in charge,' and my mother and I always waited to receive his wave, then it was back home for the day" (1996, 32). The equivalent making of a romantic folk hero out of my father is that whenever I drive by any of the many refineries that he worked at around the country, I say, "My father built that."

Jesse and I are what J. Martin Favor calls populist elitists in that we romanticize working-class folkness to make it the basis for an authenticity of identity in the present that we see as superior in some ways to our educated middle-class status (1999, 8). Applying the concept of populist elitism to a specific ethnographic case indicates that it is much more complex than simply romanticizing the folk and making negative critiques of the bourgeoisie. A built-in ambivalence exists in this position because the folkness that makes us authentic is left behind as we became more educated and middle-class, and evidence in both our lives indicates that we feel ambivalent about our class identities. We share these attitudes, but racial difference complicates the essentializing process of imagining a folk identity for ourselves and therefore makes our collaborative relationship even more complex.

Jesse associated his folkness with race and oppression, an attitude that became part of his ideology as an educated adult. In my case, I associated part of my folkness with being an oppressor, even though I leave that out of the public display of myself as folk. For instance, in my family saga I never mention relatives who were overtly racist, but I am aware of that aspect of my heritage, and southern white liberal guilt is part of who I am. We both maintained contradictory attitudes toward our folk cultural backgrounds and our current educated middle-class status: as populist elitists we could critique the bourgeoisie as lacking the earthy honesty of lower-class folk culture, as being less authentic, while at the same time cling to our middle-class comforts and educated tastes. We maintained a positive sense of what we conceive as our folk heritage, but we rejected much of the actual daily practices associated with the folk. While romanticizing agrarian practices, neither of us wanted to be out plowing a field or picking cotton.

Both of us used the romantic side of our folk background to represent ourselves as more authentically Texan in our refined educated world, but blackness and whiteness merged with folkness in different ways. Jesse's racializing of the folk gave power to his racial politics, made him a more authentic spokesperson for the racially oppressed in his civil rights activism. "Black identity, as formulated on the class basis, requires a certain quotient of oppression; second-class status is essential to racial identity" (Favor 1999, 13). I used my personal concept of folkness to identify with the downtrodden of whatever race thereby erasing difference while at the same time on another level making myself more black, patterns of thinking about race that connect me to Alan Lomax. Like Lomax, I racialized the folk as part of forming my political beliefs and practices.

In many ways Jesse is like other black scholars and intellectuals who, according to Favor, "equate the black bourgeoisie with materialism and a loss of race consciousness. The desire for wealth, it seems, often makes one 'less black,' or at least a less authentic representative of racial identity" (13). Jesse then is caught between his desire to be upwardly mobile, a trait that is culturally imagined as being white, and his desire for a folk identity associated with blackness. His use of slave metaphors is one way of imaginatively constructing himself as an oppressed folk. This is one of those points where deconstructing race could inadvertently suggest that the results of race construction are imaginary; however, pointing out that Jesse's metaphors operate on the level of imagination does not mean that his experiences of racism are not real. The way people act based on constructed ideas about race remind us that the metaphors of "slave collar" and "prisoner of war" are also historical facts.

My ambivalence about folkness is of a different kind because I am white; being upwardly mobile is assumed to be appropriate white behavior, but it still takes me away from my folk working-class roots and therefore makes me less authentic. Class and race are more specifically related together in Jesse's case while class is the focus in mine and whiteness is taken for granted, an unnoticed and usually unexamined factor. My ambivalence is less consequential, but for Jesse it could lead to an identity crisis. According to Favor, some black people "suffer from what we might call a crisis of authenticity. They have . . . been accused of being not 'truly' African American. That is . . . attitudes toward gender, and class status have somehow rendered their racial status as African Americans less 'real'" (2). This may have happened to Jesse since his doctorate, middle-class status, and long residence in the north removed him from that part of his identity that depends on his folk background in East Texas and at the same time made him more white and less black in terms of race as social construct.

The opposite is true of me: my adolescent love of African American music and my continuing fascination with black culture indicate that I, like Alan Lomax, want to be less white and more black. Jesse and I end up as racial mirrors of each other. We are similar in some ways to the fictional characters in black filmmaker Spike Lee's *Bamboozled*. According to W. J. T Mitchell, Pierre and Dunwitty "mirror each other's stereotypical roles as the Oreo and the Wannabe, the black man who wants to be white, and the white man who wants to be black" (2005, 304). The film exaggerates these stereotypes for satiric purposes; the fictional characters lack the complex ambivalence about race that Jesse and I have although the black Pierre is much more complex than the flat white character Dunwitty. Jesse is too proud of his blackness to ever consciously want to be white, but his upward mobility and education are still associated in the culture with being white. As Mitchell points out, "'assimilation' . . . continues to involve the adoption of normative whiteness and the exclusion of some form of racial otherness" (308). Therefore, every black person who culturally assimilates is adopting whiteness and excluding blackness on some level. The assimilation process is more complex though in that it does not always depend on exclusion or adoption; assimilation also includes the merging of cultural traits as "syncretism" (Herskovits 1958 [1941], xxii) or hybridization. As is often the case, Franz Fanon is insightful on this racial ambivalence: "There is no help for it. I am a white man. For unconsciously I distrust what is black in me, that is, the whole of my being" (1967 [1952], 191). Fanon is also relevant on the white man's ambivalence. His statement about the sickness of the white man who "adores the Negro" has caused me to examine my own fascination with African American culture in more depth. I have become too intellectually aware of the racializing process as a social construction of reality to let my love of black music and dance become a fetish, although it still operates on an emotional level.

Susan Gubar says, "Only when the boundaries separating black and white are perceived as demonstrably permeable does racial mutability lead to the undermining of race itself as a category" (1997, 25). This principle indicates one of the final ironies of our collaborative research across racial lines: when Jesse becomes more white and I become more black, we are both involved in "racechange," thereby proving the permeability of the racial boundaries that separate us. Even though racial difference is one of the factors that caused us to fail in our collaborative effort, inherent in our assumptions and behaviors is an idea that could potentially help us overcome the problems. The way we are both white and black at the same time indicates that racial distinctions are artificially imposed—difference between black and white is a fiction on the biological level—and this could be the basis for successful collaboration in the future. Overcoming our misunderstandings completely will be difficult because beliefs about racial difference are deeply ingrained, but that does not mean that researchers should abandon the effort and go back to our own ethnic, racial, class, gender, or national enclaves and give up communicating and trying to understand difference. For all the hurt and disappointment on both sides, I am still committed to doing research across boundaries of difference, and I hope Jesse is too. At this point, the best way to solve the problems in cross-racial field research is more collaboration.

References

Aarne, Antti. 1964. *The Types of the Folktale: A Classification and Bibliography*. Trans. and enlarged by Stith Thompson. 2nd rev. ed. Helsinki: Suomalainen Tiedeakatemia Academia Scientiarum Fennica.

Abrahams, Roger D. 1964. *Deep Down in the Jungle . . . Negro Narrative Folklore from the Streets of Philadelphia*. Hatboro, Pa.: Folklore Associates.

———. 1969. *Jump-Rope Rhymes, A Dictionary*. Austin: University of Texas Press.

———. 1970a. *Deep Down in the Jungle . . . Negro Narrative Folklore from the Streets of Philadelphia*. 1st rev. ed. Chicago: Aldine.

———. 1970b. *Positively Black*. Englewood Cliffs, N.J.: Prentice-Hall.

———. 1976. *Talking Black*. Rowley, Mass.: Newbury House.

———. 1983. *The Man-of-Words in the West Indies: Performance and the Emergence of Creole Culture*. Baltimore: Johns Hopkins University Press.

———. ed. 1985. *Afro-American Folktales: Stories from Black Traditions in the New World*. New York: Pantheon Books.

———. 1992. The Past in the Presence: An Overview of Folkloristics in the Late 20th Century. In Reimund Kvideland, ed., *Folklore Processed*, 32–51. Helsinki: Suomalaisen Kirjallisuuden Seura.

———. 1993. Phantoms of Romantic Nationalism in Folkloristics. *Journal of American Folklore* 106:3–37.

———. 2000. Mr. Lomax Meets Mr. Kittredge. *Journal of Folklore Research* 37:99–118.

———. 2002. Interview by Patrick B. Mullen. January 12, 2002. Personal collection.

———. 2005. E-mail to publore@list.unm.edu. September 2, 2005.

Albertson, Chris. 1964. Liner Notes to Lightnin' Hopkins, *Down Home Blues*. Prestige 1086.

Babcock, Barbara A.. 1984 [1977]. The Story in the Story: Metanarration in Folk

Narrative. In Richard Bauman, ed., *Verbal Art as Performance,* 61–79. Prospect Heights, Ill.: Waveland Press.

———. 1993. "At Home, No Womens are Storytellers": Potteries, Stories, and Politics in Cochiti Pueblo. In Joan Newlon Radner, ed. *Feminist Messages: Coding in Women's Folk Culture,* 221–51. Urbana: University of Illinois Press.

Baker, Houston A., Jr. 1984. *Blues, Ideology, and African American Literature: A Vernacular Theory.* Chicago: University of Chicago Press.

Banks, Ann. 1981. *First Person America.* New York: Vintage Books.

Barksdale, Richard, and Kenneth Kinnamon, eds. 1972. *Black Writers of America: A Comprehensive Anthology.* New York: Macmillan Company.

Baron, Robert, and Nicholas R. Spitzer, eds. 1992. *Public Folklore.* Washington, D.C.: Smithsonian Institution Press.

Barton, Matthew. 2005. E-mail to publore@list.unm.edu. August 31, 2005.

Bascom, William R. 1965 [1954]. Four Functions of Folklore. In Alan Dundes, ed. *The Study of Folklore,* 279–98. Englewood Cliffs, N.J.: Prentice-Hall.

Bauman, Richard. 1972. Differential Identity and the Social Base of Folklore. In Richard Bauman and Américo Paredes, eds., *Toward New Perspectives in Folklore.* Austin: University of Texas Press, 31–41.

———. 1984 [1977]. *Verbal Art as Performance.* Prospect Heights, Ill.: Waveland Press.

———. 1992. Performance. In Richard Bauman, ed., *Folklore, Cultural Performance, and Popular Entertainments: A Communication-Centered Handbook,* 41–49. New York: Oxford University Press.

Bendix, Regina. 1997. *In Search of Authenticity: The Formation of Folklore Studies.* Madison: University of Wisconsin Press.

Blank, Les. 1967. *The Blues Accordin' to Lightnin' Hopkins.* Flower Films.

Bluestein, Gene. 1972. *The Voice of the Folk: Folklore and American Literary Theory.* Amherst: University of Massachusetts Press.

Botkin, B.A., ed. n.d. *Folk Music of the United States: Negro Work Songs and Calls.* The Library of Congress Music Division. AAFS L8.

Brady, Margaret K. 1974. Gonna Shimmy Shimmy 'Til the Sun Goes Down: Aspects of Verbal and Nonverbal Socialization in the Play of Black Girls. *Folklore Annual* 6:1–16.

———. 1975. This Little Lady's Gonna Boogaloo: Elements of Socialization in the Play of Black Girls. In *Black Girls at Play: Perspectives on Child Development.* Austin: Southwest Educational Development Laboratory, 1–56.

Brewer, James Mason. 1968. *American Negro Folklore.* Chicago: Quadrangle Books.

Briggs, Charles L. 1986. *Learning How to Ask: A Sociolinguistic Appraisal of the Role of the Interview in Social Science Research.* Cambridge: Cambridge University Press.

Bronner, Simon J. 1986. *American Folklore Studies: An Intellectual History.* Lawrence: University Press of Kansas.

Brown, Sterling A., Arthur P. Davis, and Ulysses Lee, eds. 1941. *The Negro Caravan.* New York: The Dryden Press.

Burke, Kenneth. 1950. *A Rhetoric of Motives.* New York: Prentice-Hall.

Burton, Richard D. E. 1997. *Afro-Creole: Power, Opposition, and Play in the Caribbean.* Ithaca, N.Y.: Cornell University Press.

Cadaval, Olivia. 2000. "Show Trial" or "Truth and Reconciliation"? *Journal of Folklore Research* 37:185–96.

Camitta, Miriam. 1990. Gender and Method in Folklore Fieldwork. *Southern Folklore* 47:21–31.

Cantwell, Robert. 1992. Feasts of Unnaming: Folk Festivals and the Representation of Folklife. In Robert Baron and Nicholas R. Spitzer, eds. *Public Folklore,* 263–305. Washington, D.C.: Smithsonian Institution Press.

———. 1993. *Ethnomimesis: Folklife and the Representation of Culture.* Chapel Hill: University of North Carolina Press.

———. 1996. *When We Were Good: The Folk Revival.* Cambridge: Harvard University Press.

Carby, Hazel V. 1994. The Politics of Fiction, Anthropology, and the Folk: Zora Neale Hurston. In Genevieve Fabre and Robert O'Meally, eds., *History and Memory in African American Culture,* 28–44. New York: Oxford University Press.

———. 1998. *Race Men.* Cambridge: Harvard University Press.

Charters, Samuel. 1975 [1959]. *The Country Blues.* New York: DaCapo.

Clifford, James, and George E. Marcus, eds. 1986. *Writing Culture: The Poetics and Politics of Ethnography.* Berkeley: University of California Press.

Cohen, Ronald D. 2002. *Rainbow Quest: The Folk Music Revival and American Society, 1940–1970.* Amherst: University of Massachusetts Press.

Cohn, Lawrence. 1964. Liner Notes to Lightnin' Hopkins, *Hootin' the Blues.* Prestige/Folklore 14021.

Crenshaw, Kimberle, et. al., eds. 1995. *Critical Race Theory: The Key Writings That Formed the Movement.* New York: New Press.

Cross, Paulette. 1973. Jokes and Black Consciousness: A Collection with Interviews. In Alan Dundes, ed. *Mother Wit From the Laughing Barrel: Readings in the Interpretation of Afro-American Folklore,* 649–69. Englewood Cliffs, N.J.: Prentice-Hall.

Cruse, Harold. 1967. *The Crisis of the Negro Intellectual.* New York: William Morrow and Company.

Dance, Daryl Cumber. 1978. *Shuckin' and Jivin': Folklore from Contemporary Black Americans.* Bloomington: Indiana University Press.

Davis, Gerald L. 1985. *I Got the Word in Me and I Can Sing It, You Know. A Study of the Performed African-American Sermon.* Philadelphia: University of Pennsylvania Press.

———. 1992. 'So Correct for the Photograph': 'Fixing' the Ineffable, Ineluctable African American. In Robert Baron and Nicholas R. Spitzer, eds. *Public Folklore,* 105–18. Washington, D.C.: Smithsonian Institution Press.

———. 2000. Thomas Washington Talley: Early Twentieth Century African-American Folklore Theorist. *New York Folklore* 18:73–89.

Delacampagne, Christian. 1990. Racism and the West: From Praxis to Logos. In David Theo Goldberg, ed., *Anatomy of Racism,* 83–88. Minneapolis: University of Minnesota Press.

Delgado, Richard, and Jean Stefancic, eds. 1997. *Critical White Studies: Looking Behind the Mirror.* Philadelphia: Temple University Press.

———. 2001. *Critical Race Theory: An Introduction.* New York: New York University Press.

Denning, Michael. 1997. *The Cultural Front: The Laboring of American Culture in the Twentieth Century.* London: Verso.

Dorson, Richard M. 1967. *American Negro Folktales.* Greenwich, Conn.: Fawcett Books.

———. 1970. Is There a Folk in the City? *Journal of American Folklore* 83:185–216.

Dorst, John. 1987. Rereading *Mules and Men. Cultural Anthropology* 2:305–18.

Douglas, Frederick. 1962 [1892]. *Life and Times of Frederick Douglas.* New York: Collier Books.

DuBois, W. E. B. 1903. *The Souls of Black Folk.* Chicago: A. C. McClurg.

Duneier, Mitchell. 1992. *Slim's Table: Race, Respectability, and Masculinity.* Chicago: University of Chicago Press.

Dyer, Richard. 1988. White. *Screen* 29:44–64.

Eckhardt, Rosalind. 1975. From Handclap to Line Play. In *Black Girls at Play: Perspectives on Child Development.* Austin: Southwest Educational Development Laboratory, 57–101.

Ellison, Ralph. 1952. *Invisible Man.* New York: New American Library.

Evans, David. 1982. *Big Road Blues: Tradition and Creativity in the Folk Blues.* Berkeley and Los Angeles: University of California Press.

Fabian, Johannes. 1971. History, Language and Anthropology. *Philosophy of the Social Sciences* 1:19–47.

———. 1983. *Time and the Other: How Anthropology Makes Its Object.* New York: Columbia University Press.

———. 1994. Ethnographic Objectivity Revisited: From Rigor to Vigor. In Allan Megill, ed., *Rethinking Objectivity,* 81–108.

Fanon, Frantz. 1967 [1952]. *Black Skin, White Masks.* New York: Grove Press.

Farrer, Claire R., ed. 1975. *Women and Folklore.* Austin: University of Texas Press.

Faulkner, William. 1932. *Light in August.* New York: Random House.

Fauset, Arthur Huff. 1971 [1944]. *Black Gods of the Metropolis: Negro Religious Cults in the Urban North.* Philadelphia: University of Pennsylvania Press.

Favor, J. Martin. 1999. *Authentic Blackness: The Folk in the New Negro Renaissance.* Durham, N.C.: Duke University Press.

Fears, Darryl, and Claudia Deane. 2001. Biracial Pairs Say Approval and Acceptance Is Spreading. Columbus (Ohio) *Dispatch,* July 6, p. A1–2.

Feintuch, Burt, ed. 1988. *The Conservation of Culture: Folklorists and the Public Sector.* Lexington: University Press of Kentucky.

Filene, Benjamin. 1991. "Our Singing Country": John and Alan Lomax, Leadbelly, and the Construction of an American Past. *American Quarterly* 43:602–24.

———. 2000. *Romancing the Folk: Public Memory and American Roots Music.* Chapel Hill: University of North Carolina Press.

Fine, Michelle, et al., eds. 1997. *Off White: Readings on Race, Power and Society.* New York: Routledge.

Foley, John Miles. 2001. *Native American Oral Tradition: Collaboration and Interpretation.* Logan: Utah State University Press.

Fry, Gladys-Marie. 1975. *Night Riders in Black Folk History.* Knoxville: University of Tennessee Press.

Fuss, Diana. 1995. *Identification Papers.* New York: Routledge.

Gates, Henry Louis, Jr. 1985. Writing "Race" and the Difference It Makes. *Critical Inquiry* 12:1–20.

———. 1988. *The Signifying Monkey: A Theory of African-American Literary Criticism.* New York: Oxford University Press.

Gaunt, Kyra D. 1995. African American Women Between Hopscotch and Hip-Hop: "Must Be the Music (That's Turnin' Me On)." In Anghrad N. Valdivia, ed. *Feminism, Multiculturalism, and the Media: Global Diversities,* 277–308. Thousand Oaks, CA: Sage Publications.

———. 1997. Translating Double-Dutch to Hip-Hop: The Musical Vernacular of Black Girls' Play. In Joseph K. Adjaye and Andrianne R. Andrews, eds. *Language, Rhythm, and Sound: Black Popular Cultures into the Twenty-First Century,* 146–63. Pittsburgh: University of Pittsburgh Press.

———. 1998. Dancin' in the Street to a Black Girl's Beat: Music, Gender, and the "Ins and Outs" of Double-Dutch. In Joe Austin and Michael Nevin Willard, eds. *Generations of Youth: Youth Cultures and History in Twentieth-Century America,* 272–92. New York: New York University Press.

———. 2006. *The Games Black Girls Play: Learning the Ropes from Double-Dutch to Hip-Hop.* New York: New York University Press.

Gleason, Ralph J. 1966. Amazing Sounds of a Blues Accordion. San Francisco *Chronicle,* April 18, p. 53.

Goldberg, David Theo, ed. 1990. *Anatomy of Racism.* Minneapolis: University of Minnesota Press.

Grier, William H., and Price M. Cobbs. 1968. *Black Rage.* New York: Basic Books.

Gubar, Susan. 1997. *RaceChanges: White Skin, Black Face in American Culture.* New York: Oxford University Press, 1997.

Gundaker, Grey. 1998. *Signs of Diaspora, Diaspora of Signs: Literacies, Creolization, and Vernacular Practice in African America.* New York: Oxford University Press.

Hacker, Andrew. 1992. *Two Nations: Black and White, Separate, Hostile, Unequal.* New York: Scribner's.

Hajdu, David. 2003. Authenticity Blues. *New Republic*. 228 (23): 38–41.

Hand, Wayland D. 1967. Newbell Niles Puckett (1898–1967). *Journal of American Folklore* 80:341–42.

Hand, Wayland D., Anna Casetta, and Sondra B. Thiederman, eds. 1981. *Popular Beliefs and Superstitions: A Compendium of American Folklore*. Boston: G. K. Hall.

Handler, Richard, and Jocelyn Linnekin. 1984. Tradition, Genuine or Spurious. *Journal of American Folklore* 97:273–90.

Hannerz, Ulf. 1969. *Soulside: Inquiries into Ghetto Culture and Community*. New York: Columbia University Press.

Hathaway, Rosemary V. 2004. The Unbearable Weight of Authenticity: Zora Neale Hurston's *Their Eyes Were Watching God* and a Theory of "Touristic Reading." *Journal of American Folklore* 117:168–98.

Hellmann, John. 2006. Personal correspondence.

Hemenway, Robert E. 1977. *Zora Neale Hurston: A Literary Biography*. Urbana: University of Illinois Press.

———. 1978. Introduction. In Zora Neale Hurston, *Mules and Men*, xi–xxviii. Bloomington: Indiana University Press.

Herskovits, Melville J. 1927. Review of *Folk Beliefs of the Southern Negro*. *Journal of American Folklore* 40:310–12.

———. 1958 [1941]. *The Myth of the Negro Past*. Boston: Beacon.

Hirsch, Jerrold. 1987. Folklore in the Making: B.A. Botkin. *Journal of American Folklore* 100:3–38.

———. 1988. Cultural Pluralism and Applied Folklore: The New Deal Precedent. In Burt Feintuch, ed. *The Conservation of Culture: Folklore and the Public Sector*, 46–67. Lexington: University Press of Kentucky.

———. 1992. Modernity, Nostalgia, and Southern Folklore Studies: The Case of John Lomax. *Journal of American Folklore* 105:183–207.

hooks, bell. 1990. *Yearning: Race, Gender, and Cultural Politics*. Boston: South End Press.

———. 1992. *Black Looks: Race and Representation*. Boston: South End Press.

Horton, John. 1972. Time and Cool People. In Thomas Kochman, ed., *Rappin' and Stylin' Out: Communication in Urban Black America*. Urbana: University of Illinois Press, 19–31.

Hufford, David J. 1995. The Scholarly Voice and the Personal Voice: Reflexivity in Belief Studies. *Western Folklore* 54:57–76.

Hughes, Langston, and Arna Bontemps, eds. 1958. *The Book of Negro Folklore*. New York: Dodd, Mead and Company.

Hurston, Zora Neale. 1978 [1935]. *Mules and Men*. Bloomington: Indiana University Press.

———. 1978 [1937]. *Their Eyes Were Watching God*. Urbana: University of Illinois Press.

Hyatt, Harry M. 1970–78. *Hoodoo-Conjuration-Witchcraft-Rootwork: Beliefs, Accepted by Many Negroes and White Persons These Being Orally Recorded Among Blacks and Whites*, 5 vols. N.P.: Memoirs of the Alma Egan Hyatt Foundation.

Jackson, Bruce, ed. 1967. *The Negro and His Folklore in Nineteenth-Century Periodicals*. Austin: University of Texas Press.

———. 1974. *"Get Your Ass in the Water and Swim Like Me": Narrative Poetry from Black Oral Tradition*. Cambridge: Harvard University Press.

———. 2002. Remembering Alan Lomax, January 31, 1915–July 19, 2002. *Buffalo Report* 7.26 (2002): January 9, 2006, http://www.buffaloreport.com/ 020726 lomax .html.

Johnson, Charles S. 1926a. More About Superstitions and Health. *Opportunity: A Journal of Negro Life* 4 (45): 271.

———. 1926b. Review of *Folk Beliefs of the Southern Negro*. *Opportunity: A Journal of Negro Life* 4:324–25.

———. 1926c. Superstitions and Health. *Opportunity: A Journal of Negro Life* 4:206–7.

Johnson, James Weldon, ed. 1922. *The Book of American Negro Poetry*. New York: Harcourt, Brace and Company.

Jones, Bessie. 1983. *For the Ancestors: Autobiographical Memories*. Collected and edited by John Stewart. Urbana: University of Illinois Press.

Jones, Bessie, and Bess Lomax Hawes. 1972. *Step It Down: Games, Plays, Songs, and Stories from the Afro-American Heritage*. New York: Harper and Row.

Jordan, Rosan Augusta. 1992. Not into Cold Space: Zora Neale Hurston and J. Frank Dobie as Holistic Folklorists. *Southern Folklore* 49:109–31.

Jordan, Rosan A., and Susan J. Kalcik, eds. 1985. *Women's Folklore, Women's Culture*. Philadelphia: University of Pennsylvania Press.

Keil, Charles. 1966. *Urban Blues*. Chicago: University of Chicago Press.

Knapp, Mary, and Herbert Knapp. 1976. *One Potato, Two Potato . . . The Secret Education of American Children*. New York: Norton.

Kodish, Debora. 1993. On Coming of Age in the Sixties. *Western Folklore* 52:193–207.

Koskoff, Ellen, ed. 1989. *Women and Music in Cross-Cultural Perspective*. Urbana: University of Illinois Press.

Kummer, George. 1981. Newbell Niles Puckett ('Barry'), 1897–1967: An Appreciation. In Wayland D. Hand, Anna Casetta, and Sondra B. Thiederman, eds. *Popular Beliefs and Superstitions: A Compendium of American Folklore*, 3:1533–36. Boston: G. K. Hall.

Lawless, Elaine J. 1992. "I Was Afraid Someone Like You . . . an Outsider . . . Would Misunderstand": Negotiating Interpretive Differences Between Ethnographers and Subjects. *Journal of American Folklore* 105:302–15.

———. 2000. "Reciprocal" Ethnography: No One Said It Was Easy. *Journal of Folklore Research* 37:197–206.

Legman, G. 1963 [1949]. *Love and Death: A Study in Censorship*. New York: Hacker Art Books.

———. 1964. *The Horn Book: Studies in Erotic Folklore and Bibliography*. New Hyde Park, NY: University Books.

Levine, Lawrence W. 1977. *Black Culture and Black Consciousness: Afro-American Folk Thought from Slavery to Freedom*. Oxford: Oxford University Press.

Lhamon, W.T., Jr. 1998. *Raising Cain: Blackface Performance from Jim Crow to Hip Hop*. Cambridge: Harvard University Press.

Lieberman, Robbie. 1989. *"My Song is My Weapon": People's Songs, American Communism, and the Politics of Culture, 1930–1950*. Urbana: University of Illinois Press.

Liebow, Elliot. 1967. *Tally's Corner: A Study of Negro Streetcorner Men*. Boston: Little, Brown and Company.

Lindfors, Bernth, ed. 1999. *Africans on Stage: Studies in Ethnological Show Business*. Bloomington: Indiana University Press.

Lipsitz, George. 1990. *Time Passages: Collective Memory and American Popular Culture*. Minneapolis: University of Minnesota Press.

Lloyd, Timothy. 1997. Whole Work, Whole Play, Whole People: Folklore and Social Therapeutics in 1920s and 1930s America. *Journal of American Folklore* 110:239–59.

Lomax, Alan. 1946. The Functional Approach. *Journal of American Folklore* 59:507–10.

———. 1958. *Texas Folk Songs Sung by Alan Lomax*. Tradition Records. TLP 1029.

———. 1960. *Folk Songs of North America*. Garden City, N.Y.: Doubleday.

———. 1968. *Folk Song Style and Culture*. Washington, D.C.: American Association for the Advancement of Science, Publication No. 88.

———. 1993. *The Land Where the Blues Began*. New York: Delta.

———. 1997 [1960]. Saga of a Folksong Hunter: A Twenty-Year Odyssey with Cylinder, Disc and Tape. *The Alan Lomax Collection Sampler*. Rounder CD 1700, 42–57.

———. 1998a. *Appalachian Journey—From the Original Ballad of Tom Dooley to the Origins of Bluegrass*. Vestapol Video 13079.

———. 1998b. *Dreams and Songs of the Noble Old*. Vestapol Video 13080.

———. 1998c. *The Land Where the Blues Began*. Vestapol Video 13078.

———. 2003a. *Alan Lomax: Selected Writings, 1934–1997*. Ed. Ronald D. Cohen. New York: Routledge.

———. 2003b. *Blues in the Mississippi Night*. Rounder CD 82161-1860-2.

———. n.d. *Roots of the Blues*. Atlantic 1348.

Lomax, John A. 1940. Field recording. Archive of Folk Culture. The American Folklife Center. The Library of Congress, Washington, D.C.

———. 1947. *Adventures of a Ballad Hunter*. New York: Macmillan.

———. n.d. *The Ballad Hunter, Parts VII and VIII: Spirituals and Railroad Songs*. The Library of Congress Music Division. AAFS L52.

Lomax, John A., and Alan Lomax. 1934. *American Ballads and Folk Songs*. New York: Macmillan.

Lott, Eric. 1993. *Love and Theft: Blackface Minstrelsy and the American Working Class*. New York: Oxford University Press.

Mailer, Norman. 1957. *The White Negro.* San Francisco: City Lights Books.

Malinowski, Bronislaw. 1979 [1931]. The Role of Magic and Religion. In William A. Lessa and Evon Z. Vogt, eds., *Reader in Comparative Religion: An Anthropological Approach,* 37–46. New York: Harper and Row.

Malone, Jacqui. 1996. *Steppin' on the Blues: The Visible Rhythms of African American Dance.* Urbana: University of Illinois Press.

Marcus, George E., and Michael M. J. Fischer. 1986. *Anthropology as Cultural Critique: An Experimental Moment in the Human Sciences.* Chicago: University of Chicago Press.

McCormick, Mack. 1959. Liner notes to Lightnin' Hopkins, *Country Blues.* Tradition TLP 1035.

———. 1960a. Liner notes to Lightnin' Hopkins, *Autobiography in Blues.* Tradition TLP 1040.

———. 1960b. Sam 'Lighnin' Hopkins—A Description, *Sing Out* 1, 4–8.

———. 1962. Lightnin' Hopkins: Blues. In Martin T. Williams, ed. *Jazz Panorama,* 311–18. Crowell-Collier: New York.

———. n.d. Liner notes to Lightnin' Hopkins, *Blues in My Bottle.* Prestige/Bluesville BV 1045.

McNutt, James Charles. 1982. Beyond Regionalism: Texas Folklorists and the Emergence of a Post-Regional Consciousness. Ph.D. dissertation, University of Texas.

Meisenhelder, Susan. 1996. Conflict and Resistance in Hurston's *Mules and Men. Journal of American Folklore* 109:267–88.

Merrill-Mirsky, Carol. 1988. "Eeny Meeny Pepsadeeny: Ethnicity and Gender in Children's Musical Play." Ph.D. dissertation, University of California, Los Angeles.

Mills, Margaret. 1993. Feminist Theory and the Study of Folklore: A Twenty-year Trajectory toward Theory. *Western Folklore* 52:173–92.

Mitchell, W. J. T. 2005. *What Do Pictures Want? The Lives and Loves of Images.* Chicago: University of Chicago Press.

Morrison, Toni. 1987. *Beloved.* New York: Alfred A. Knopf.

———. 1992. *Playing in the Dark.* Cambridge: Harvard University Press.

Mullen, Patrick B. 1970. A Negro Street Performer: Tradition and Innovation. *Western Folklore* 29:91–103.

———. 1972. Folk Songs and Family Traditions. In Francis Edward Abernethy, ed. *Observations and Reflections on Texas Folklore,* 49–63. Austin, Tx.: Encino Press.

———. 1978. *I Heard the Old Fishermen Say: Folklore of the Texas Gulf Coast.* Austin: University of Texas Press. Rpt. 1988. Logan: Utah State University Press.

———. 1997. The Prism of Race: Two Texas Folk Performers. *Southern Folklore* 54:13–25.

———. 1979–81. Black Consciousness in Afro-American Children's Rhymes: Some Ohio Examples from the Early 1970s. *Ohio Folklife: Journal of the Ohio Folklore Society* 6:1–20.

———. 1992. *Listening to Old Voices: Folklore, Life Stories, and the Elderly.* Urbana: University of Illinois Press.

———. 1999 Race and Ethnographic Allegory. *Fabula: Journal of Folktale Studies* 40:17–25.

———. 2000a. The Dilemma of Representation in Folklore Studies: The Case of Henry Truvillion and John Lomax. *Journal of Folklore Research* 37:155–74.

———. 2000b. Collaborative Research Reconsidered. *Journal of Folklore Research* 37:207–14.

———. 2000c. Belief and the American Folk. *Journal of American Folklore.* 113 (448): 119–43.

Murray, Albert. 1970. *The Omni-Americans: New Perspectives on Black Experience and American Culture.* New York: Outerbridge and Dienstfrey. Rpt. 1983. New York: Vintage Books.

Myerhoff, Barbara. 1984. Rites and Signs of Ripening: The Intertwining of Ritual, Time, and Growing Older. In David I. Kertzer and Jennie Keith, eds., *Age and Anthropological Theory,* 305–30. Ithaca, N.Y.: Cornell University Press.

Newell, William Wells. 1963 [1903]. *Games and Songs of American Children.* New York: Dover.

O'Connor, Bonnie Blair. 1995. *Healing Traditions: Alternative Medicine and the Health Professions.* Philadelphia: University of Pennsylvania Press.

O'Connor, Flannery. 1971. Everything That Rises Must Converge. In *The Complete Stories of Flannery O'Connor.* New York: Farrar, Straus and Giroux.

Oliver, Paul. 1960. *Blues Fell This Morning: The Meaning of the Blues.* London: Cassell.

Ong, Walter J. 1967. *The Presence of the Word: Some Prolegomena for Cultural and Religious History.* New Haven, Conn.: Yale University Press.

Opie, Iona, and Peter Opie. 1959. *The Lore and Language of Schoolchildren.* London: Oxford University Press.

Outlaw, Lucius. 1990. Toward a Critical Theory of Race. In David Theo Goldberg, ed. *Anatomy of Race,* 58–82. Minneapolis: University of Minnesota Press.

Parrish, Lydia. 1965 [1942]. *Slave Songs of the Georgia Sea Islands.* Hatboro, Pa.: Folklore Associates.

Parsons, Elsie Clews. 1923. *Folklore of the Sea Islands, South Carolina.* New York: G. E. Stechert and Company.

Pearson, Barry Lee. 1984. *"Sounds So Good to Me": The Bluesman's Story.* Philadelphia: University of Pennsylvania Press.

———. 1990. *Virginia Piedmont Blues: The Art and Lives of Two Virginia Bluesmen.* Philadelphia: University of Pennsylvania Press.

Pearson, Barry Lee, and Bill McCulloch. 2003. *Robert Johnson: Lost and Found.* Urbana: University of Illinois Press.

Portelli, Allessandro. 1997. *The Battle of Valle Giulia: Oral History and the Art of Dialogue.* Madison: University of Wisconsin Press.

Porterfield, Nolan. 1996. *Last Cavalier: The Life and Times of John A. Lomax, 1867–1948.* Urbana: University of Illinois Press.

———. 2000. Telling the Whole Story: Biography and Representation. *Journal of Folklore Research* 37:175–84.

Pound, Louise. 1927. Review of *Folk Beliefs of the Southern Negro. Journal of American Folklore* 40:101–2.

Puckett, Newbell Niles. 1931. Religious Folk Beliefs of Whites and Negroes. *Journal of Negro History* 16:9–35.

———. 1934. Negro Character as Revealed in Folklore. *Publications of the American Sociological Society* 28:12–23.

———. 1969 [1926]. *Folk Beliefs of the Southern Negro.* New York: Dover Publications.

———. 1973 [1926]. Race Pride and Folklore. In Alan Dundes, ed. *Mother Wit from the Laughing Barrel: Readings in the Interpretation of Afro-American Folklore,* 3–8. Englewood Cliffs, N.J.: Prentice-Hall.

———. n.d. Unpublished manuscript. Newbell Niles Puckett Memorial Gift, Special Collections, Cleveland (Ohio) Public Library.

Ramsey, Frederic. 1960. *Been Here and Gone.* New Brunswick, N.J.: Rutgers University Press.

Riddell, Cecelia. 1990. Traditional Singing Games of Elementary School Children in Los Angeles. Ph.D. dissertation, University of California, Los Angeles.

Roberts, John W. 1989. *From Trickster to Badman: The Black Folk Hero in Slavery and Freedom.* Philadelphia: University of Pennsylvania Press.

———. 2000. African-American Folklore in a Discourse of Folkness. *New York Folklore* 18:73–89.

Robinson, Beverly J. 1990. Africanisms and the Study of Folklore. In Joseph E. Holloway, ed. *Africanisms in American Culture,* 211–24. Bloomington: Indiana University Press.

Roediger, David R. 1991. *The Wages of Whiteness: Race and the Making of the American Working Class.* London: Verso.

Rogin, Michael. 1996. *Blackface, White Noise: Jewish Immigrants in the Hollywood Melting Pot.* Berkeley: University of California Press.

Seward, Adrienne Lanier. 1983. The Legacy of Early Afro-American Folklore Scholarship. In Richard M. Dorson, ed., *Handbook of American Folklore,* 48–56. Bloomington: Indiana University Press.

Skoog, Lawrence C. 1968. Liner notes to *George Coleman, Bongo Joe.* Arhoolie 1040.

Sowell, Thomas. 1997. Excuses and "Understanding" Harm Those Who Need Help. *The Columbus* (Ohio) *Dispatch* June 27, 9A.

Spivak, Gayatri Chakravorty, and Ellen Rooney. 1993. In a Word: Interview. In Spivak, *Outside in The Teaching Machine,* 1–23. New York: Routledge.

Stancil, Cassandra A. 2000. An Early Model for the Study of African-American Folklore: Carter G. Woodson. *New York Folklore* 18:73–89.

Staub, Michael. 1994. *Voices of Persuasion: Politics of Representation in 1930s America.* Cambridge: Cambridge University Press.

Steele, Shelby. 1990. *The Content of Our Character.* New York: St. Martin's Press.

Stewart, John O. 1989. *Drinkers, Drummers, and Decent Folk: Ethnographic Narratives of Village Trinidad.* Albany: State University of New York Press.

Sumner, William Graham. 1906. *Folkways: A Study of the Sociological Importance of Usages, Manners, Customs, Mores, and Morals.* Boston: Ginn.

Sykes, Charles J. 1992. *A Nation of Victims: The Decay of the American Character.* New York: St. Martin's Press.

Szwed, John. 1969. An American Anthropological Dilemma: The Politics of Afro-American Culture. In Dell Hymes, ed. *Reinventing Anthropology,* 153–81. New York: Random House.

———. 1971. Introduction. In Arthur Huff Fauset, *Black Gods of the Metropolis: Negro Religious Cults in the Urban North,* v–x. Philadelphia: University of Pennsylvania Press.

Talbot, Margaret. 1999. Review of *The Crime of Sheila McGough. New York Times Book Review,* February 7, p. 6.

Tate, Greg. 2003. *Everything But the Burden: What White People Are Taking from Black Culture.* New York: Broadway Books.

Talley, Thomas W. 1968 [1922]. *Negro Folk Rhymes, Wise and Otherwise.* New York: MacMillan Company.

Thompson, Stith, ed. 1953. *Four Symposia on Folklore.* Bloomington: Indiana University Press.

Titon, Jeff Todd. 1980. The Life Story. *Journal of American Folklore* 93:276–92.

———. 1987. History and Fiction in Blues Biography: The Case of John Lomax and Huddie Ledbetter. Paper presented at the annual meeting of the Organization of American Historians, Philadelphia.

———. 1993. Reconstructing the Blues: Reflections on the 1960s Blues Revival. In Neil V. Rosenberg, ed. *Transforming Tradition: Folk Music Revivals Examined,* 220–40. Urbana: University of Illinois Press.

Toomer, Jean. 1923. *Cane.* New York: Boni and Liveright.

Torgovnick, Marianna. 1990. *Gone Primitive: Savage Intellects, Modern Lives.* Chicago: University of Chicago Press.

Truvillion, Jesse G. 1995. Interview by Patrick B. Mullen. Personal collection.

———. 1996. Henry Truvillion of the Big Thicket: A Song Worth Singing. In Francis E. Abernethy, Patrick B. Mullen, and Alan B. Govenar, eds. *Juneteenth Texas: Essays in African-American Folklore,* 21–38. Denton: University of North Texas Press.

———. 2000a. A Child of the Big Thicket. *Journal of Folklore Research* 37:123–54.

———. 2000b. Singing a New Song: Notes on Redemption. *Journal of Folklore Research* 37:215–26.

Valentine, Bettylou. 1978. *Hustling and Other Hard Work.* New York: The Free Press.

Walker, Alice. 1983. *In Search of Our Mother's Gardens.* San Diego: Harcourt Brace Jovanovich.

Ware, Vron, and Les Back. 2002. *Out of Whiteness: Color, Politics, and Culture.* Chicago: The University of Chicago Press.

Weingarten, Marc. 2005. Book Says Alan Lomax Neglected Black Scholars. *New York Times,* August 29, p. B1,6.

West, Cornell. 1994. *Race Matters.* New York: Vintage.

Wheat, John. 1996. Lightnin' Hopkins: Blues Bard of the Third Ward. In Francis E. Abernethy, Patrick B. Mullen, and Alan B. Govenar, eds. *Juneteenth Texas: Essays in African-American Folklore,* 255–71. Denton: University of North Texas Press.

Whisnant, David. 1983. *All That is Native and Fine: The Politics of Culture in An American Region.* Chapel Hill: University of North Carolina Press.

Whitten, Norman E., Jr. 1974. *Black Frontiersmen: A South American Case.* New York: Schenkman.

Wiegman, Robyn. 1995. *American Anatomies: Theorizing Race and Gender.* Durham, N.C.: Duke University Press.

Wiggins, William H., Jr. 1987. *O Freedom!: Afro-American Emancipation Celebrations.* Knoxville: University of Tennessee Press.

———. 1988. Afro Americans as Folk: From Savage to Civilized. In William M. Clements, ed., *100 Years of American Folklore Studies: A Conceptual History,* 29–32. Washington, D.C.: The American Folklore Society.

Williams, Patricia J. 1991. *The Alchemy of Race and Rights: Diary of a Law Professor* Cambridge: Harvard University Press.

Wilson, Russ. 1996. Fascinating Blues Display. Oakland *Tribune,* April 16, p. 11b.

Wilson, William A. 1989 [1973]. Herder, Folklore and Romantic Nationalism. In Elliot Oring, ed., *Folk Groups and Folklore Genres: A Reader,* 21–37. Logan: Utah State University Press.

Wolfe, Charles, and Kip Lornell. 1992. *The Life and Legend of Leadbelly.* New York: Harper Collins.

Work, John W. 2005. *Lost Delta Found: Rediscovering the Fisk University-Library of Congress Coahoma County Study, 1941–42.* John W. Work, Lewis Wade Jones, Samuel C. Adams, Jr.; edited by Robert Gordon and Bruce Nemerov. Nashville: Vanderbilt University Press.

Wright, Richard. 1938. *Uncle Tom's Children, Four Novellas.* New York: Harper and Brothers.

———. 1940. *Native Son.* New York: Harper and Brothers.

Index

Abrahams, Roger D.: attraction to African American culture, 9, 12, 99; and folksong revival, 144–45; influence on scholarship by, 4, 19, 61, 71, 151, 179; interpretations of folklore by, 24, 32, 168; and leftist politics, 125, 130, 131–32, 141–46, 148–49; and orality/literacy, 140–41, 146–48; and performance approach, 132–32, 137–43; and psychoanalytic approach, 133–38; and reflexive ethnography, 149–50; and urban research, 131–32; and white innocence, 145–46

African American folklore: animal tales, 31–34; children's rhymes, 112–13, 151–76; folk belief, 40–47, 52–53; in general, 4–5; jokes, 22–24; signifying, 128–30; toasts (narrative poems), 30–32, 139

Africanism, 7–8, 81–87, 91

authenticity, 14–15, 83–84, 100, 120–25, 139–41, 189–91

blackface minstrelsy, 12–13, 93, 99–104

blackness: as Africanism, 7–8, 81–87, 91; dynamic with whiteness, 6–8, 27,

48–49, 96–98, 109–16; and racial politics, 131–32, 141–46, 148–49, 190–92; and white desire, 9–10, 94–96, 99–104, 114–15

blues: cultural representations of, 117–25, 126–28, 142–43; and sexuality, 112, 114; white mimicry of, 12–13, 99–102; white response to, 80, 144–45

collaborative research, 11, 39, 109, 152–53, 176, 177–92

critical race theory: and Africanist persona, 81–87; as black/white dynamic, 27, 30, 48–49, 53, 61, 70, 93, 96–98, 109–16, 148–49, 190–92; history and principles of, 6–10, 16; in racial politics, 143–44

cultural evolution, 8, 43–48, 62, 64, 88, 141

cultural relativism, 44, 88–89

cultural representation: of black children, 151–52, 155–56, 164, 168–69, 174; as "fictionalized," 81–82; of the folk, 83–87, 117–30; as pathological, 2–3, 61, 62–64, 70–71, 83, 85–86; of race relations, 181–82, 184–85; and racial poli-

PATRICK B. MULLEN is a Professor Emeritus of English and folklore at Ohio State University. He is author of *Listening to Old Voices: Folklore, Life Stories, and the Elderly; I Heard the Old Fishermen Say: Folklore of the Texas Gulf Coast;* and *Lake Erie Fishermen: Work, Identity, and Tradition* (with Timothy Lloyd).

The University of Illinois Press
is a founding member of the
Association of American University Presses.

_____

Composed in 10.5/13 Adobe Minion Pro
with FontFont Meta display
by Jim Proefrock
at the University of Illinois Press.
Manufactured by Cushing-Malloy, Inc.

University of Illinois Press
1325 South Oak Street
Champaign, IL 61820-6903
www.press.uillinois.edu